TEACHER'S GUIDE

GRADE 10

Authors:

Robert Pavlik

Richard G. Ramsey

Great Source Education Group

a Houghton Mifflin Company
Wilmington, Massachusetts
www.greatsource.com

Authors

Dr. Richard G. Ramsey is currently a national educational consultant for many schools throughout the country and serves as president of Ramsey's Communications. He has been a teacher and a principal for grades 1–12 for 23 years. Dr. Ramsey has also served on the Curriculum Frameworks Committee for the State of Florida. A lifelong teacher and educator and former principal, he is now a nationally known speaker on improving student achievement and motivating students.

Dr. Robert Pavlik taught high school English and reading for seven years. His university assignments in Colorado and Wisconsin have included teaching secondary/content area reading, chairing a reading/language arts department, and directing a reading/learning center. He is an author of several books and articles and serves as director of the School Design and Development Center at Marquette University.

CONSULTANT **Catherine McNary** of Proviso West High School in Illinois is a reading specialist who works with teachers of struggling readers. She has been an invaluable consultant during the development of the *Sourcebook* series. She is currently pursuing a doctorate in reading.

International Standard Book Number: 0-669-47139-9

5 6 7 8 9 10 06 05

Readers and Reviewers

Marsha Besch
Literacy/Secondary Curr. Coordinator ISD #196
Rosemount, Minnesota

Tim McGee
Worland High School
Worland, Wyoming

Mary Grace
Marshall Middle School
Janesville, Wisconsin

Shelly L. Fabozzi
Holmes Middle School
Colorado Springs, Colorado

Jim Burke
Burlingame High School
San Francisco, California

Phyllis Y. Keiley-Tyler
Education Consultant
Seattle, Washington

Jenny Sroka
Learning Enterprise High School
Milwaukee, Wisconsin

Glenda Swirtz
Flint Southwestern Academy
Flint, Michigan

Jeff Wallack
Learning Enterprise High School
Milwaukee, Wisconsin

Jay Amberg
Glenbrook South High School
Glenview, Illinois

Sherry Nielsen
Curriculum and Instruction
Saint Cloud, Minnesota

Deborah Schroeder
Harlan Community Academy
Chicago, Illinois

Richard Stear
Central Office
Rochester, New York

Hilary Zunin
Napa High School
Napa, California

William Weber
Libertyville High School
Libertyville, Illinois

Beverly Washington
Fenger High School
Chicago, Illinois

Lyla Fox
Loy Norrix High School
Kalamazoo, Michigan

Eileen Davis
Banneker Academic High School
Washington, D.C.

Christine Heerlein
Rockwood Summit High School
Fenton, Missouri

Barbara Ellen Pitts
Detroit, Michigan

Kimberly Edgeworth
Palm Beach Lakes High School
West Palm Beach, Florida

Jeffrey Hicks
Whitford Middle School
Beaverton, Oregon

Mark Tavernier
Norfolk, Virginia

Gina La Manna
Southeast Raleigh High School
Raleigh, North Carolina

Jennifer Sharpe-Salter
Southern Nash Sr. High School
Bailey, North Carolina

Elizabeth Dyhouse
Longfellow Middle School
Flint, Michigan

Rose Chatman
Dayton Public Schools
Dayton, Ohio

Gereldine Conaway
Mumford High School
Detroit, Michigan

Barb Evans
Lorain City Schools
Lorain, Ohio

Deborah Gonzalez
Puget Sound Education School District
Burien, Washington

Rosita Graham
Winter Halter Elementary School
Detroit, Michigan

Elaine Hanson
Mounds View School District
Saint Paul, Minnesota

Barbara Heget
Milwaukee, Wisconsin

Patrick Horigan
Milwaukee, Wisconsin

Rose Hunter
Whittier Middle School
Flint, Michigan

Ray Kress
Wilson Middle School
Newark, Ohio

Evelyn McDuffie
Beaubien Middle School
Detroit, Michigan

Robin Milanovich
Jefferson High School
Edgewater, Colorado

Dr. Howard Moon
Kenosha School District
Kenosha, Wisconsin

Jeanette Nassif
Central High School
Flint, Michigan

Dr. Joe Papenfuss
Racine Unified School District
Racine, Wisconsin

Lori Pfeiffer
West Bend School District
West Bend, Wisconsin

Evelyn Price
Milwaukee, Wisconsin

Karen Rano
Educational Consultant
River Forest, Illinois

Karen Ray
Darwin Elementary School
Chicago, Illinois

Renetha Rumph
Flint Southwestern High School
Flint, Michigan

Sarike Simpson
Racine, Wisconsin

Branka Skukan
Chopin School
Chicago, Illinois

Stephanie Thurick
Minneapolis Public Schools
Minneapolis, Minnesota

Gloria Tibbets
Curriculum Institute
Flint, Michigan

Anita Wellman
Northwestern High School
Detroit, Michigan

Barb Whaley
Akron City Schools
Akron, Ohio

Ray Wolpow
Western Washington University
Bellingham, Washington

Robin Gleason
Wilson Elementary School
Wauwatosa, Wisconsin

Kay Briske
Janesville School District
Janesville, Wisconsin

Table of Contents

Introduction to Program

Strategy Handbook

Table of Contents

PUPIL'S EDITION SKILLS AND STRATEGIES

The chart below identifies the strategies for each part of each pupil's edition lesson.

Selection	I. Prereading	II. Response Notes	Comprehension	III. Prewriting
1. **High School: The Bad and the Good** (nonfiction)	anticipation/reaction guide	highlight	directed reading	group discussion
2. **Finding Patrick** (nonfiction)	read-aloud	visualize	double-entry journal	narrowing a topic
3. **It's Quiet Now** (fiction)	word web	clarify	story map	personal response
4. **Survival** from (autobiography)	skim	question	reciprocal reading	summarize
5. **How It Feels to Be Colored Me** (autobiography)	preview	mark	word attack	topic sentence and details
6. **The Eatonville Anthology** (fiction)	think-pair-and-share	react	directed reading	compare and contrast
7. **Visit to Africa** (autobiography)	read-aloud	prediction	predict	main idea and supporting details
8. **Dear Tía and Papa** (poetry)	word web	react and connect	double-entry journal	brainstorming
9. **The Guest Who Ran Away** (folktale)	preview	clarify/predict	reciprocal reading	character attribute map
10. **The Price of Pride and How Si' Djeha Staved Off Hunger** (folktales)	predict	read-aloud/predict	retell	sequencing a plot
11. **Puerto Rican Paradise** (autobiography)	picture walk	mark	sequence	narrowing a topic
12 **If You Ain't Got Heart, You Ain't Got Nada** (autobiography)	quickwrite	react and connect	graphic organizer	group discussion
13. **Her Life Was Not a Joke** (nonfiction)	anticipation guide	question	prediction	graphic organizer
14. **One Morning** (autobiography)	think-pair-and-share	visualize	storyboard	research
15. **The Knight in Person** (nonfiction)	K-W-L	mark or highlight	directed reading	main idea and details
16. **The Victorious Feudal Knight** (nonfiction)	preview	react and connect	graphic organizer	topic sentence and details
17. **Forgetfulness and An Unwritten Letter** (autobiography)	read-aloud	questions	reader's log	brainstorming
18. **A Man Reserves a Seat and Justice** (autobiography)	word web	visualize	predict	sequence/storyboard
19. **Ancestry** (autobiography)	anticipation guide	prediction	retell	opinion and support
20. **Rosa Parks** (interview)	skim	question	reciprocal reading	outlining
`21. **A Taste of War** (fiction)	picture walk	react	time line/sequence	brainstorming
22. **War Comes to Our Island** (fiction)	walk-through	question	story frame	topic sentence and supporting details
23 **Frustration** (fiction)	word web	question	reciprocal reading	quickwrite
24. **Hints** (essay)	web	mark	word attack	brainstorming

IV. Writing	Grammar/Usage	V. Assessment
paragraph	capitalization	understanding
descriptive paragraph	end punctuation	meaning
journal entry	articles	enjoyment
letter	commas	ease
personal narrative	fragments	depth
dialogue	punctuation and indents	style
summary	easily confused words	meaning
poem	easily confused words	understanding
story beginning	comma splices	enjoyment
story ending	run-ons	ease
autobiographical paragraph	capitalization	style
narrative paragraph	consistency	depth
character sketch	verbs	understanding
article	apostrophes	meaning
summary	commas	ease
expository paragraph	commas	enjoyment
anecdote	adjectives and adverbs	style
story	subject-verb agreement	depth
persuasive paragraph	commas	meaning
3-paragraph essay	abbreviations	understanding
story beginning	subject-verb agreement	depth
review	titles	style
journal entry	commas	ease
science-fiction story	capitalization	enjoyment

TEACHER'S GUIDE SKILLS AND STRATEGIES

The chart below identifies the strategies for each part of each teacher's edition lesson.

Selection	Vocab	Prereading	Comprehension
1. **High School: The Bad and the Good** (nonfiction)	antonyms	a) anticipation/reaction guide b) picture walk	a) directed reading b) graphic organizer
2. **Finding Patrick** (nonfiction)	context clues	a) read-aloud b) think-pair-and-share	double-entry journal
3. **It's Quiet Now** (fiction)	context clues	a) word web b) quickwrite	story map
4. **Survival** (autobiography)	context clues	a) skimming b) preview	a) reciprocal reading b) prediction
5. **How It Feels to Be Colored Me** (autobiography)	context clues	a) preview b) preview chart	a) word attack b) double-entry journal
6. **The Eatonville Anthology** (fiction)	homophones	a) think-pair-and-share b) K-W-L	a) directed reading b) story frame
7. **Visit to Africa** (autobiography)	synonyms	a) read-aloud b) picture walk	a) stop and predict b) graphic organizer
8. **Dear Tía and Papa** (poetry)	Mexican Spanish	a) word web b) read-aloud	a) double-entry journal b) graphic organizer
9. **The Guest Who Ran Away** (folktale)	irregular verbs	a) preview b) quickwrite	a) reciprocal reading b) graphic organizer
10. **The Price of Pride and How Si' Djeha Staved Off Hunger** (folktales)	suffixes	a) predict b) preview	a) storyboard b) story frame
11. **Puerto Rican Paradise** (autobiography)	root words	picture walk	sequence graphic organizer
12. **If You Ain't Got Heart, You Ain't Got Nada** (autobiography)	word analysis	quickwrite	graphic organizer
13. **Her Life Was Not a Joke** (nonfiction)	suffixes	a) anticipation guide b) picture walk	a) prediction b) double-entry jounral
14. **One Morning** (autobiography)	synonyms	a) think-pair-and-share b) quickwrite	a) storyboard b) directed reading
15. **The Knight in Person** (nonfiction)	pronunciation	a) K-W-L b) picture walk	a) directed reading b) graphic organizer
16. **The Victorious Feudal Knight** (nonfiction)	context clues	preview	graphic organizer
17. **Forgetfulness and An Unwritten Letter** (autobiography)	Greek prefix	read-aloud	a) reader's log b) double-entry journal
18. **A Man Reserves a Seat and Justice** (autobiography)	root words	word web	a) predict b) directed reading
19. **Ancestry** (autobiography)	prefixes	a) anticipation guide b) K-W-L	retell
20. **Rosa Parks** (interview)	synonyms	a) skim b) preview	reciprocal reading
21. **A Taste of War** (fiction)	idioms	picture walk	a) time line/sequence b) directed reading
22. **War Comes to Our Island** (fiction)	prefixes and suffixes	a) walk-through b) picture walk	a) story frames b) predictions
23. **Frustration** (fiction)	prefixes	a) word web b) read-aloud	a) reciprocal reading b) double-entry journal
24. **Hints** (essay)	word analysis	a) web b) quickwrite	a) word attack b) directed reading

Questions	Literary Skill	Prewriting	Assessment
a) comprehension b) critical thinking	expository nonfiction	a) narrowing a topic b) group discussion	multiple-choice test
a) comprehension b) critical thinking	tone	narrowing a topic	multiple-choice test
a) comprehension b) critical thinking	point of view	a) personal response b) group discussion	multiple-choice test
a) comprehension b) critical thinking	autobiography	summarize	multiple-choice test
a) comprehension b) critical thinking	metaphor	gather details	multiple-choice test
a) comprehension b) critical thinking	characterization	a) compare and contrast b) brainstorming	multiple-choice test
a) comprehension b) critical thinking	setting	a) main idea and supporting details b) group discussion	multiple-choice test
a) comprehension b) critical thinking	free verse	brainstorming	multiple-choice test
a) comprehension b) critical thinking	folktale	a) character attribute map b) brainstorming	multiple-choice test
a) comprehension b) critical thinking	conflict	a) sequencing a plot b) graphic organizer	multiple-choice test
a) comprehension b) critical thinking	tone	a) narrowing a topic b) storyboard	multiple-choice test
a) comprehension b) critical thinking	vernacular	a) group discussion b) cause and effect	multiple-choice test
a) comprehension b) critical thinking	author's purpose	a) graphic organizer b) topic sentence and details	multiple-choice test
a) comprehension b) critical thinking	chronological order	a) retell b) narrowing a topic	multiple-choice test
a) comprehension b) critical thinking	inference	a) main idea and details b) topic sentence	multiple-choice test
a) comprehension b) critical thinking	details	topic sentence and details	multiple-choice test
a) comprehension b) critical thinking	stream-of-consciousness	a) brainstorming b) anecdotes	multiple-choice test
a) comprehension b) critical thinking	theme	a) plot sequence b) storyboard	multiple-choice test
a) comprehension b) critical thinking	word choice	a) opinion and support b) group discussion	multiple-choice test
a) comprehension b) critical thinking	point of view	a) outlining b) graphic organizer	multiple-choice test
a) comprehension b) critical thinking	dialect	a) brainstorming b) story beginning	multiple-choice test
a) comprehension b) critical thinking	climax	topic sentence and supporting details	multiple-choice test
a) comprehension b) critical thinking	science fiction	a) summarize b) quickwrite	multiple-choice test
a) comprehension b) critical thinking	humor	brainstorming	multiple-choice test

CORRELATION TO *WRITERS INC @2001*

Like the *Writers INC* handbook, the *Sourcebook* will appeal to teachers who believe that writing is a way of learning or a means of discovery and exploration. Students pursue ideas and interpretations in the *Sourcebook*. They jot notes, create organizers, plan and brainstorm compositions, and write drafts of their work. The *Sourcebook* is one way students clarify in their minds what they have read and how they respond to it. And, in the end, students learn how to write different kinds of compositions—a paragraph, a description, a letter, a character sketch, a persuasive paragraph, or review.

Students are also invited to revise their compositions in a feature called Writers' Checklist. These features, found in Part IV Writing, highlight two or three critical questions and explain some aspect of grammar, usage, and mechanics. These features are brief mini-lessons. They invite students to look back at their writing and apply some aspect of grammar, usage, or mechanics to it.

In the *Sourcebooks*, both the kinds of writing and the mini-lessons on grammar, usage, and mechanics afford the best opportunities to use the *Writers INC* handbook as a reference. To make this convenient, both the writing activities and the mini-lessons are correlated below to the ©2001 *Writers INC* handbook.

Selection Title	Writing Activity/ Writers INC Reference (pages)	Writers' Mini-Lesson/ Writers INC Reference (pages)
1. High School: The Bad and the Good	paragraph 95–104	capitalization 475–477
2. Finding Patrick	descriptive paragraph 156–157	ending sentences with punctuation 455, 467
3. It's Quiet Now	journal entry 144–146	articles
4. Survival	letter 297–308	commas 457–461.3
5. How It Feels to Be Colored Me	personal narrative 140, 147–151	fragments 83–84
6. The Eatonville Anthology	dialogue 175, 468.3	punctuation
7. Visit to Africa	summary 403–404	easily confused words 491–500
8. Dear Tia *and* Papa	poem 179–184	easily confused words 491–500
9. The Guest Who Ran Away	story beginning 55	comma splices 84
10. The Price of Pride and How Si'Djeha Staved Off Hunger	story ending 58	run-on sentences 84
11. Puerto Rican Paradise	autobiographical paragraph	capitalization 475–477
12. If You Ain't Got Heart, You Ain't Got Nada	narrative paragraph 140, 147–151	consistency
13. Her Life Was Not A Joke	character sketch 156–157	verbs 507–512
14. One Morning	article 105–113	apostrophes 472–473
15. The Knight in Person	summary 403–404	commas 457–461.3
16. The Victorious Feudal Knight	expository paragraph 105–113	commas 457–461.3
17. Forgetfulness *and* An Unwritten Letter	anecdote 168–173 152–153	commas 457–461.3
18. A Man Reserves A Seat *and* Justice	story 168–173	subject-verb agreement 526–527

Selection Title	Writing Activity/ Writers INC Reference (pages)	Writers' Mini-Lesson/ Writers INC Reference (pages)
19. Ancestry	persuasive paragraph 98	commas 457–461.3
20. Rosa Parks	three-paragraph essay 227–232	abbreviations
21. A Taste of War	story beginning 55	subject-verb agreement 526–527
22. War Comes to Our Island	review 143–154	titles 468.1–470.2
23. Frustration	journal entry 144–146	commas 457–461.3
24. Hints	science fiction story 167–172	capitalization 475–477

OVERVIEW

The *Sourcebook* is directed to struggling readers. These students seldom receive adequate help, partly because they need so much. They need to be motivated. They need quality literature that they can actually read. They need good instruction in strategies that will help them learn how to transform a mass of words and lines into a comprehensible text. They need help with getting ready to write; with grammar, usage, and mechanics; and with writing different kinds of texts themselves—letters, journal entries, summaries, and so forth.

A Comprehensive Approach

Because of the multitude and enormity of their needs, struggling readers all too often are subjected to a barrage of different remedies. It is too easy simply to say "This doesn't work" and turn to yet another text or strategy. The *Sourcebook* takes a holistic approach, not a piecemeal one. Through a five-part lesson plan, each *Sourcebook* lesson walks the student through the steps needed to read actively and to write well about literature.

The five-part lesson plan is:

I. **BEFORE YOU READ** (prereading)

II. **READ** (active reading and responding to literature)

III. **GATHER YOUR THOUGHTS** (prewriting)

IV. **WRITE** (writing, revising, grammar, usage, and mechanics)

V. **WRAP-UP** (reflecting and self-assessment)

Through a comprehensive, structured approach, students can see the whole process of reading and writing. By following a consistent pattern, students can internalize the steps in the process, and they can move forward and experience success along the way, on a number of different fronts at once. See also the book and lesson organization on pages 18–22.

A Strategy-Intensive Approach

The *Sourcebook* is a strategy-intensive approach. Each *Sourcebook* builds students' repertoire of reading strategies in at least three areas.

1. To build motivation and background, prereading strategies are used to get students ready to read and to help them see the prior knowledge they already bring to their reading experiences.

2. To build active readers, each *Sourcebook* begins with an overview of interactive reading strategies (called response strategies), explicitly showing students six ways to mark up texts. Then, at least one of these strategies is used in each lesson.

3. To build comprehension, each *Sourcebook* uses six to nine different comprehension strategies, such as prediction, reciprocal reading, retelling, and using graphic organizers. By embedding these strategies in the literature, the *Sourcebook* shows students exactly which strategies to use and when to use them, building the habits of good readers.

A Literature-based Approach

Above all, the *Sourcebook* takes a literature-based approach. It presents 24 selections of quality literature of various genres by a wide range of authors. Some selections focus on literature; others are cross-curricular in emphasis, taking up a subject from history or geography; and others focus on issues of importance and relevance to today's students.

An Interactive Approach

The *Sourcebook* is, in addition, an interactive tool. It is intended to be a journal for students, where they can write out their ideas about texts, plan and write out compositions, and record their progress throughout the year. Students should "own" their *Sourcebooks*, carrying them, reading in them, marking in them, and writing in them. They should become a record of their progress and accomplishments.

On a day-to-day basis when teaching each lesson, teachers and students should use the Readers' Checklist for assessment:

UNDERSTANDING Did you understand the reading?

Was the message or point clear?

Can you restate what the reading is about?

Asking a different combination of 2-3 questions from the Readers' Checklist will help students become increasingly clear about why and how they are reading.

On a monthly basis, one of the best measures of student progress will be a student's marked up Sourcebook. Teacher-student conferences can use the following questions to reflect on the quality of a student's written responses among lessons:

a. In what ways has the content of your written responses improved?
   (e.g., accuracy, clarity, amount of comprehension)

b. In what ways has the structure of your written responses improved?
   (e.g., organization, coherence, neatness, spelling, punctuation)

c. In what ways is your reading improving?

d. What new reading habits are you finding useful? Why?

WHO IS THIS BOOK FOR?

Struggling Learners

Frequently high schools have classes specifically designed for students who consistently rank in the lower 50 percent of the class. Instead of the usual focus on literary masterworks, these classes focus on improving reading and writing skills and often are labeled with anonymous-sounding names, such as English I, Applied Communication, or Fundamentals of Reading and Writing. The *Sourcebook* was designed with such courses in mind. It offers a comprehensive program of student-appropriate literature, strategy building, writing, and revising. Quite often teachers in these classes pull an exercise from one text on the shelf, a reading from another, and a blackline master activity from still another. The materials are a patchwork, with the teachers making the best of the meager offerings available.

Each *Sourcebook* has a comprehensive network of skills (see pages 6–9) that brings together the appropriate literature, reading strategies for that literature, and prewriting, writing, and revising activities. Students who work through even two or three entire selections will benefit greatly by seeing the whole picture of reading actively and writing about the text. They will also benefit from the sense of accomplishment that comes through completion of a whole task and that results in creative, original work of their own—perhaps some of the first they have accomplished.

Reading Classes

Students who clearly are reading two or more levels below grade often are put into "special reading" courses. Quite often these classes feature a great number of blackline masters on discrete skills, such as "main idea and details," "analogies," and the like. Such classes are ideal for the *Sourcebook*. Instead of covering one discrete skill, each *Sourcebook* selection offers students reading strategies that they can use on any text, and it offers them high-quality literature. All too often students in reading classes are given "high-interest" materials. The materials have regulated vocabulary and short sentences and are on topics that range from natural disasters to biographies of rock divas. The *Sourcebook* focuses on high-quality literature that is also high interest because it addresses questions and issues of significance to students.

With the *Sourcebook*, a better choice exists. The literature was chosen specifically with struggling readers in mind. It offers compelling subjects, such as knights and chivalry, school days, and discrimination, and offers a worthy challenge for students.

ESL Classes

Students for whom English is a second language can also benefit from the *Sourcebook*, even though the *Sourcebook* is not an ESL program. The literature selections in the *Sourcebook* vary in difficulty level. The level for each selection is given on the first page of the *Teacher's Guide* lesson. But the subjects of the literature—immigrants, being an outsider, understanding different cultures—are ones that will naturally appeal to ESL students.

In addition, summaries of each selection appear in Spanish in the *Teacher's Guide*, along with additional help with vocabulary and comprehension. So, while not explicitly for ESL students, the program offers good support for them and may be more appropriate than some of the other materials they are currently using.

Alternative Settings

Many school systems also have whole schools or classes that are called "alternative" for students who for a variety of reasons are not mainstreamed. The *Sourcebook* is appropriate for these students as well, if only because of its literature selections, which focus on themes of identity, prejudice, and separateness, about which many alternative students will have a natural interest.

Summary

The ***Sourcebook*** cannot reach every struggling student. It is not a panacea. It will be helpful with struggling readers, especially those who are reading a grade level or two below their academic grade. The challenges struggling readers face, especially those reading more than two grades below their academic grade level, ought not be underestimated or minimized. Reading and writing deficits are hard, almost intractable problems for high school students and require a great amount of effort—on the part of the teacher and the student—to make any real improvement. The ***Sourcebook*** is one further tool in helping create better readers and writers.

FREQUENTLY ASKED QUESTIONS

Because the *Sourcebooks* were extensively reviewed by teachers, a number of commonly asked questions have surfaced already, and the answers to them might be helpful in using the program.

1. Why is it called a *Sourcebook*?

The word *Sourcebook* captures a number of connotations and associations that seemed just right. For one, it is published by Great Source Education Group. The word *source* also had the right connotation of "the place to go for a real, complete solution," as opposed to other products that help in only a limited area, such as "main idea" or "analogies." And, lastly, the term *Sourcebook* fits nicely alongside *Daybook*, another series also published by Great Source that targets better readers and writers who need help in fluency and critical reading, as opposed to this series, which targets struggling readers.

2. Can students write in the *Sourcebook*?

Absolutely. Only by physically marking the text will students become truly active readers. To interact with a text and truly read as an active reader, students *must* write in the *Sourcebook*. The immediacy of reading and responding right there on the page is integral to the whole idea of the *Sourcebook*. By writing in the text, students build a sense of ownership about their work that is impossible to match through worksheets handed out week after week. The *Sourcebook* also serves, in a sense, as the student's portfolio and can become one of the most tangible ways of demonstrating a student's progress throughout the year.

3. Can I photocopy these lessons?

No, you cannot. Each page of the pupil's book carries a notice that explicitly states "copying is prohibited." To copy them illegally infringes on the rights of the authors of the selections and the publishers of the book. Writers such as Maya Angelou, Piri Thomas, Bob Greene, and others have granted permission to use their work in the *Sourcebook*, but have not granted the right to copy it.

You can, however, copy the blackline masters in this *Teacher's Guide.* These pages are intended for teachers to photocopy and use in the classroom.

4. Can I skip around in the *Sourcebook*?

Teachers will naturally wish to adjust the *Sourcebook* to their curriculum. But a logical— that is, the optimum—order of the book is laid out in the table of contents. The difficulty of the literary selection, the kind and difficulty of writing assignments, the amount of scaffolding provided for a specific reading strategy—all are predicated on where they occur in the text. Easier assignments and selections, naturally, tend to cluster near the beginning of the *Sourcebook*; in the back half of the book, both the assignments and selections challenge students with more rigorous demands.

5. Where did the strategies used throughout the book come from?

Most of the reading strategies used are commonplace in elementary classrooms throughout the country. They are commonly described in the standard reading education textbooks, as well as at workshops, conferences, and in-services. What is unusual in the *Sourcebook* is the way these strategies have been applied to high school–appropriate literature.

6. Why did you label the strategies with names such as "stop and think" when it is really just directed reading or some other reading technique?

The pupil's edition of the *Sourcebook* uses student-friendly terms, such as "stop and think," "retell," or "stop and record." Throughout, an attempt was made to motivate students, not hammer them with pedagogical terms. Leaden-sounding names for reading strategies (for example, "directed reading strategy" or "reciprocal reading") seemed counterproductive for students, even while being perfectly descriptive to teachers. The same logic explains why such student-friendly titles as "Before You Read" were used instead of "Prereading." In the *Teacher's Guide*, reference is frequently made to the more formal pedagogical term ("directed reading") alongside the friendlier student term ("stop and think").

7. Has anyone told you that the *Sourcebook* doesn't follow the textbook definition of a number of strategies?

Yes, absolutely. Teachers who reviewed the *Sourcebooks* were quick to mention that "textbook" definitions and application of strategies were not followed. One clear example is reciprocal reading. It is an intervention strategy where a reading partner or teacher works with a student to clarify, question, predict, and summarize; but the *Sourcebook* is a text, not a walking-and-breathing reading tutor. As a result, the questioning strategy of reciprocal reading is employed in the *Sourcebook*, with full knowledge that the technique cannot be perfectly replicated using a book. Yet the force of these strategies seemed too potent simply to discard, so, like any good teacher, the *Sourcebook* authors adapted a strategy to fit their particular needs.

8. How were the selections chosen and what is their readability?

The decision to use "real" or "quality" literature by well-known authors was, in fact, made by teachers. They selected the authors they wanted to use with their students. They insisted that the quality and force of the literature itself—not its readability—become the primary selection criteria for the literature. Especially when a selection would become the focal point of an extended lesson, the literature had to be primary. "If my students are going to spend several days on a lesson, the literature needs to be worth spending time and attention on it," one early reviewer said.

Plus, they insisted that their struggling readers be challenged. Among teachers of struggling readers, a consistent appeal was that the literature challenge their students, yet also give them lots of support. Challenge and support were the watchwords that guided the development of the *Sourcebook* program. Choosing high-quality literature was the first consideration; secondarily, the syntactical difficulty, sentence length, and vocabulary level were also considered.

9. How can I know if my students can read this literature?

Teachers have a number of ways to know how well their students can read the selections. For one, they can simply try out a lesson or two.

Second, teachers can also use a 20- or 30-word vocabulary pretest as a quick indicator. For each selection, randomly select 20 words. Ask students to circle the ones they know and underline the ones they don't know. If students know only one to 5 or 6 to 9 words, then the selection will probably be frustrating for them. Spend some time preteaching the key vocabulary.

10. What if my students need even more help than what's in the book?

This *Teacher's Guide* has been designed as the next level of support. Extra activities and blackline masters on vocabulary, comprehension, prewriting, and assessment are included here so that they can be used at the teacher's discretion. Parts of each lesson could have been scaffolded for five to ten more pages, but at a certain point more worksheets and more explanation become counterproductive. Teachers advised the authors again and again to give students worthwhile literature and activities and let the students work at them. Students' work will not be perfect, but, with the right tools, students will make progress.

ORGANIZATION

Book Organization

Each **Sourcebook** has 24 selections organized into three general categories:

1. Contemporary Issues
2. Cross-curricular Subjects
3. Literature

The purpose of this organization is to provide selections that are relevant and purposeful in students' lives. By pairing selections, students can take the time to build extended background on a topic or idea (for example, Apartheid, Arab folktales), building upon knowledge they gained in earlier selections. Each of the 12 units in the **Sourcebook** is introduced by an opener that helps teachers build background on the subject. Ways to teach and introduce each opener are included in the **Teacher's Guide**.

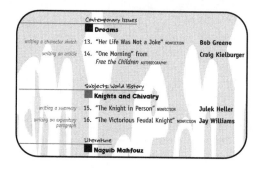

Lesson Organization

Each lesson in the **Sourcebook** has five parts:

I. Before You Read

- Each lesson begins with **I. Before You Read** to emphasize to students how important prereading is. The lesson starts with an introductory statement that draws students into the lesson, often by asking a provocative question or making a strong statement.

- The prereading step—the critical first step—builds background and helps students access prior knowledge. Among the prereading strategies (see page 6) included in Part I of this **Sourcebook** are:

  - Think-Pair-and-Share
  - K-W-L
  - Anticipation Guide
  - Preview or Walk-through
  - Skimming
  - Picture Walk
  - Quickwrite
  - Word Web

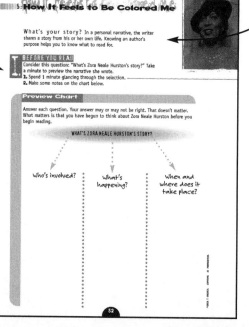

II. Read

- The reading step, called **II. Read,** begins with an invitation to read and suggestions for how to respond to the literature and mark up the text. An example is provided.

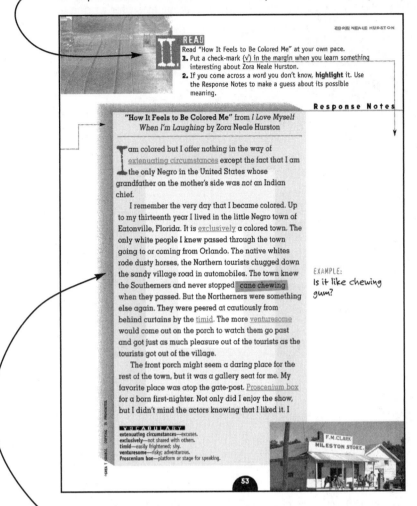

- The selection follows, with the difficult vocabulary highlighted throughout the selection and defined at the bottom of the page.

- Then, within the selection, a powerful comprehension strategy is embedded to help build in students the habits of good readers. Among the comprehension strategies included (see also page 50 in Part II of this **Sourcebook**) are these:

  - Predict

  - Stop and Think (directed reading)

  - Stop and Clarify, Question, Predict (reciprocal reading)

  - Storyboard (using graphic organizers)

  - Double-entry Journal

  - Retelling

  - Story Frame

III. Gather Your Thoughts

- The prewriting step is called **III. Gather Your Thoughts**. It starts with the literature selection. Through two or three carefully sequenced activities, the prewriting step helps students go back into the literature in preparation for writing about it.

Among the more common prewriting activities are these:

- Character Map

- Main Idea and Supporting Details

- Brainstorming

- Building a Topic Sentence

- Forming an Opinion

- Supporting a Main Idea

IV. Write

- The writing step begins with step-by-step instructions for building a writing assignment. Taken together, these instructions form the writing rubric for students to use in building the assignment. Among the writing assignments students are asked to write are these:

  - Paragraph with Topic Sentence and Supporting Details

  - Narrative Paragraph

  - Expository Paragraph

  - Compare and Contrast paragraph

  - Paragraph of Reflection

  - Autobiographical Paragraph

  - Journal Entry

  - Story

  - Character Sketch

  See page 7 for a full list.

WRITE
Use Hurston's writing as a model to write a **personal narrative** about an experience.
1. Use the topic sentence and details you developed on the previous page.
2. Use the Writers' Checklist to help you revise.

Title:

WRITERS' CHECKLIST

FRAGMENTS
❏ Did you avoid writing sentence fragments? A sentence fragment is a group of words that may start with a capital letter and finish with an end punctuation mark but is not a complete sentence.
To fix a fragment you may need to add a subject or a verb, eliminate or add words, or combine the fragment with another sentence.
EXAMPLES: The girls laughing on the porch. (fragment) The girls laughed on the porch. (sentence) The girls laughing on the porch seemed happy. (sentence)

62

- Each **IV. Write** also includes a **Writers' Checklist**. Each one is a brief mini-lesson on a relevant aspect of grammar, usage, or mechanics. The intent of the **Writers' Checklist** is to ask of the students appropriate questions after they write, instilling the habit of going back to revise, edit, and proof their work. The **Writers' Checklist** also affords teachers the opportunity to teach relevant grammar, usage, and mechanics skills at a teachable moment.

V. Wrap-up

- The last step of each lesson is to reflect. Students are asked a question about their reading and writing experience from the **Readers' Checklist**. This "looking back" is intended to help students see what they learned in the lesson. They are intentionally asked more than simply, "Did you understand?"

- For good readers, reading is much, much more than "Did you get it?" Good readers read for pleasure, for information, for the pure enjoyment of reading artfully written material, for personal curiosity, for a desire to learn more, and countless other reasons. So that students will begin to see that reading is worthwhile to them, they need to believe the payoff is more than "Did you get it?" on a five-question multiple-choice test.

- The **Sourcebook** attempts with **V. Wrap-up** to help students ask the questions good readers ask of themselves when they read. It attempts to broaden the reasons for reading by asking students to consider six reasons for reading:

  - Meaning

  - Enjoyment

  - Understanding

  - Style

  - Ease

  - Depth

Organization

TEACHER'S LESSON PLANS

Each lesson plan for the teacher of the **Sourcebook** has eight pages:

PAGE 1 Overview and Background

- The chart at the beginning of each lesson plan gives an "at-a-glance" view of the skills and strategies, plus the difficulty level of the reading and five key vocabulary words.

- Background on the author and selection and a graphic are included.

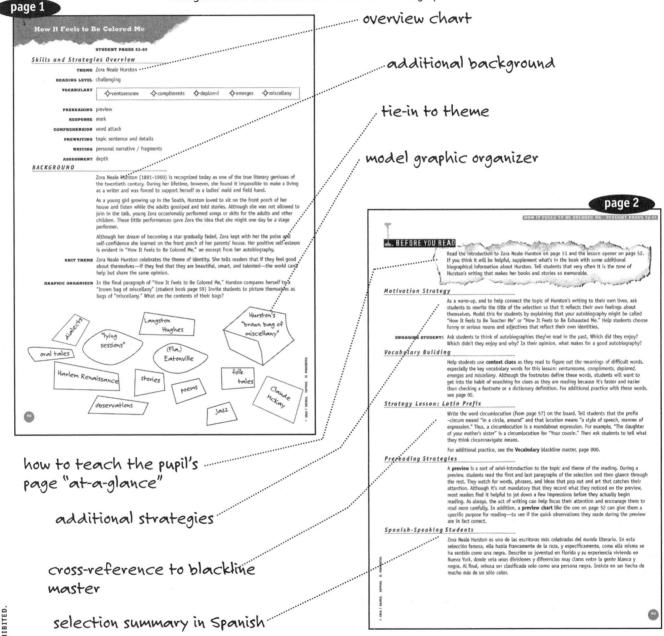

overview chart

additional background

tie-in to theme

model graphic organizer

how to teach the pupil's page "at-a-glance"

additional strategies

cross-reference to blackline master

selection summary in Spanish

PAGE 2 Before You Read

- The first page of the teacher's plan begins with a motivation strategy and a suggestion for vocabulary building. Additional prereading strategies are suggested, along with a summary of the selection in Spanish.

Each lesson plan in the **Sourcebook Teacher's Guide** follows the pupil's lesson step-by-step.

PAGE 3 **Read**

- The response strategy gives students one way to interact with the text as they read.

- Additional comprehension strategies are suggested, along with a *Comprehension* blackline master found later in the lesson.

- The discussion questions cover both literal and interpretative levels of thinking.

- A literary skill is suggested for each selection, allowing teachers to build literary appreciation as they provide basic support with reading comprehension.

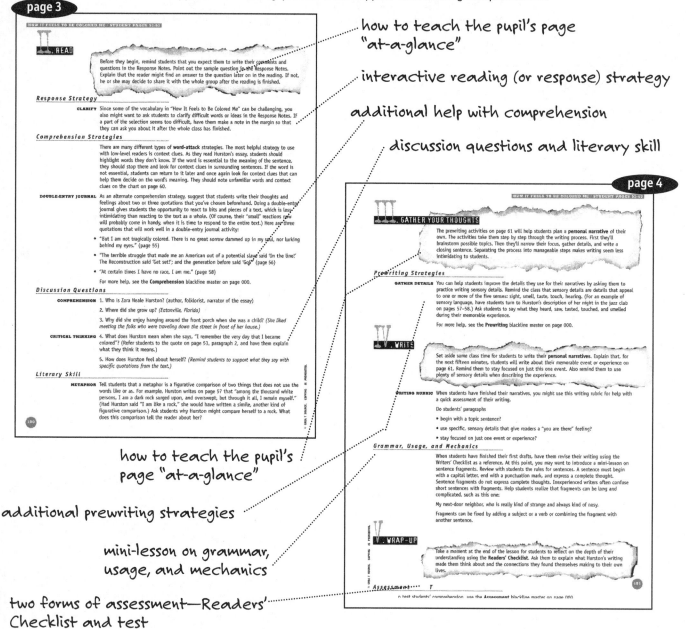

how to teach the pupil's page "at-a-glance"

interactive reading (or response) strategy

additional help with comprehension

discussion questions and literary skill

how to teach the pupil's page "at-a-glance"

additional prewriting strategies

mini-lesson on grammar, usage, and mechanics

two forms of assessment—Readers' Checklist and test

PAGE 4 **Gather Your Thoughts, Write, Wrap-up**

- The page begins with additional help with prewriting and references another blackline master that offers additional support.

- Next, the students write and are directed to the **Writers' Checklist** in the pupil's book, which gives the grammar, usage, and mechanics mini-lesson.

- The writing rubric gives teachers a way to evaluate students' writing.

- The lesson ends with reference to the **Readers' Checklist** in the pupil's book, encourages students to reflect on what they have read, and cross-references the **Assessment** blackline master.

Each lesson plan in the *Sourcebook Teacher's Guide* has four blackline masters for additional levels of support for key skill areas.

PAGE 5 Vocabulary

- Each **Vocabulary** blackline master helps students learn the meanings of five words from the literature selection and focuses on an important vocabulary strategy, such as understanding prefixes, root words, and word families.

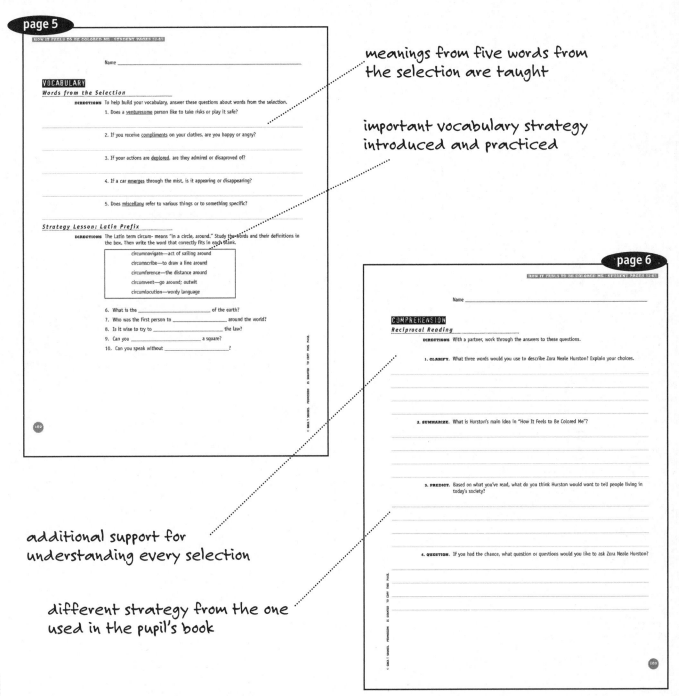

meanings from five words from the selection are taught

important vocabulary strategy introduced and practiced

additional support for understanding every selection

different strategy from the one used in the pupil's book

PAGE 6 Comprehension

- Each **Comprehension** blackline master affords teachers still another way to build students' understanding of the selection, using a different strategy from the one found in the *Sourcebook*.

PAGE 7 Prewriting

- Occasionally students will need even more scaffolding than appears in the pupil's lesson as they prepare for the writing assignment.
- The "extra step" in preparing to write is the focus of the **Prewriting** blackline master.

PAGE 8 Assessment

- Each lesson in the *Sourcebook* ends with the opportunity for students to reflect on their reading with the **Readers' Checklist**. This self-assessment is an informal inventory of what they learned from the reading.
- The **Assessment** blackline master gives a multiple-choice test on the selection and suggests a short-essay question for a more formal assessment.

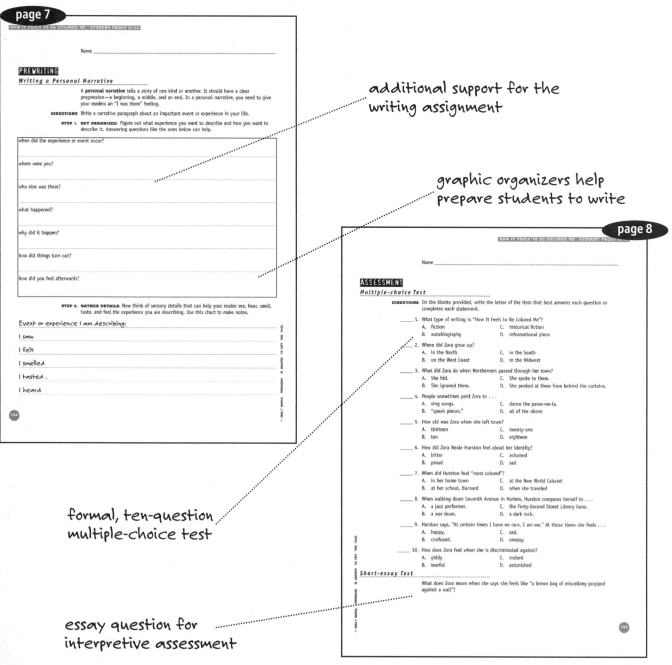

additional support for the writing assignment

graphic organizers help prepare students to write

formal, ten-question multiple-choice test

essay question for interpretive assessment

Teaching Struggling Readers

BY DR. RICHARD G. RAMSEY

What It Means to Teach

I enjoy being an educator. . . . We have the best job in the world, because we touch the future every day. We are in the business of making dreams come true for children. . . . And every day that I get up I'm excited about just going to work because now I know I have an opportunity to touch another life. . . . We have so many kids right now in our country coming to us from all walks of life, walking through our school doors every single day. When they walk through those doors, they're looking for one thing: they have open eyes, open minds, and open hearts seeking your validation. . . . The last thing children need to have done to them when they walk into your classroom is to be discouraged. They need hope, they need to be inspired by you every single day. . . .

The names of those who practice our profession read like a hall of fame for humanity: Booker T. Washington, Buddha, Confucius, Ralph Waldo Emerson, Leo Buscaglia, and many, many others. . . . Through and through the course of being a teacher, I've been called upon to be an actor, a nurse, a doctor, a coach, a finder of lost articles, a money lender, a taxicab driver, and also a keeper of the faith. I'm a paradox and I speak loudest when I listen the most to my students. I, as a teacher, am the most fortunate person who labors. A doctor is allowed to bring life into the world in one magic moment, but I, as a teacher, I am allowed to see that life is reborn each and every day with new questions, ideas, and friendship. I'm a warrior doing battle every single day against peer pressure, negativity, fear, conformity, and prejudice. . . .

Elements of Teaching

ATTITUDE But there are three things I always say that a teacher has to have to be able to survive: The first thing you have to have is the proper attitude. . . . I say attitudes are contagious, is yours worth catching? . . . Our attitude plays a big role when we're dealing with children and I tell myself to come to school smiling every day, be happy. . . . Children are looking for you to be that positive example for them. . . . Every day we have two choices. . . . You can complain about your job every day and let children fail or you can begin to love what you do every single day and make sure that every child has the opportunity to be successful. . . .

Life is a challenge. We are challenged with diverse populations that we're not accustomed to working with. Life is a gift. Teach our children that you only go around one time and it's not a practice run. Respect the gift of life. Life is an adventure. . . . Life is also a saga . . . and teach our kids that there will be a better tomorrow if they just hold on and don't quit. Life is also a tragedy; unfortunately we are going to lose kids to homicide, drug abuse, and all kinds of dreadful diseases. And I say, hold on to those that we have because they are our future. Life is also a duty; you have a duty as a teacher to teach every child the way you would want somebody to teach yours, and if you do that, you've done your duty for that day. Life is also a game; be the best player so you can help children. Life is an opportunity; take advantage of it and make sure that the children understand that opportunities in life only come one time. Life is also a struggle; fight it with every ounce of energy that you have to do the best with children. Life is also a goal; set goals for yourself, set goals for the children. But more importantly, make sure that you work with them so they can achieve the goals they've set. Finally, life is a puzzle; but if all of us today take back what we have and work together as a team, we can solve that puzzle and make sure that children are successful in life. To teach is to heal, to teach is to love, to teach is to care, to teach is to set high expectations. You are a teacher. There are many kids waiting for you and looking in your eyes every day and saying, "I need your help, I need your motivation." But remember, you don't motivate with fear. You may get compliance, but you certainly won't get commitment.

CARE Good teaching, as I tell my teachers all the time, does not come from behind the desk, it comes from behind the heart. . . . And kids know whether you care about them, and kids can be successful because excellence can be obtained if you just care more than other people think is wise, risk more than others think is safe, dream more than others think is practical, and expect out of your students more than others think is possible. An unspoken belief can teach young minds what they should be. You as a teacher can make that difference. . . . Remember, good teachers explain, superior teachers demonstrate. The great teachers, they inspire their students every single day. And if a kid can be inspired by you, he's going to want to come to your class every day, he's going to give you his best or her best every single day. . . .

COMMITMENT I'm going to tell a little story to you called, "Three Letters of Teddy."

"Teddy's letter came today and now that I've read it, I will place it in my cedar chest with the other things that are important in my life. I, as a teacher, had not seen Teddy Starlin since he was a student in my fifth-grade class 15 years ago. It was early in my career and I had only been teaching for 2 years. From the first day he stepped into my class, I disliked him. Teachers are not supposed to dislike any child, but I did and I showed my dislike to this young boy."

Any teacher would tell you it's more of a pleasure to teach a bright child. It's definitely more rewarding to one's ego with any teacher, with their credentials, a challenge working with a bright child and keeping them challenged and learning while they spend a major effort for those students who need help. Any teacher can do this, most teachers do, but she said she didn't, not that year. In fact, she concentrated on her best students and let the others follow along the best they could. Ashamed as she is to admit it, she took pleasure in using her red pen. And every time she came to Teddy's paper, the cross marks, and they were many, were always a little larger and a little redder than necessary. While she didn't actually ridicule the boy, her attitude, ladies and gentlemen, was obvious and quite apparent to the whole class for he quickly became the class goat, the outcast, the unlovable and the unloved child in that classroom. He didn't know why she didn't like him, nor did she know why she had such an intent dislike for this boy. All he wanted was somebody just to care about him, and she made no effort on his behalf. . . .

She knew that Teddy would never catch up in time to be promoted to the sixth-grade level. She said he would be a repeater. And to justify herself, she went to his folder from time to time. He had very low grades for the first 4 years but not failures. How he had made it, she said, she didn't know. But she closed her mind to all of the personal remarks in Teddy's folder. It said: first grade—Teddy shows promise by working attitude but has poor home situation. Second grade—Teddy could do better but his mother is terminally ill and he receives no help at home. Third grade—Teddy's a pleasant boy, helpful but too serious, slow learner. His mother, she passed away at the end of the year. Fourth grade—very slow but well behaved. His father shows no interest at all. She said, well, they passed him four times but he would certainly repeat the fifth grade, she said, it would do him good.

And then the last day before the holidays arrived, the little tree on the reading table supported paper and popcorn chains and many gifts were underneath the tree awaiting a big moment. Teachers always get several gifts at Christmas, she said, but hers that year were more elaborate than ever. Every child had brought her a gift and each unwrapping brought squeals of delight and the proud giver received profusive thank yous. His gift wasn't the last one she picked up; in fact, it was in the middle of the pile. Its wrapping was a brown paper bag and he had colored Christmas trees and red bells all over it and it was stuck together with masking tape. And it read "for Ms. Thompson, from Teddy, I love you." The group was completely silent, and for the first time she felt very embarrassed because all of the students stood there watching her unwrap that gift. And as she removed the last bit of masking tape, two items fell to her desk, a gaudy rhinestone bracelet with several stones missing and a small bottle of dime store cologne half empty. She heard the snickers and the whispers from the students and she wasn't even sure that she could hold her head up and look at Teddy, but she said, "Isn't this lovely." And she asked Teddy to come up to help her fasten the clasp. He smiled as he fixed the clasp on her arm and then there were finally a few hesitant oohs and ahs from the students. But as she dabbed the cologne behind her ears, all the little girls got up to get a dab behind theirs. She continued to open the gifts until she reached the bottom of the pile. They ate their refreshments and the bell rang. The children filed out and shouted, "See you next year, Merry Christmas," but Teddy, he waited at his desk. When they all had left, he walked toward her clutching his books and his gift to his chest with tears streaming down his face and he said to her, you smell just like my mom, her bracelet looks real pretty on you, too. I'm glad you like it. He left quickly. She got up and locked the door, sat at her desk, and wept resolvedly to make Teddy what she had deprived him of, to be a teacher who cared.

She stayed every afternoon with Teddy until the last day of school. Slowly but surely, he caught up with the rest of the class. Gradually, there was a definite upward curve in his grades. He didn't have to repeat the fifth grade; in fact, his average was among the highest in the class. Even though he was moving next year with his father, she wasn't worried because Teddy had reached a level that would serve him anywhere, because her teaching training had taught her that success deals success. She didn't hear from Teddy until seven years later when his first letter appeared in the mailbox. It said, "Dear Ms. Thompson, I want you to be the first to know that I'll be graduating second in my class next month, very truly yours, Teddy Starlin." She sent him a congratulatory card, wondering what he would do after graduation. Four years later she received another letter. It said, "Dear Ms. Thompson, I want you to be the first to know that I was just informed that I will be graduating first in my class. The university hasn't been easy; however, I liked it." She sent him silver monogrammed cufflinks and a card, so proud of him that she could burst. The final note came from him. It said, "Dear Ms. Thompson, I want you to be the first to know that as of today I am Theodore J. Starlin, M.D., how about that?" He said, "I'm going to be married in July, to be exact, and I want to ask you if you would come and do me a big favor, I would like you to come to my wedding and sit where my mom would have been if she was alive. I have no family now because my dad died last year. Ms. Thompson, you are all I have left, please come to my wedding, very truly yours, Teddy Starlin." She said, "I'm not sure what kind of gift one sends to a doctor on completion of medical school and state board; maybe I'll just wait and take a wedding gift," but she said, "my note cannot wait." It said, "Dear Ted, congratulations, you made it, you did it yourself. In spite of those like me and not because of us, this day has come for you. God bless you and I'll be at your wedding with bells on."

You have a lot of students like that in your classroom right now; all they need is a push. These kids are coming to us and they're looking for that special person to be there for them. . . .

RESPONSIBILITY We have a responsibility to touch the lives of children. But the question is: "Are we walking away from the children who need us, or are we coming to them and picking them up when they fall down? Children are not responsible for their parents, they are not responsible for where they live, they're only trying to make it with the conditions that they have. . . . Don't quit on children. Let them know they can be somebody. . . .

NOTE The article above is a transcript adapted from a lecture.

BY DR. ROBERT PAVLIK

REFLECTIONS • What was one of your most valuable learning experiences that involved reading and writing?

• What made the learning experience so valuable? So memorable?

Defining Expert Readers and Writers

Experts in various professions have extensive content knowledge and efficient skills:

> . . . experts have acquired extensive knowledge that affects what they notice and how they organize, represent, and interpret information in their environments. This, in turn, affects their abilities to remember, reason, and solve problems. (Bransford, Brown, and Cocking, 1999)

Novices, in contrast, lacking extensive content knowledge and efficient skills, tend to make confusing interpretations, record and retrieve information laboriously, and solve problems inaccurately.

The overall goal of the *Sourcebook* is to build expert readers and writers, learners who develop extensive content knowledge and efficient skills for using reading and writing to meet their needs within and beyond school. Expert readers and writers also develop their own "voices" for interacting within and among families, fellow learners, and community members. Far too many high school students, especially those at the lower end of the academic spectrum, lack extensive content knowledge or efficient skills. As a result, they can become confused, confusing, inefficient, and ineffective when attempting to use reading and writing to meet their needs. In addition, far too many high school students do not develop their own "voices."

REFLECTIONS • For which school subjects were you a novice or an expert reader? A novice or expert writer? How did you know?

• How would you describe your "voice" in high school today?

• Which of your recent/current students would you describe as novice or expert readers? As novice or expert writers? How do you know?

• How would you describe the "voices" of your students?

Using Culturally Diverse Literature

Rapidly changing national demographics require us to reconsider what fiction and nonfiction literature we include in our curricula. In essence, to what extent do we study the literature from and about people who helped shape the United States, and to what extent do we study the literature from and about people who shape the United States today and are shaping the future of the United States?

The *Sourcebook* provides fiction and nonfiction selections that represent current demographics of high school students. Approximately 60 percent of the selections represent traditional ideas and values, while the remaining 40 percent represent the ideas and values of several other cultures. This range of culturally diverse literature provides optional selections for meeting students' needs to

• understand themselves.

• understand the worldviews and culture of the United States.

• understand others.

• understand the worldviews and cultures of other countries.

For students, this range of culturally diverse literature provides meaningful, authentic opportunities to read and write and to learn new and familiar vocabulary in a variety of contexts. In addition, the breadth and depth of the selections can inspire further student reading, student-teacher discussions, and student-student discussions.

REFLECTIONS
- How culturally diverse was the fiction you studied as a high school student? The nonfiction?

- How valuable was the literature you studied in high school for the four needs cited above?

- What are the demographics of your students?

- What cultures and "voices" must your literature selections address?

Using an Interactive Instructional Approach

Current approaches for improving the reading and writing of high school students range

- from telling students to "practice, practice, practice" their reading and writing. In essence, teachers tell students to read a lot to become better readers and write a lot to become better writers.

- to identifying a student's level of skill mastery for reading and writing and, then, organizing students into groups for appropriate reading and writing skills instruction.

- to inviting students to discover their own strategies through teacher-guided discussions.

- to creating stimulating environments and meaningful projects around significant themes that motivate students to build and refine their uses of reading, writing, speaking, listening, and viewing.

All of these approaches to instruction have proven effective in recent decades, especially with populations of similar students. However, increasing numbers of high school students represent diverse cultures, perform well below their potential, speak English only in school, and attend school irregularly.

Vygotsky's thinking (1978) inspires and informs much of our approach to instruction. We believe that today's high school students can become expert readers and writers despite the challenges confronting them. To do so, students need

- meaningful, authentic fiction and nonfiction.

- an approach to instruction that respects how they are trying to learn within their fragmented, often chaotic lives.

- teachers and materials that direct and guide them to form, state, and test strategies for reading with peers and adults.

Therefore, our overall instructional approach involves modeling what expert readers and writers do as they negotiate with fiction and nonfiction and, then, inviting students to adapt what they learn from the modeling to their own reading and writing strategies. In the process, students can build and refine their thinking with others in order to apply the strategies on their own as needed.

For example, the *Sourcebook* opens with a feature entitled **"Responding to Literature"** that directs and invites students to

- see examples of written responses to ideas in a short selection from an expert reader-writer.

- engage a strategy sheet for making similar responses.

- make similar responses to a short selection on their own.

We apply this overall instructional approach throughout the *Sourcebook*.

• What instructional approaches did your teachers apply to improve your reading and writing?

• Which approaches did you as a high school student find valuable? Not valuable?

• As a teacher, what instructional approaches have you found effective and why? Ineffective and why?

Teaching Meaning-making Strategies

Research studies on expert readers and writers reveal two important insights:

• Expert readers and writers will use a variety of strategies automatically when they encounter new and difficult tasks—strategies that novice readers and writers would not use.

• A number of reading and writing strategies have been developed and can be taught (Paris, Wasik, and Turner, 1991; Dahl and Farnan, 1998).

Within our five-part lesson framework for each piece of fiction and nonfiction, students apply several meaning-making strategies to become expert readers and writers.

Part I. Before You Read

Struggling novice readers tend to avoid most types of reading in and outside of school. Even some expert readers often choose to spend only a few minutes each day reading in and outside of school, on either assigned or independent reading. The reasons why high school students choose not to read range from having poor reading skills to responding to peer pressure and even gender expectations.

The *Sourcebook* addresses these avoidance behaviors by presenting two prereading strategies per selection and guiding students to apply the strategies successfully. We assign specific strategies for each selection to get students doing something before they read, e.g., asking their opinions, engaging with a sample from the selection to read, or responding to a quick survey about their expectations. Our prereading strategies applied among the selections include these:

• Walking through a selection

• Using an anticipation guide

• Using K-W-L

• Using word webs

• Using a read-aloud

• Using a think-pair-and-share

• Previewing

• Skimming and scanning

Initially, engaging students in the prereading strategies motivates them to "get into" any selection. Eventually, students apply these prereading strategies to build background, activate prior knowledge, or raise questions that become part of the purpose for reading. With consistent practice, coaching, and guided reflection over the use of prereading strategies, students can build and refine their own lifetime prereading strategies.

Part II. Read

Novice readers usually do not choose to read with pencil in hand and mark up the text. Their reasons range from fearing to write in the text to not having a personal system of symbols for their responses, to fearing to make their "thinking tracks" public, to not having accurate language for describing the author's content and structure in annotations. Expert readers typically mark up a text, though not always. They will often mark up texts in which they find new or difficult information. They will rarely mark up texts in which they find familiar, easy-to-access or easy-to-remember information.

The *Sourcebook* addresses these varying comfort levels by presenting one or more interactive reading strategies per selection and guiding students to apply the strategies successfully. Our goal is to get students actually to write in their texts. The interactive reading strategies include these:

- Marking and highlighting

- Questioning

- Clarifying

- Visualizing

- Predicting

- Reading and connecting

The major purposes of these interactive reading strategies are to help students learn how and when to mark up texts and how to focus on specific content or structures of texts. Later, as their abilities develop for describing, labeling, commenting on, and reorganizing the information they read, students may find that these strategies slow down rather than accelerate their reading—a behavior indicating that they are becoming more expert readers.

Struggling novice readers often find themselves reading with no understanding or, even worse, reading with their eyes closed and imagining they are making sense of a piece of fiction or nonfiction. Expert readers develop new levels of understanding each time they read whole texts or parts of texts. They have learned where to pause and reread and how to apply any of several strategies to help understand what they read.

The comprehension strategies applied in the *Sourcebook* include these:

- Directed reading

- Predicting

- Using graphic organizers

- Using reciprocal reading questions

- Retelling

- Making double-entry journals

We assign one of these tried-and-true strategies to the appropriate types of fiction and nonfiction. Our goal is to model how expert readers come to understand a text. Ultimately, after students experiment with a variety of comprehension strategies, they will modify the strategies for their purposes until the strategies are no longer recognizable as they are developed in the *Sourcebook*—another indication of an expert reader in the making.

Part III. Gather Your Thoughts

Struggling novice writers usually do not choose to engage in any prewriting activities when they have a choice. Expert writers, while they vary widely in the breadth and depth of their prewriting strategies, view prewriting activities as the time when personally significant learning takes place. Prewriting activities provide the time and the means for engaging in critical and creative thinking.

Part III of the *Sourcebook* presents one or more prewriting strategies per selection. Students receive step-by-step guidance for applying each strategy successfully. The prereading strategies we apply among the selections include these:

- Discussing in pairs and small groups

- Clustering details

- Drawing a place

- Brainstorming

- Quickwriting

- Using anecdotes

- Comparing and contrasting

- Using a graphic organizer

- Using storyboards

Most of these prewriting activities involve two or more persons. Most thinking is social, according to Vygotsky; group interactions following various learning experiences, including reading and before writing, provide students with valuable opportunities to develop, refine, and internalize their purposes and plans for writing.

Part IV. Write

Struggling novice writers often think of completing a writing assignment as involving a two-step, one-time process—just sit down and write. They often postpone completing writing assignments, thinking that once they sit down and write, they can complete the assignment in one work session. Expert writers think of completing a writing assignment as involving several steps, e.g., narrowing the topic, planning, gathering data, drafting, revising one or more times, sharing, and publishing; personalizing ways to complete each of the steps; and involving more than one work session.

The *Sourcebook* invites students to engage in several small writing tasks. Note the types of writing listed in the Table of Contents to the left of each selection title. The writing tasks become increasingly larger so that students come to view the writing process as a series of recursive, interlocking steps. When students present and reflect on their best writing samples, they come to understand how the writing process varies among types of writing and among students—another indication of an expert writer.

Part V. Wrap-up

Being able to answer such reflection questions as these indicates how well readers and writers understand the fiction and nonfiction selections they study.

1. UNDERSTANDING Did I understand? How do I know?

Is the message or point clear?

Can I restate what it was about?

2. EASE Was it easy to read?

Was I able to read it smoothly and without difficulty?

3. MEANING Did I learn something or take away something from it?

Did it affect me or make an impression?

4. STYLE Did I find it well written?

Was the writing well crafted? Were the sentences well constructed? Were the words well chosen?

Does it show me how to be a better writer?

5. DEPTH Did it make me think about things?

Did it set off thoughts beyond the surface topic?

What are the immediate implications for me? Others?

What are the long-term implications for me? Others?

6. ENJOYMENT Did I like it?

Was the experience pleasurable?

Would I want to reread it or recommend it to someone?

Answering such questions as these honestly and consistently for a wide variety of texts and purposes indicates that a learner is becoming an expert reader.

REFLECTIONS What strategies do you find personally valuable

- for prereading?

- for reading?

- for gathering your thoughts?

- for writing?

- for reflecting on your reading and writing?

• What are your roles when using the *Sourcebook* to build expert readers and writers? How might your roles change during this school year?

• How can you create the most significant learning experiences when your students use reading and writing?

REFERENCES Bransford, J. D., A. L. Brown, and R. R. Cocking, eds. *How People Learn: Brain, Mind, Experience and School*. Washington, D.C.: National Academy Press, 1999.

Cawelti, G., ed. *Handbook of Research on Improving Student Achievement*. 2nd ed. Arlington, Va.: Educational Research Service, 1999.

Graves, M., and B. Graves. *Scaffolding Reading Experiences: Designs for Student Success*. Norwood, Mass.: Christopher-Gordon Publishers, 1994.

BY CATHERINE MCNARY

The Situation in High School

In high school, strategic reading is an essential learning tool. Unlike grade school, in which the learning environment is child-centered and focused on learning to learn, the high school is departmentalized and focused on the learning of subject area content. Two primary learning mediums are used to disseminate information—classroom lecture and textbook reading. The high school student is expected to have sufficient vocabulary, background knowledge, metacognitive strategies, and motivation to translate textbook print into usable, applicable information.

For some students, the expectations are realistic. For many, they are not. (The 1998 NAEP assessment stated that 31 percent of fourth graders, 33 percent of eighth graders, and 40 percent of twelfth graders attained a proficient level of reading [Donahue, Voelkl, Campbell, & Mazzeo, 1999].) What happens with the 67 percent of students in eighth grade and the 60 percent of students in twelfth grade who are not proficient readers? What strategies and teaching methods have been proven to provide this group with the best possible instruction in reading so that they, like their more able peers, may keep pace with the high school curriculum?

In the literature, five traits have been identified that provide readers with the cognitive tools to learn from text: general cognitive capacity, reader strategies and metacognition, inferential and reasoning abilities, background knowledge, and basic reading skills (Van Den Broek & Kremer, 2000). Most high school students, even those reading two years below grade level, have adequate basic skills, and general cognitive capacity is beyond the purview of the high school. However, the remaining abilities are integral to an instructional program at the high school level and include these:

- reader strategies and metacognition

- inferential and reasoning ability

- background knowledge

Best Practices to Use with High-Risk Students

Dr. Norman Stahl has suggested ten recommendations for programs from research for teaching high-risk college students (Stahl, Simpson & Hayes, 1994). Dr. Stahl's list can be consolidated into four components that are relevant to high school reading programs and that match the five traits for success outlined by Taylor and others.

Best practices for a high school reading program should reflect instruction in these four components:

1. develop background knowledge

2. model metacognitive strategies and promote their independent usage

3. incorporate writing into the curriculum

4. develop vocabulary

Develop Background Knowledge

The importance of developing background knowledge has been emphasized by several researchers (Alvermann & Moore, 1996). Because reading is thought to be a construction of meaning in which the reader not only absorbs information from the text but also combines that information with his or her own prior knowledge, background is essential. The reader cannot interact with the text without prior understanding of the content. He or she would have no anchor upon which to build.

Teachers use several strategies to build background before reading. These include field trips, films, guest speakers, discussions, short articles, library research and projects, anticipation guides, K-W-L, brainstorming, quickwrites, DRTA, simulations, questionnaires, structured overviews, and advance organizers.

The *Sourcebook* is organized with a prereading activity at the beginning of each selection. These prereading activities include quickwrites, K-W-L, anticipation guides, previews, and other sound activities. Not only do these lessons serve as models for prereading strategies, they also provide strategic practice for students.

Other important prereading practices that go hand-in-hand with background building are setting purpose and previewing. Just as a reader must have background information to interact with text, a reader must also have a clear understanding of why he or she is reading a selection. Purpose can be set by teacher direction. Instead of suggesting, "Read Chapter Five for a quiz on Tuesday," the teacher should probably say, "Read Chapter Five to find three reasons why or how a problem was solved. Concentrate on the sequence of the solution." This small change gives a concrete purpose to the reading and helps students to focus on the main idea.

Previewing is another strategy that directs a student to discover the main idea of the text. Previewing activities include looking at titles, subheadings, chapter questions, photos, and captions. The information gathered acts as a director for how the student approaches the information.

These strategies are not new to teachers. The challenge is the number of times students must practice the strategy before it is internalized, until it can be done independently. The *Sourcebook* provides numerous opportunities for practicing each strategy. Repeated practice helps the student make the strategy automatic. The *Sourcebook* also provides the student with a written record of his or her strategy development. This record allows the student to monitor his or her own progress.

Model Metacognitive Strategies

It is clear from the literature that strategic readers comprehend print more efficiently (Paris, Wasik, & Turner, 1996) than those readers without strategies. Typically, the less-able reader has no plan for attacking print—he or she just reads every word, each with the same emphasis. He or she skips problematic words or passages or rereads them in exactly the same manner—with no strategies for monitoring the effectiveness of his or her comprehension. The goal of strategic reading instruction is to model a variety of strategies to students (both teacher- and student-generated), to give students sufficient guided and independent practice to incorporate the strategies into his or her own portfolio, and to observe the student using these strategies in his or her own independent reading. This instruction will then allow students to monitor the effectiveness of their own reading—and adjust if the reading has not been sufficient.

For many high school readers, self-monitoring of comprehension is a new concept. Explicit instruction and practice are necessary for these students to develop self-monitoring techniques. Several strategies are available. While a student reads, he or she should mark up the text, underlining and highlighting information. In addition, note-taking of text during reading is also suggested. Students should be taught to write down the questions that come up while reading; write down issues that need clarification or that they wish to discuss; draw pictures of characters they need to visualize; note any parts or quotes within the selection that provoke a reaction; and graph any process or sequence that seems important. The *Sourcebook* is excellent for modeling and providing students with the opportunity to practice student-generated during-reading strategies.

In the space called "**Response Notes**," students record questions, clarifications, pictures, and graphic representations. Highlighting and underlining are also modeled. In addition, students can write in their books. Reading teachers are often at a disadvantage in teaching self-monitoring because students do not own the books and cannot write in the books they are reading. Consequently, these strategies are ignored or modified beyond recognition. With the *Sourcebook,* these activities can be practiced as they are meant to be—in the book. This is an opportunity for both teacher monitoring and self-monitoring of strategy acquisition.

Many of the during-reading strategies are teacher generated. These include K-W-L, DRTA, and study guides. Two of the teacher-generated strategies the *Sourcebook* encourages during reading are **stop and think** questions and the **double-entry journal. Stop and think** (directed reading) activities function like a within-text study guide. Text is broken, at a strategic place, with a question box. Students are expected to stop and answer the question and then continue reading.

The location of the **stop and think**, within text, is of great value. This proximity helps to keep students connected to text to evaluate both their response and the place in text that referenced it. The repeated usage of **stop and think** in the *Sourcebook* permits students the practice to make the connection from text to response, as well as to establish a habit of questioning to check for understanding while reading.

The **double-entry journal** also appears within text. The student is required to stop reading and respond to a quote. This strategy not only emphasizes the importance of closely attending to text but also brings the student's experience and prior knowledge into the reading process. The strategy is quite useful in helping students learn how to interpret text, especially when they later write about it.

Many activities are used to assess knowledge of a selection after reading. These include dramatizations, debates, tests, and group and individual projects. These culminating activities reflect the use of many strategies but are not a single strategy themselves. Any unit in the *Sourcebook* lends itself to the development of a culminating activity. For example, after reading "A Taste of War," a culminating activity might be for groups in the class to choose an aspect about the Civil War on which to present. After-reading strategies that reflect the reader's process of organizing and applying his thoughts about the selection can be exemplified by content mapping, summarizing, discussion, and guided writing.

The *Sourcebook* uses the strategies of content mapping and summarizing, as well as journaling and webbing to encourage student reflection. The content mapping, which is text structure sensitive, is a particularly good way for students to "gather their thoughts" after reading. In this manner, graphic organizers are modeled and made available for practice.

One of the most powerful strategies for showing an understanding of main idea and subsequent detail is the ability to summarize. Summarization is not an easy task. Several activities that include mapping main idea and detail, both graphically and in prose, accompany summary writing activities in the *Sourcebook.* Graphic and prose organizers are explained in a step-by-step fashion. Repeated practice, paired with these several instructional models, is a valuable practice.

Incorporate Writing into the Curriculum

In reviewing the literature on writing, one statement summarizes the current thinking:

> We believe strongly that in our society, at this point in history, reading and writing, to be understood and appreciated fully, should be viewed together, learned together, and used together (Tierney & Shanahan, 1996).

Writing and reading complement each other. Each can be used as a strategy to strengthen the other. **Quickwrites** at the beginning of a selection can bring up background and focus purpose for reading. During reading, note-taking and questioning can increase metacognitive awareness and enhance comprehension. After reading, summarizing, journaling, and paragraph and theme writing can extend thought and enhance higher-order thinking.

The *Sourcebook* is an excellent resource for presenting reading and writing in tandem. Writing is integrated into before, during, and after reading instruction. Journal responses, paragraph and theme writing, summarization, quickwrites, and the graphic organizers are integrated seamlessly with the reading, creating a complete, fully integrated lesson.

Develop Vocabulary

Several researchers have shown that direct instruction in vocabulary does enhance comprehension (Beck & McKeown, 1996). It is known that effective vocabulary instruction connects prior knowledge to new words (Lenski, Wham, & Johns, 1999) and provides instructional strategies that promote the active processing of words (Beck & McKeown, 1996). Examples of strategies that do this are list-group-label, concept mapping, semantic feature analysis, synonym clustering, semantic mapping, and word sorts. Each of these strategies is involved in mapping word relationships. For example, a synonym cluster begins with a word and attaches three synonyms to that word. Attached to those three synonyms are three more synonyms, and so on.

All the above strategies can be used independently with a word journal or a word box, in pairs or small groups with a word box or a word journal, or as a whole-class activity with a word box or a word wall. It is most effective if new vocabulary is highly visible and used.

The *Sourcebook* best enhances vocabulary instruction by making the student aware of the need for growth in vocabulary. Each selection has difficult vocabulary words highlighted in the text and defined at the bottom of the page. In addition, the *Teacher's Guide* includes practice on selected words from the lesson and introduces students to a vocabulary strategy.

Conclusion

The teaching of secondary reading is not an easy endeavor. Pressures by other teachers, students, and administrators are apparent daily. Not only is the reading teacher faced with the classroom challenges of students with diverse and serious issues but also with unrealistic expectations and goals from other teachers and administrators.

Because students in the classroom are diverse in their educational needs, the secondary reading teacher is constantly juggling curriculum and time to focus on the individual needs of his or her students. Each reading teacher is his or her own research assistant, constantly reviewing the literature for best practices and strategies, to motivate and engage the reluctant reader. He or she is forever combing the teacher store for materials that are relevant, strategic, and appropriate.

The *Sourcebooks* are a fine resource. Not only do they model strategies at the cutting edge of research, they are also made up of good-quality, highly motivating literature, both narrative and expository. Selections from authors such as Mark Mathabane, Zora Neale Hurston, Piri Thomas, and Naguib Mahfouz reflect the populations of our classes and their multicultural nature.

Here is a quick guide to the main prereading, comprehension, and reflecting strategies used in the *Sourcebooks*. In order to help students internalize these strategies, the number and use of them was limited so that students could encounter them repeatedly throughout the book.

Overview

PREREADING STRATEGIES
Picture Walk

What It Is

A picture walk is a prereading activity in which students look at the images from a selection to get a sense of what the selection will be about. Other strategies may be more powerful, but a picture walk is a necessary strategy for all students to have in their repertoire. Once they become more skilled readers, they will most likely use it in conjunction with other prereading strategies—for example, skimming.

How to Introduce It

Have students page through the selection and look at the images.

Ask them questions such as the ones below to help them reflect on the images.

- How do the images make you feel?
- Based on the images, what do you think the selection will be about? Why?

Read the selection.

Encourage students to generate other questions of their own.

After reading, invite students to return to the images to discuss the accuracy of their predictions.

Example

The photo of . . .	tells me . . .

The photo of . . .	tells me . . .

Why It Works

Picture walks get students, especially visual learners, actively involved in the prereading process. Questions about the images spark students' interest, activate prior knowledge, and encourage prediction.

Comments and Cautions

As an extension to the activity, invite students to add a new image, either before reading (to illustrate their prediction) or after.

Picture walks work well with both fiction and nonfiction material. You can also use a modified version for selections involving graphic sources, such as maps and diagrams.

What It Is

K-W-L is a pre- and post-reading strategy designed to facilitate students' interest in and activate their prior knowledge of a topic before reading nonfiction material. The letters *K*, *W*, and *L* stand for "What I **K**now," What I **W**ant to Know," and "What I **L**earned."

Look at the example of a K-W-L chart from Lesson 15, "The Knight In Person."

Example

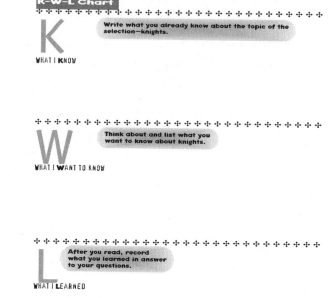

K-W-L Chart

K — Write what you already know about the topic of the selection—knights.
WHAT I KNOW

W — Think about and list what you want to know about knights.
WHAT I WANT TO KNOW

L — After you read, record what you learned in answer to your questions.
WHAT I LEARNED

How to Introduce It

For students unfamiliar with the strategy, you might try to introduce K-W-L as a whole-class activity. Once students are familiar with the strategy, they can complete the charts on their own.

Ask students what they know about the topic. List their answers in the *K* column.

Discuss what students hope to learn about the topic from reading the selection. Write their questions in the *W* column.

Read the selection.

Return to the chart and list what students learned in the *L* column.

Why It Works

Brainstorming (the *K* part) activates prior knowledge. What sets K-W-L apart from other prereading strategies is that K-W-L also encourages students to ask questions (the *W* component), thereby setting meaningful purposes for their reading. Returning to the chart (the *L* component) brings closure to the activity and demonstrates the purposefulness of the task.

Comments and Cautions

Don't worry about the accuracy of the answers under the *K* column; this is a brainstorming activity; students can correct any errors later during the *L* part of the activity.

After brainstorming, have students categorize their lists into three or four general groups.

You might add a fourth column, "What I Still Need to Learn," for questions that aren't answered in the text or that arise after reading the material.

Anticipation Guide

What It Is

An anticipation guide is a series of statements to which students respond, first individually and then as a group, before reading a selection. For example, in Lesson 13, "Her Life Was Not A Joke," students are asked to mark statements about life in the late 19th century true or false.

Example

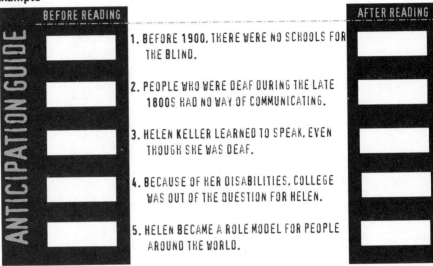

ANTICIPATION GUIDE

BEFORE READING

AFTER READING

1. BEFORE 1900, THERE WERE NO SCHOOLS FOR THE BLIND.

2. PEOPLE WHO WERE DEAF DURING THE LATE 1800S HAD NO WAY OF COMMUNICATING.

3. HELEN KELLER LEARNED TO SPEAK, EVEN THOUGH SHE WAS DEAF.

4. BECAUSE OF HER DISABILITIES, COLLEGE WAS OUT OF THE QUESTION FOR HELEN.

5. HELEN BECAME A ROLE MODEL FOR PEOPLE AROUND THE WORLD.

How to Introduce It

Have students read the statements. (When making your own guides, keep the number of statements to fewer than 10. More than that makes it difficult to discuss in detail.)

Discuss the students' responses. This is the point of an anticipation guide—to discuss. Build the prior knowledge of one student by adding to it the prior knowledge of other students, which can be done through discussion. The discussion of anticipation guide statements can also be a powerful motivator, because once students have answered the statements, they have a stake in seeing if they are "right."

Encourage students to make predictions about what the selection will be about based on the statements.

Then read the selection.

After reading the selection, have students return to their guides and re-evaluate their responses based on what they learned from the selection.

Why It Works

Anticipation guides are useful tools for eliciting predictions before reading both fiction and nonfiction. By encouraging students to think critically about a series of statements, anticipation guides raise expectations and create anticipation about the selection.

Comments and Cautions

This is a motivational activity. Try not to allow the class discussion to become divisive or judgmental; the teacher's role is that of a facilitator, encouraging students to examine and re-examine their responses. The bigger stake students have in an opinion, the more they will be motivated to read about the issue.

The focus of the guides should not be whether students' responses are "correct" or not but rather the discussion that ensues after completing the guides individually.

Anticipation guides work well in counteracting stereotypes and prejudice, as in Lesson 1, "High School: The Bad and the Good."

You can turn the entire anticipation guide process into a whole-group activity by having students respond with either "thumbs up" or "thumbs down."

Preview or Walk-through

What It Is

Previewing is a prereading strategy in which students read the title and first paragraph or two of a selection and then reflect on a few key questions. It asks the students to "sample" the selection before they begin reading and functions very much like the preview to a movie. Occasionally it is simply referred to as a *walk-through* and is a less formal variation of skimming and scanning.

How to Introduce It

Previewing can be done as an individual or group activity. You might introduce it to the group and in later lessons encourage students to work on their own.

Read aloud, or have students read to themselves, the first paragraph or two of a selection.

Have students respond to four or five questions about the selection. Their responses will be predictions based on their initial sampling of the piece. Questions might include these:

- What is the selection about?
- When does it take place?
- Who is in it?
- How will the selection end?

Read the rest of the selection.

Return to the questions and discuss the accuracy of students' predictions. Were they surprised at how the selection turned out based on their initial preview? Why or why not?

Example

Preview

What did you find out from reading the title and author's name?

What did you learn by reading the first paragraph?

What characters are involved?

What do you think this story will be about?

Why It Works

Previews work because they provide a frame of reference in which to understand new material. Previews build context, particularly when students read about unfamiliar topics. Discussing the questions and predicting before reading helps students set purposes for reading and creates interest in the subject matter.

Comments and Cautions

Previews work best with more difficult reading selections, especially texts with difficult vocabulary. Previewing helps students to understand a context for a selection—what's the subject? Where's the story located? Who's involved?

Once students are familiar with previews, you might ask them to generate their own list of questions and have a partner respond to them.

Quickwrite

What It Is

A quickwrite is just what the name implies, a short, one- to ten-minute activity in which students write down their thoughts about a topic. Quickwriting is impromptu writing, without concern for spelling and grammatical conventions. It is intended to help students articulate some of the prior knowledge they have on a subject.

How to Introduce It

Provide students with a topic on which to focus.

Invite students to write about whatever comes to mind regarding the topic.

Encourage students to share their quickwrites in a small group. Discuss their similarities and differences.

Ask students to predict what they think the selection will be about based on their quickwrites.

Read the selection.

Discuss the connections between students' quickwrites and the selection.

Example

> **QUICKWRITE**
>
> NOW QUICKWRITE. WHAT DO YOU THINK ABOUT THE WRITER AND STORY? SHARE YOUR RESPONSE WITH A PARTNER.

Why It Works

Quickwriting works as a prereading strategy on a number of levels. For one, the very process of writing without regard to writing conventions frees up students to write from a deeper level of understanding. Quickwriting encourages students to make connections between their own lives and the reading material, activates prior knowledge, and sparks interest. Quickwriting can also help correct misconceptions about a topic.

Comments and Cautions

As an extension to the activity, have students quickwrite again after reading the selection and compare their two quickwrites to see what they've learned from reading the material.

Skimming

What It Is

Skimming is a prereading strategy in which students look over the entire selection to get a sense of what it will be about. It is one of the best prereading strategies and best known. Much of the time, however, students never learn how to skim effectively and what to look for.

How to Introduce It

Skimming is a useful tool, both for prereading and content area reading, but one that many students have difficulty mastering. Therefore, introduce skimming as a whole-group activity; teacher modeling might work best for the initial activity. Skimming involves these activities:

• Examining the table of contents

• Reading the first and last paragraph

• Checking the selection's length and reading difficulty

• Reading any captions

• Looking over illustrations

• Noting section headings, diagrams, and other graphic sources

Example

SKIM FOR KEY WORDS AND PHRASES

names

repeated words

phrases from beginning and end of each paragraph

Who and what is "Survival" about?

To help students master the technique of skimming, provide them with a series of questions to answer about the selection, as in the example above. Questions such as these provide a clear purpose for skimming and help students focus their attention on the key parts of the selection.

Why It Works

Skimming is an excellent tool for setting purposes and activating prior knowledge before reading nonfiction material. Like a picture walk, skimming draws students into a selection.

Comments and Cautions

Skimming works best when students have a clear purpose for going through a selection. Direct students, for example, to underline one to two words in each line of the first and last paragraph, or to circle names or words that appear a number of times.

Teach a clear method for skimming and try not to assume students will know what it means.

Think-Pair-and-Share

What It Is

Think-pair-and-share is a prereading strategy that encourages group discussion and prediction about what students will read. Students work in pairs to discuss sentences selected from the text.

How to Introduce It

Break students into groups of two or three. Present three to six sentences from the selection. Ask group members to read the sentences and discuss what they mean and in what order they appear in the text.

Encourage groups to make predictions and generate questions about the reading.

Then read the selection.

Have groups discuss the selection and the accuracy of their think-pair-and-share sentences. How many were able to correctly predict the order in which they appeared? How many could predict what the selection was about?

Example

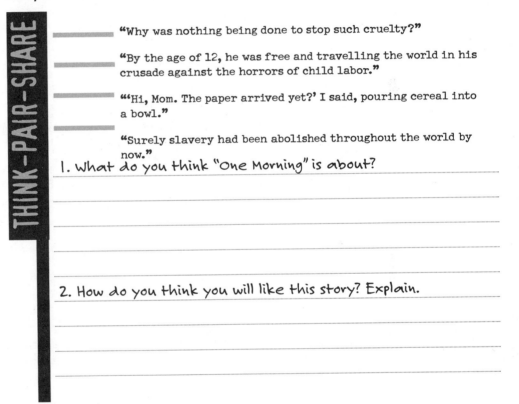

THINK-PAIR-SHARE

"Why was nothing being done to stop such cruelty?"

"By the age of 12, he was free and travelling the world in his crusade against the horrors of child labor."

"'Hi, Mom. The paper arrived yet?' I said, pouring cereal into a bowl."

"Surely slavery had been abolished throughout the world by now."

1. What do you think "One Morning" is about?

2. How do you think you will like this story? Explain.

Why It Works

Think-pair-and-share can be a powerful tool for getting students motivated to read. Small-group work such as this gives students the chance to discover that they don't always have to come up with all the answers themselves; sometimes two or three heads *are* better than one. Working in groups also provides reluctant readers with the understanding that all readers bring different skills and schema to the reading task. The activity also begins the critical process of "constructing meaning" of the text.

Comments and Cautions

Enlist students in building the think-pair-and-share activity. Have each group member write one sentence from the text on a file card. Then ask groups to exchange file cards—one group pieces together the sentences of another group.

The active, social nature of this activity stimulates students, which can be highly motivational and beneficial if properly channeled into purposeful activity.

Word Web

What It Is

A word web is a prereading activity in which students brainstorm and make connections to a key concept from the reading material.

Example

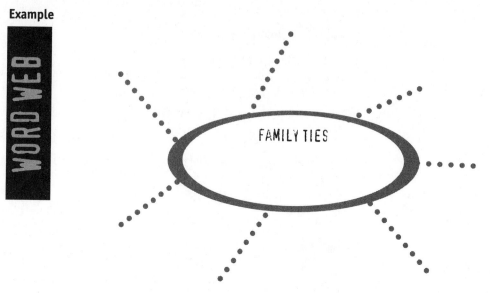

How to Introduce It

Word webs can be done independently or as a whole-group activity. You might want to do the initial word webs with the whole group and assign later word webs for independent learning.

Write a key concept in a circle. For example, in Lesson 8, "Dear Tía" and "Papa," the concept is family ties.

Have students brainstorm words related to the concept on spokes coming out of the circle.

Discuss with students how the key word is connected to the reading material.

Read the selection.

Return to the word web and add any new ideas brought about by reading the selection.

Why It Works

Word webs are excellent tools for developing students' conceptual knowledge. They tap into students' prior knowledge and help students make connections between what they know and what they will learn.

Comments and Cautions

Even though this is a brainstorming activity, do challenge incorrect assumptions about the concept, particularly when using the word web with a whole group. You want to be sure that students go into the reading assignment with an accurate impression of the concept.

If students get "stuck," encourage them to write down words, phrases, examples, or images they associate with the concept.

RESPONSE STRATEGIES

The response strategies are introduced at the beginning of each *Sourcebook* (pages 8–10). They are the heart of the interactive reading students are asked to do throughout the book. In Part II of each lesson, one or two response strategies are suggested to help teach students how to mark up a text and become active readers.

Struggling readers do not naturally know how to interact with a text, so these strategies are designed to help them get started. Examples are also provided in each lesson to model the strategy. The intent is to build the habit of reading with a pen in hand and marking up the text until it becomes a natural way to read.

Response Strategies

1. Mark or highlight

2. Question

3. Clarify

4. Visualize

5. Predict

6. React and Connect

Example

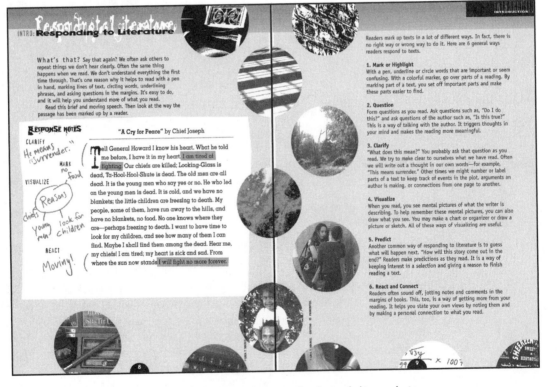

The purpose of these response strategies in each lesson is to

1. help students learn how to mark up a text

2. help students focus on specific aspects of a text and find the information they need

3. build lifelong habits for students by repeating good reading practices

COMPREHENSION STRATEGIES
Directed Reading

What It Is

Directed reading is a structured activity designed to guide students through a reading selection. Directed reading is composed of a series of steps, including readiness, directed silent reading, comprehension check and discuss, oral rereading, and follow-up activities. In the *Sourcebook*, students gain readiness in Part I, read silently in Part II, and then encounter questions that check their comprehension throughout the selection. Teachers are encouraged to have students go back through selections with this strategy and read the selection a second time. Repeated reading of a selection often increases reading fluency, which in itself often increases comprehension.

How To Introduce It

First, help students get ready to read by activating their prior knowledge, creating interest, and setting purposes. The prereading strategies described in Part I of the lesson offer suggestions for activities that promote reading readiness.

Next, have students read the selection silently. Guide them as they read by providing stopping points, such as the stop and think sections in the *Sourcebook*. Encourage them to focus on the purpose for reading that they established in Part I.

Example

STOP AND THINK

What world events caused harassment of Muslim students?

STOP AND THINK

After students have read the selection, take a moment to engage them in a discussion about what they read.

During or directly after the discussion, have students orally reread the selection to answer any remaining questions or clear up any confusion about the reading material.

During the discussion and oral rereading stages, you can get a sense of what kind of difficulties students are having with the material. Use follow-up activities to work on these areas of weakness and to extend students' understanding of the material, or use the additional comprehension activities included in each *Teacher's Guide* lesson. Follow-up activities range from direct skill instruction designed for individual or small-group work to response activities, such as those found in the *Sourcebook*.

Why It Works

Directed reading enhances students' ability to think critically and reflectively about the reading material. It helps them ask the questions good readers ask themselves as they read. The structured format ensures that students of all reading levels will be asking the right kinds of questions needed to comprehend the text.

Comments and Cautions

As with any comprehension strategy, directed reading needs to be modified to fit the needs of individual students.

Directed reading can be overly prescriptive, and overuse can contribute to passive reading if it is relied on exclusively. Including activities that require student speculation and higher-level thinking will foster more active reading.

Prediction

What It Is

Prediction is both a comprehension strategy and a prereading strategy, but in the *Sourcebooks* it is formally used mostly as a comprehension strategy. Nearly all of the prereading strategies used in the *Sourcebooks* involve some level of prediction, but prediction is categorized as a comprehension strategy. When students predict during reading, they rely on information they have already read in the selection.

How to Introduce It

Break the selection into three or four parts.

Have students read to the first stopping point and then ask them to predict what they think will happen. Predictive questions include these:

- What will happen to the character?
- How do you think the problem will be resolved?
- How do you think the selection will end?

Example

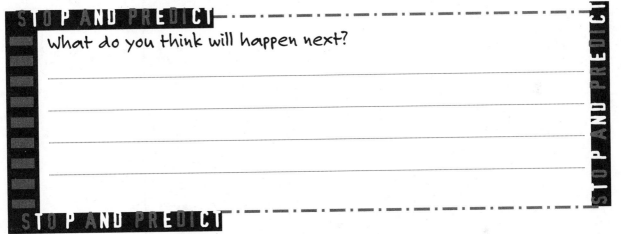

STOP AND PREDICT

What do you think will happen next?

As students read on, encourage them to reflect on their predictions and modify them as further information is provided.

After reading, discuss the accuracy of students' predictions, not to determine if the predictions were "correct," but to provide closure to the activity and validate students' responses. Reflecting on the predictions will also help students see the information they might have used from the selection to predict but did not.

Why It Works

Because of the students' assertions about "what will happen," predicting gives students a stake in what they read. Their opinion is on the line, and this helps students set purposes for reading.

Comments and Cautions

Look for natural stopping points in texts; obvious spots to stop and predict what will happen next usually occur before episodes, or events, that occur in the story.

Prediction is best used with fiction, although it can also be applied to nonfiction with readers skilled at making predictions.

Graphic Organizers

What It Is

A graphic organizer is a visual representation of the key information for a reading selection. Graphic organizers can be as simple as two-column charts or as complicated as multi-dimensional diagrams. They come in many sizes and shapes, such as plot charts, cause-effect charts, and character maps.

How to Introduce It

Begin by explaining the purpose of the graphic and the kind of information students should put into each of its parts.

Invite students to fill in the graphic organizer as they read, and then review it and make any modifications after completing the selection. For example, on page 155 in "The Victorious Feudal Knight," students use the graphic organizer to arrange what they have learned about feudalism.

Examples

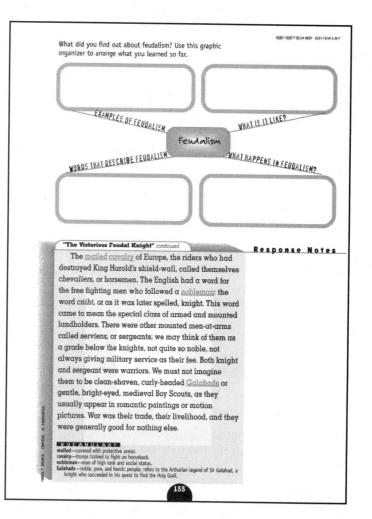

Examples

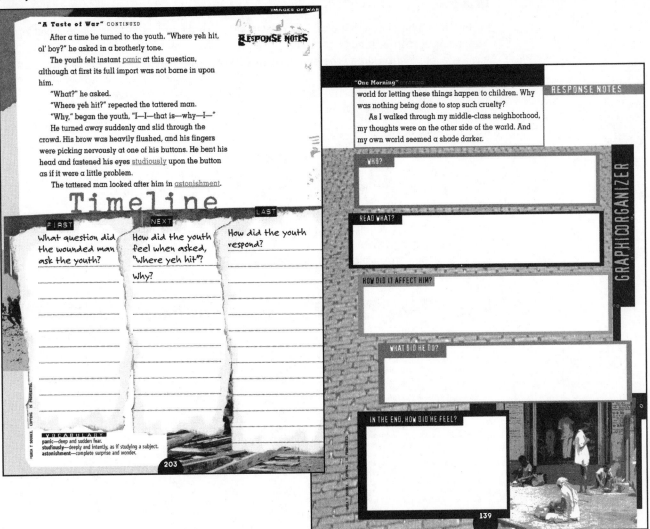

Why It Works

A graphic organizer is a useful tool for helping students to structure what they understand from their reading. It also helps students make connections among ideas, especially in flow charts or cause-effect charts.

Comments and Cautions

Some of the more common graphic organizers are these:

- Venn diagram for showing comparison and contrast

- Cause-and-effect chart for demonstrating causal relationships

- Sequence map for keeping track of a series of events

- Problem-solution map for identifying the problem and its solution(s)

- Word web for representing information about a particular concept

Graphic organizers are excellent tools for all students but are especially helpful for visual learners.

Reciprocal Reading

What It Is

Reciprocal reading is a small-group activity in which students take turns reading aloud to each other or with a tutor. It is such a powerful reading strategy that it has been modified for use in the *Sourcebooks*. The power of the questions generated does not diminish when reciprocal reading is taken out of the group work or tutor/pupil setting and transferred to a pupil-and-text relationship. The strategy is characterized by asking students to ask questions, clarify, predict, and summarize.

How to Introduce It

Take a moment to introduce the strategy to the whole class. Explain that this strategy involves working with a partner or reading tutor and asking four kinds of questions: clarifying ones, predicting ones, exploratory ones, and summarizing ones.

Invite one student to read the title and opening paragraphs aloud. At the first question point and ask for a volunteer to answer the question. Work through the entire selection with students as a group. Then, ask students to reread the selection again in pairs, taking turns asking and then answering the questions.

Example

Why It Works

Reciprocal reading can be an excellent tool for both reinforcing listening skills (an often-overlooked skill) and improving reading fluency. It structures the work of students working with a reading partner and naturally helps them ask useful questions—the kinds good readers automatically ask—about a text.

Comments and Cautions

To ensure that the activity doesn't turn into a word-attack session, go over unfamiliar vocabulary before reading.

For reciprocal reading to be successful, it is important to introduce the idea to the whole class before turning students loose with a reading partner. Taking the time to walk through the process will prove beneficial later on when students are asked to work with their reading partners, because they will have a structured routine to fall back on.

Double-Entry Journal

What It Is

A double-entry journal is an adaptation of the more familiar response journal. Typically, the left column includes quotes or facts from a selection, while the right column offers students the opportunity to respond to the quotation or idea. It is a very good strategy to build students' ability to comprehend and interpret a text.

How to Introduce It

Begin by having students list quotations from the selection that interests them, or you can pull out some quotations yourself, as is done in the *Sourcebook*. The benefits of selecting the quotations for students are that the focus is then on interpreting passages of the text and that the task is simplified, making it easier for students to succeed.

Invite students to reflect on the meaning of each quotation and write their thoughts in the right column.

Example

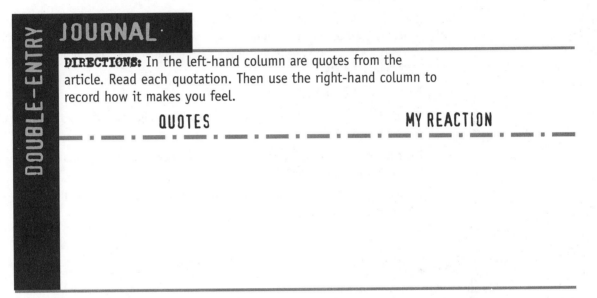

DOUBLE-ENTRY JOURNAL

DIRECTIONS: In the left-hand column are quotes from the article. Read each quotation. Then use the right-hand column to record how it makes you feel.

QUOTES   MY REACTION

Why It Works

Double-entry journals encourage students to become more engaged in what they are reading by focusing on just one part of the text at a time. With this kind of journal, students naturally make connections between the literature and their own lives. Double-entry journals expand on students' understanding of the material and build an initial interpretive response. By beginning the interpretation of literature, students will find writing about a text easier if they focus on the quotations they (or you) selected and their interpretations of them.

Comments and Cautions

Even if you structure the activity by selecting quotations, invite students to add those that have particular meaning to themselves as well.

Encourage students to use double-entry journals in other reading situations, including content-area reading.

What It Is

Retelling is a comprehension strategy and assessment tool in which students retell a selection. It works best with chronological selections as a means of checking whether students followed the sequence of events.

How to Introduce It

Before reading the selection, let students know that they will be asked to retell or summarize their reading in their own words.

Either at the end of the selection or at certain stopping points within the selection (as done in the *Sourcebook*), have students retell what they have read as if they are telling it to a friend who has never heard it before.

Have students compare their retellings to examine each other's interpretations of the reading material.

Why It Works

Because retelling allows students to respond in their own words to what they've read, it increases both the quality and quantity of what is comprehended. Retelling also helps students make the text more personally meaningful and provides a deeper understanding of the reading material.

Comments and Cautions

You might have students tape-record the retellings and let students listen and assess their own work.

For fictional selections, try having students retell the story from another character's point of view to provide a different perspective to the tale.

A student's retelling offers a window into the student's thinking and is, therefore, a valuable assessment tool as well.

stop + retell

Retell in your own words what has happened so far. Think about these questions:

- Who is telling about the events?
- What has he described?

Story Frame

What It Is

A story frame or story map is a visual representation of one or more of the key elements of a story: character, setting, plot, or theme. It helps students graphically construct the main elements of a story.

How to Introduce It

First, explain the idea of a story frame and its elements: plot, setting, characters, and themes. Be sure students understand that story frames can organize events, too. Just as there are many kinds of stories, students need to understand that there are many kinds of story frames.

Example

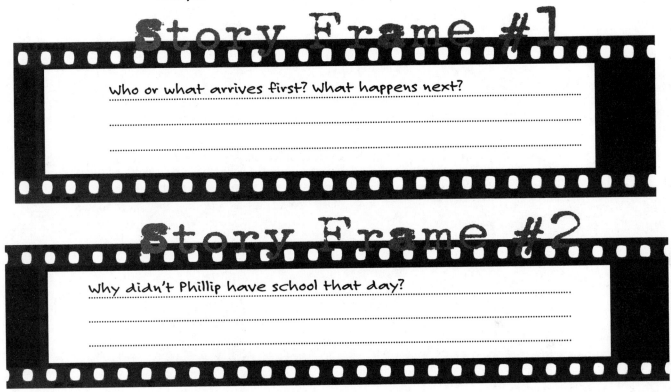

Story Frame #1

Who or what arrives first? What happens next?

Story Frame #2

Why didn't Phillip have school that day?

After completing the frame, have students use it as the basis for discussion about the selection or to help in their written responses.

Comments and Cautions

Story frames come in all shapes and sizes. Modify the frame to fit the needs of the students and the focus of the material. For instance, in "War Comes to Our Island," the story frame focuses on the sequence of events; others focus on character development throughout a story. Other frames might focus on theme or other story elements.

For students who need more guidance filling in their frames, provide them with question prompts, such as "What happened first?" "What happened next?" "Who did it happen to?" Let students know this is a strategy they are free to experiment with and use in whatever way they find is most helpful.

REFLECTIVE READING STRATEGIES

The reflective reading strategies occur in **Part V** of each lesson. They help students take away more from what they read. All too often students are asked, "Did you get it?" Reading seems like a code they have been asked to decipher but cannot. They feel stupid and think they have failed.

How can we turn around struggling readers if the only payoff for reading is "getting it"? Good readers read for a variety of reasons: to entertain themselves, to expand their understanding of a subject or develop their thinking in an area, or simply because they have to read. Yet good readers naturally take away more from what they read. For example:

- We read novels by Nobel Prize winners because of their writing **style**.

- We read sports pages because they are **enjoyable**.

- We read philosophy or religious meditations to add more **depth** to how we think about things.

- We read about such topics as Lamaze child-bearing techniques or natural foods because they are personally **meaningful** to us.

- We read cartoons and *People* magazine because they are **easy** to browse through.

- We read directions about setting up a computer because we **have to**; we need to have that particular understanding.

We read, in other words, for a variety of reasons. As teachers, we need to help struggling readers see that—and not just that they did not "get it" on the multiple-choice test. So, **Part V** of each lesson in the *Sourcebook* is a "reflective" assessment, a looking back, so students can see what they *gained* from the lesson, not what they failed to understand.

Example

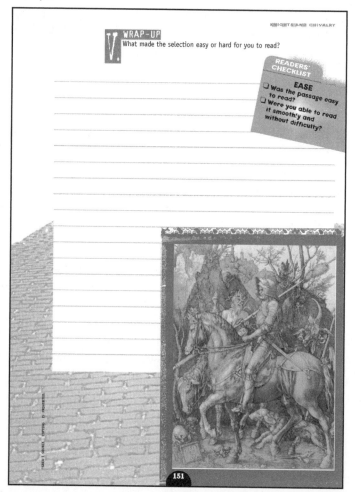

The purpose of the **Readers' Checklist** in each lesson is to:

1. model for students the questions good readers ask of themselves after reading.

2. expand the reasons for which students want to read.

3. build lifelong habits for students by repeating best reading practices.

Reflective Assessment

1. **Understanding**

   Did you understand the reading?

   Was the message or point clear?

   Can you restate what the reading is about?

2. **Ease**

   Was the passage easy to read?

   Were you able to read it smoothly and without difficulty?

3. **Meaning**

   Did you learn something from the reading?

   Did it affect you or make an impression?

4. **Style**

   Did you find the passage well written?

   Are the sentences well constructed and the words well chosen?

   Does the style show you how to be a better writer?

5. **Depth**

   Did the reading make you think about things?

   Did it set off thoughts beyond the surface topic?

6. **Enjoyment**

   Did you like the reading?

   Was the reading experience pleasurable?

   Would you want to reread the piece or recommend it to someone?

   Invite students regularly to provide examples and reasons for their answers to these questions.

School Days

Unit Background   **SCHOOL DAYS** (pages 11–32)

This unit includes two nonfiction selections—one about the experiences of Muslim students in American high schools, the other about Patrick Ntutu, a member of the Masai people in Kenya, who was brought to the United States on a college scholarship awarded by the Michael Jordan Foundation.

Teaching the Introduction

The photographs on page 11 illustrate four benefits of school.

1. Ask students to discuss what distinguishes a good school experience from a bad one.

2. Ask students whether they feel their school is free of prejudice. Have them support their opinions.

3. Find out whether any students have gone to school outside of the United States. If so, ask them to tell about the school.

4. Ask: How would you react if, for some reason, you were told you could not go to school any more?

Opening Activity

Students might be divided into several small groups to prepare, distribute, analyze, and "publish" results of a questionnaire measuring class attitudes about school. For example, a questionnaire might ask students to rate on a scale what they most enjoy about school, how friendly the school is, and so on. All replies should be anonymous.

High School: The Bad and the Good

STUDENT PAGES 12-19

Skills and Strategies Overview

THEME School Days

READING LEVEL easy

VOCABULARY

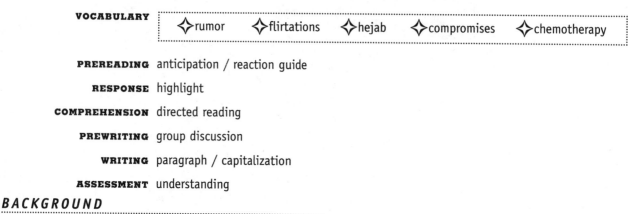

◇rumor ◇flirtations ◇hejab ◇compromises ◇chemotherapy

PREREADING anticipation / reaction guide

RESPONSE highlight

COMPREHENSION directed reading

PREWRITING group discussion

WRITING paragraph / capitalization

ASSESSMENT understanding

BACKGROUND

"High School: The Bad and the Good" is an excerpt from a book about the prejudice people of Middle-Eastern descent encounter in the United States today. However, rather than focus on the problem as a whole, Richard Wormser limits the scope of his discussion to the problems Muslim students face in our nation's schools.

Wormser interviewed several students for his book *American Islam: Growing Up Muslim in North America*. The teenagers he spoke with explained the pull they experienced from two different cultures and explored how defenseless they felt in the face of American prejudice. Although they tried to shrug off their fellow classmates' insulting questions and observations, they were clearly hurt by others' comments.

This selection and the one that follows ("Finding Patrick," student pages 20–32) present an excellent opportunity to discuss coping strategies with students. A problem-solution-refined solution organizer such as the one below can help you lead this discussion.

UNIT THEME Richard Wormser reveals that prejudice is a serious problem in American schools.

GRAPHIC ORGANIZER **Problem-solution-refined solution**

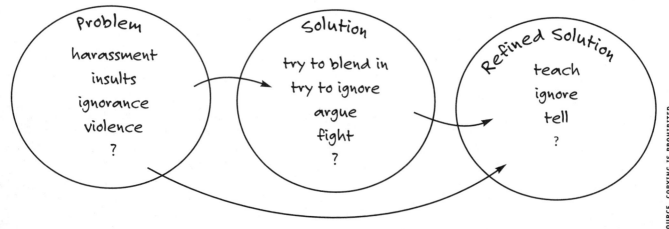

BEFORE YOU READ

Read through the introduction to the lesson on page 12 with students. The purpose of the page is to motivate and focus students. The art has been chosen with the aim of drawing students in and showing them the universality of this theme.

Next introduce the prereading activity, an **anticipation/reaction guide**. (Refer to the **Strategy Handbook** on page 40 for more help.)

Motivation Strategy

In "High School: The Bad and the Good," Richard Wormser explores what it feels like to be alienated because of one's family heritage. Ask students to tell about a time they witnessed or heard about an act of prejudice in their school or community. Encourage them to think of examples involving students their own age.

ENGAGING STUDENTS Explain that Wormser presents readers with the question that is at the heart of many teen dilemmas: "Is it better to fit in and keep the peace, or stand up for what you believe in—even if it causes argument?" Have students debate this question, suggesting pros and cons for each side. Later, after they have finished reading the selection, students can discuss the question again. Have their attitudes changed? If so, how and why?

Vocabulary Building

Help students use **context clues** as they read to figure out the meanings of difficult words, especially key vocabulary for this lesson: *rumor, flirtations, hejab, compromise,* and *chemotherapy.* Tell students to circle these words in the text. Model using context and then checking your ideas against the footnote so that students begin to have an idea of the kinds of clues they should look for when defining in context.

For additional practice with these words, see the **Vocabulary** blackline master, page 66.

STRATEGY LESSON: ANTONYMS Remind students that sometimes learning the synonym or antonym of a word is a shortcut to understanding the word. Give students a list of words that relate to the selection, such as *explosion, escalate, petty, complaints*, and *vicious*. Have volunteers suggest antonyms for each word. Students can use these antonyms to help them better understand the selection.

For additional practice on this strategy, see the **Vocabulary** blackline master, page 66.

Prereading Strategies

The purpose of an **anticipation/reaction guide** is to explore students' ideas about a theme, both before and after reading. The statements on the guide have been chosen to pique students' interest, while at the same time help them begin thinking about theme. Once they've finished reading, students will look back to the "after reading" column and once again say whether they agree or disagree with the statements. After they've marked their new set of answers, point out to students that what we read really *can* change our attitudes and beliefs. In fact, one of the reasons we read is to enlighten ourselves about new ideas and opinions.

PICTURE WALK As an alternate prereading strategy, ask students to do a picture walk. Have them begin with art on the unit opener (page 11) and then look carefully at the art on pages 12–19. Ask students to make predictions about the article based on what they see in the photographs. Have them tell you what they think the topic of the selection is and then predict whether or not they'll find it difficult to read.

Spanish-speaking Students

"El colegio: lo malo y lo bueno" da luz al prejuicio que la gente musulmana frecuentemente se encuentra durante la adolescencia. Aunque muchos estudiantes musulmanes nacen en los Estados Unidos, se sienten lazos muy fuertes a su religión, cultura, y patria. Han tenido que aguantar acosamiento y comentario grosero solo porque son diferentes de sus compañeros de clase. Esta selección muestra la pena e injusticia que resultan de un desrepeto por otros.

READ

Explain how important it is for students to **mark** or **highlight** words they don't understand, circle phrases and sentences that they think are important or interesting, and write comments in the margins. Reading with a pencil in hand keeps students focused on the selection and intent on their first-pass goal of comprehending the author's words.

Response Strategy

VISUALIZE As an alternative strategy, have students sketch pictures of incidents they read about.

Comprehension Strategies

Directed reading (stop and think) can help reluctant or low-level readers better understand what they are reading. In a directed reading, the teacher or group leader reads the selection aloud, pausing occasionally to ask comprehension questions that can assist students in understanding the sequence, characters, setting, and so on. Even the simplest stop and think questions, such as, "Who is the author talking about here?" can help clear up student confusion. Be prepared to ask these types of questions along with the questions written in the student book.

GRAPHIC ORGANIZER As an alternate comprehension strategy, work with students to create a graphic organizer that lists the names of the students Wormser interviewed, in addition to the comments these students make about prejudice against people of Middle-Eastern descent. You might post the organizer on the board and turn to it each time a new student "speaks" in the article.

For more help, see the **Comprehension** blackline master on page 67.

Discussion Questions

COMPREHENSION 1. Why does Anam remove her hejab? *(It sets her apart and draws attention to her heritage, which in turn causes those around her to make ugly, prejudicial comments.)*

2. What effect does the Trade Center bombing have on Sadeck? *(Sadeck's fellow students begin making anti-Muslim comments to her and others, although they clearly had nothing to do with the bombing.)*

3. What are Muslim children taught about fighting? *(Avoid fights if possible, but avoid losing if there must be a fight.)*

CRITICAL THINKING 4. What do you think these students want most from their peers? *(Accept reasonable responses. Remind students to support what they say with evidence from the selection or evidence from their own lives.)*

5. What does the title "High School: The Bad and the Good" mean"? *(Point out to students that "bad" comes before "good" in the title, which is not the usual arrangement when these two words are paired. What is the significance of this arrangement?)*

Literary Skill

EXPOSITORY NONFICTION To introduce a literary skill with this lesson, you might discuss with students the characteristics of expository nonfiction. Remind the class that expository nonfiction is a straightforward recitation of facts, information, and ideas, with little or no editorializing on the part of the author. Expository nonfiction appears in newspaper articles, encyclopedias, textbook pages, and so on. In contrast, narrative nonfiction, which is also factual, is a recitation of events from one person's viewpoint. "How It Feels to Be Colored Me" (student pages 52–63) is an example of narrative nonfiction.

III. GATHER YOUR THOUGHTS

The goal of these prewriting activities is first to help students collect what they learned from reading the selection, and then to build a topic to write about. Use the first prewriting activity to help students explain how and why their attitudes have changed as a result of reading the selection. Use the second prewriting activity (**discuss**) to give students the chance to voice their own opinions about the topic. Before they begin, you might tell students that these two activities will help them with the writing assignment in Part IV.

Prewriting Strategies

TOPIC SENTENCES You might want to review with students the procedure for writing a topic sentence for a paragraph. Remind the class that a topic sentence must clearly state the subject of the paragraph. In addition, it must state a feeling or attitude about the subject. Have students use this simple formula when writing topic sentences:

A specific topic + a specific feeling = a good topic sentence.

Have students use the **Prewriting and Writing** blackline master on page 68.

IV. WRITE

Set aside plenty of time for students to write their **paragraphs**. Remind the class that they are writing in response to one of the discussion questions on page 17. After they have finished writing, ask them to revise using the **Writers' Checklist**.

WRITING RUBRIC Use the writing rubric to help students focus on the assignment requirements and for help with a quick assessment of their writing.

Do students' paragraphs

- begin with a topic sentence that clearly answers one of the discussion questions?

- contain details that support the topic sentence?

- stay focused on *their* answers to the questions (rather than other people's answers)?

Grammar, Usage, and Mechanics

You might use this opportunity to teach a mini-lesson on capitalization. Review with students the rules for capitalizing the first word in every sentence, proper nouns, proper adjectives, and the pronoun *I*. If you like, put some practice sentences on the board. Have students edit each for capitalization errors. For example:

when i first heard about the fights at temple mall, i called

tia louise, who lives in philadelphia, pennsylvania.

V. WRAP-UP

Take a moment at the end of the lesson for students to reflect using the **Readers' Checklist** for **understanding**. These questions are the ones that good readers ask themselves either consciously or unconsciously at the end of every reading. Encourage students to get into the habit of asking these types of questions each time they finish reading a selection.

Assessment

To test students' comprehension, use the **Assessment** blackline master on page 69.

Name _____

VOCABULARY

Words from the Selection

DIRECTIONS Answer these questions that use words from the selection. Explain your answers.

1. If you hear a <u>rumor</u>, can you trust that the story is true?

_____

2. If you engage in <u>flirtations</u>, are you showing interest or disinterest in another person?

_____

3. If you are wearing a <u>hejab</u>, are you wearing it on your head or your arms?

_____

4. When you make <u>compromises</u>, are you starting an argument or trying to solve one?

_____

5. When you receive <u>chemotherapy</u>, is it for your body or your emotions?

_____

Strategy Lesson: Antonyms

An antonym is a word that means the opposite of another word. For example, *stop* is an antonym for *go*.

DIRECTIONS Find the word in column B that is the opposite of the word in column A. Then draw a line between the two words. If there's a word you don't know, skip it and come back to it when you've finished the whole column.

Column A	Column B
6. explosion	important
7. escalate	kind
8. petty	decrease
9. complaints	implosion
10. vicious	compliments

Name _____

COMPREHENSION
Directed Reading

DIRECTIONS With a partner, work through the answers to these questions.

1. Why are students like Sadeck, Muhammad Jihad, and Tehani El-Ghussein teased and insulted?

_____

_____

_____

2. What do their fellow Americans do that makes these students feel angry and unhappy?

_____

_____

_____

3. What effect did the Pan Am explosion over Scotland and the World Trade Center bombing have on these students?

_____

_____

_____

4. If you could give these students some advice, what would it be?

_____

_____

my advice for Sadeck: _____

_____

my advice for Muhammad Jihad: _____

_____

my advice for Tehani El-Ghussein: _____

_____

Name _____

PREWRITING AND WRITING
Writing a Topic Sentence and Details

DIRECTIONS Every paragraph you write must have a topic sentence. A topic sentence tells the subject of the paragraph and how you feel about the subject. You can use this formula to help you write a topic sentence.

A specific topic + a specific feeling = a good topic sentence.

Now follow these steps to write a topic sentence and supporting details.

1. WRITE A TOPIC SENTENCE ABOUT PREJUDICE IN YOUR SCHOOL AND HOW TO GET RID OF IT.

prejudice in my school + _____ = _____.
(how to get rid of it)   (my topic sentence)

2. NEXT PLAN DETAILS TO SUPPORT YOUR TOPIC SENTENCE.

Your details will be examples from your own life. They will give readers more information on how you think your school can end prejudice.

detail #1: _____

_____

_____

detail #2: _____

_____

_____

detail #3: _____

_____

_____

3. WRITE A CONCLUDING SENTENCE THAT IS A RESTATEMENT OF YOUR TOPIC SENTENCE.

My concluding sentence: _____

_____

_____

Name _____

ASSESSMENT

Multiple-Choice Test

DIRECTIONS   On the blanks provided, write the letter of the item that best answers each question or completes each statement.

_____ 1. Anam's family came from which country?
  A. Ireland
  B. Pakistan
  C. India
  D. America

_____ 2. Who was arrested and charged with the World Trade Center bombing?
  A. terrorists
  B. Anam's Family
  C. Muslim fundamentalists
  D. Sadeck

_____ 3. What major decision does Anam make?
  A. She decides to draw attention to herself.
  B. She won't go to school anymore.
  C. She won't wear her hejab in public.
  D. She will start flirting with men.

_____ 4. How are Muslim students taught to handle harassment?
  A. avoid fighting
  B. if you fight, avoid losing
  C. both A. and B.
  D. none of the above

_____ 5. Why do Muslim women cover their heads and faces?
  A. for religious reasons
  B. for personal safety
  C. The U.S. President tells them to.
  D. all of the above

_____ 6. Where do the Muslim students find danger?
  A. in their yards
  B. on the way home from school
  C. in school
  D. all of the above

_____ 7. If a problem escalates, it means that the problem . . .
  A. is solved.
  B. goes away on its own.
  C. grows larger.
  D. none of the above

_____ 8. The Muslim students are harassed because . . .
  A. kids think they are mean.
  B. kids think they take American jobs.
  C. kids think they tease others.
  D. kids think they are different.

_____ 9. What is a hejab?
  A. a head and face covering
  B. a weapon
  C. a Muslim organization
  D. none of the above

_____ 10. When Tehani's friend says, "Aren't we supposed to hate each other?", Tehani feels . . .
  A. scared.
  B. disappointed.
  C. mad.
  D. happy.

Short-Essay Test

What advice do you have for Anam?

Skills and Strategies Overview

THEME	School Days
READING LEVEL	average
VOCABULARY	◆ herdsman ◆ departure ◆ marathon ◆ management ◆ development
PREREADING	read-aloud
RESPONSE	visualize
COMPREHENSION	double-entry journal
PREWRITING	narrowing a topic
WRITING	descriptive paragraph / end punctuation
ASSESSMENT	meaning

BACKGROUND

"Finding Patrick" was originally published as a feature article in the *Chicago Tribune*. The reporter, Paul Galloway, conducted extensive interviews with Patrick Ntutu (who at the time was enrolled in the government program at Roosevelt University in Chicago) and with the many people who helped Patrick make a life for himself in the United States.

Patrick, a native of Kenya and the recipient of a college scholarship from the Michael Jordan Foundation, had recently left his small Masai village in order to study abroad. The chance to study in the United States felt like a miracle to Patrick, who had resigned himself to living as a herdsman for the rest of his life.

In "Finding Patrick," Galloway describes the life Patrick led before coming to the United States. He also describes the changes that have occurred in Patrick's life as a result of his scholarship. Patrick says that his life has changed for the better, although he admits that there are some who feel he has put his small rural village at risk for "Westernization," which the Masai and other small African tribes have been fighting for generations. Patrick, who understands his people's concerns, admits that he, too, is worried about his culture, and says: "There are good things about our Masai way of life. . . . I hope I can help to keep the good things of our culture."

UNIT THEME   "Finding Patrick" is about someone who has struggled his whole life for the opportunity to attend school. This article gives students the chance to see that what they take for granted—the right to attend school—is something that some children have to fight for day in and day out.

GRAPHIC ORGANIZER   A sequence organizer can help students keep track of events.

Patrick Ntutu learns he will not be able to attend college.

↓

He resigns himself to life as a herdsman.

Deloris Johnson and others arrive in Kenya in the fall of 1993.

↓

Group visits Ololulunga, home of the Ntutu clan.

Chicago group and Ntutu family meet.
Jordan offers scholarship to Beatrice, who declines.
Beatrice suggests Patrick as an alternate.
Patrick accepts scholarship and prepares to leave for the United States.
Patrick leaves Africa for Roosevelt University in Chicago.

BEFORE YOU READ

Ask a volunteer to **read aloud** the introduction on page 20. Be sure students understand how to **visualize** as they read. Explain that the mental pictures they make can help them better understand the people and places the author describes. Then turn to the prereading activity, a **read-aloud** and **listener's guide**. (Refer to the **Strategy Handbook** on page 40 for more help.)

Motivation Strategy

Tell the class that "Finding Patrick" is about a young man who will do just about anything so that he can go to school each day. Ask students: "Is it a right or a privilege to go to school in the United States?" How would students feel if they were denied the right to attend school? These questions will help students connect their own lives and experiences to the topic of Galloway's article.

ENGAGING STUDENTS "Finding Patrick" concerns one boy's dreams for his future. Ask students to explain or write what they'd like to be doing two years, five years, or even ten years from now. What will they do to help their dreams come true?

Vocabulary Building

As students read, point out key vocabulary words for this lesson: *herdsman, departure, marathon, management,* and *development.* Have students circle these words in the text. Explain that three of these words have a suffix. Tell them that the suffixes *–ment* and *–ure* change a word from a verb to a noun and mean "act of." The word *herdsman* is a compound word made up of two separate English words. Ask someone to find the origin of *marathon* in a dictionary. For additional practice with these words, see page 74.

STRATEGY LESSON: CONTEXT CLUES Although many of the more difficult words in the article are footnoted, students should get into the habit of using context clues to define words they don't know. Model using context clues. "I've never seen the word *manyatta.* I notice, however, that it is defined in the sentence. It's a one-room dwelling."

For additional practice on this strategy, see the **Vocabulary** blackline master on page 74.

Prereading Strategies

A **read-aloud** can be a terrific strategy to use with reluctant or low-level readers. Many times it's easier to understand a selection if it is read aloud at the appropriate pace. Remind your reader to read slowly and with expression so that listeners can clearly hear the different speakers in the article. Also be sure to have students follow along in their books as they are listening. When the reader has finished the opening paragraphs, ask students to pause for a few moments and complete the **listener's guide** on page 20.

THINK-PAIR-AND-SHARE As an alternate prereading strategy, ask students to work together on a think-pair-and-share for this selection. Pull four or five quotations from the text that relate to the theme of school days. Write the quotes on the board and then ask students to guess which quote comes first, which comes next, and so on. When they've finished, ask each student to write a one-sentence prediction about the article. This activity will help students become involved in the topic and theme before they begin reading.

Spanish-speaking Students

"Descubriendo a Patrick" viene de un artículo originalmente publicado en el *Chicago Tribune.* Cuenta como un pastor africano, Patrick, ganó una beca académica en Chicago. Un muchacho inteliegente, trabajador, y pobre, Patrick tenía el deseo pero no el dinero para continuar sus estudios en África. Gracias a la fundación de Michael Jordan, guiada por su madre, Deloris, y a la organización de los Chicago Bulls, Patrick Ntutu se trasladó a Chicago y pronto ingresó en la universidad. Su vida ha cambiado mucho desde que fue descubierto por la gente de Chicago.

The directions on page 21 ask students to read the article with a partner, although you may want to conduct a whole-class **read-aloud** of the selection. Explain how important it is for students to **visualize** as they follow along in their books, making sketches of the people, setting, and events that Galloway describes. Their sketches will help them stay actively involved in the article.

Response Strategy

VISUALIZE   Ask students to compare their sketches of the setting and people when the whole class has finished the article.

Comprehension Strategies

A **double-entry journal** gives students the chance to give their reactions to parts of a reading that are interesting, puzzling, or thematically important. In the left side of each double-entry journal box, there is a quotation from the article. Students should read the quotation carefully and then explain their thoughts and feelings in the right-hand box. Later, you might enlarge on this activity by having students choose one or two quotations to respond to on their own. Remind them to choose quotes that they think are particularly interesting or important.

For more help, see the **Comprehension** blackline master on page 75.

Discussion Questions

COMPREHENSION   1. Where is Patrick from? *(a small village in Kenya)*

2. Why does he come to the United States? *(to go to college)*

3. How does he feel about his experience in the United States? *(He calls it a "miracle.")*

CRITICAL THINKING   4. Does Patrick intend to return home after he graduates? *(Yes, although perhaps with some reluctance.)*

5. What three words would you use to describe Patrick? *(Answers will vary. Ask students to support what they say with evidence from the article.)*

Literary Skill

TONE   Tone is an author's attitude or feeling about the topic or the audience. An author's tone can be serious, humorous, satiric, and so on. In "Finding Patrick," Galloway's tone reveals the admiration he feels for Patrick, Deloris Jordan, and the Michael Jordan Foundation. (His admiration is particularly evident in the final paragraph of the article.) Point out to students that even in writing that is supposed to be completely unbiased, such as a newspaper or textbook article, it's always possible to find some clues about tone. Most of these clues can be found in the author's word choices.

III. GATHER YOUR THOUGHTS

On page 30, students are asked to practice **narrowing the focus** of a writing topic. This activity will be enormously helpful to most students because inexperienced writers tend to try to cover too broad a topic in a single piece of writing. If students need help, work as a class to complete the pie chart in the middle of the page. Refer students to the sample pie in the upper-right corner of the page if they get stuck.

Prewriting Strategies

TOPIC SENTENCE After students narrow their topics, you may want to help them write topic sentences that they can use for the writing assignment on page 31. Remind the class that a topic sentence must clearly state what the paragraph is about. In addition, it must state a feeling or attitude about the topic. Keep this formula for writing topic sentences posted on the board:

A specific topic) + a specific feeling = a good topic sentence.

For additional practice, have students use the **Prewriting** blackline master on page 76.

IV. WRITE

On page 31, students are asked to write a **descriptive paragraph** about one of the subtopics they created on page 30. In a descriptive paragraph, the writer describes something by sharing details of an experience. The best paragraphs pull readers into the story and keep them wondering what will happen next.

Before they begin writing, remind students to start their paragraphs with a topic sentence and to use sensory details that can help their readers "see" and "hear" everything they describe. When students have finished their first drafts, ask them to read the **Writers' Checklist** and revise their writing with those questions in mind.

WRITING RUBRIC When students have finished revising, you can use the writing rubric for help with a quick assessment of their writing.

Do students' paragraphs

- begin with a topic sentence?
- use specific, sensory details that help pull readers into the story?
- stay focused on just one event or experience?

Grammar, Usage and Mechanics

At this point, you might want to introduce a mini-lesson on punctuation. Review with students the rules for end punctuation: periods, question marks, and exclamation points. If you have time, you might post a few sentences on the board that are incorrectly punctuated and ask students to edit them on their own.

V. WRAP-UP

At the end of the lesson, allow time for students to reflect on what they have learned and accomplished. As students answer the questions about the **meaning** of the article, encourage them to make connections between their lives and families and the people Galloway describes.

Assessment

To test students' comprehension, use the **Assessment** blackline master on page 77.

Name _____

VOCABULARY
Words from the Selection

DIRECTIONS From the list of words at the right, choose the word that fits the sentence and write it on the appropriate blank.

1. Patrick did not want to be a _____ on his father's cattle ranch.

2. We had intended to _____ at noon, but our _____ was delayed one hour.

3. We have run in a _____ every year.

4. If he learns to _____, he can soon rise to a _____ level in business.

5. He wanted to _____ his skills so he could help _____ in his own country.

departure

herdsman

depart

development

manage

management

marathon

develop

Strategy Lesson: Context

DIRECTIONS Use context clues to figure out which word fits in each sentence. Write the correct word on the blank.

6. When Patrick learned he could not enroll in a university as he had hoped, he was _____.
   (a) devastated (b) relieved (c) happy (d) excited

7. By showing the most improvement in grades and attendance, six sixth-graders were _____ with a trip to Africa.
   (a) pleased (b) rewarded (c) punished (d) compelled

8. Since there was no running water, villagers _____ their water to the village from a river.
   (a) found (b) drank (c) hauled (d) purified

9. Because they disliked being a British colony, the Masai later _____ Westernization.
   (a) wanted (b) resisted (c) prized (d) explored

10. The challenges Patrick faced are a _____ to those Americans who complain about how tough their lives are.
    (a) bore (b) gift (c) satisfaction (d) rebuke

Name _____

COMPREHENSION
Venn Diagram

DIRECTIONS An important part of reading is making a connection between yourself and the characters or people the author describes. Use this Venn diagram to compare and contrast yourself to Patrick Ntutu. Refer to the text if you can't remember specific details about Patrick.

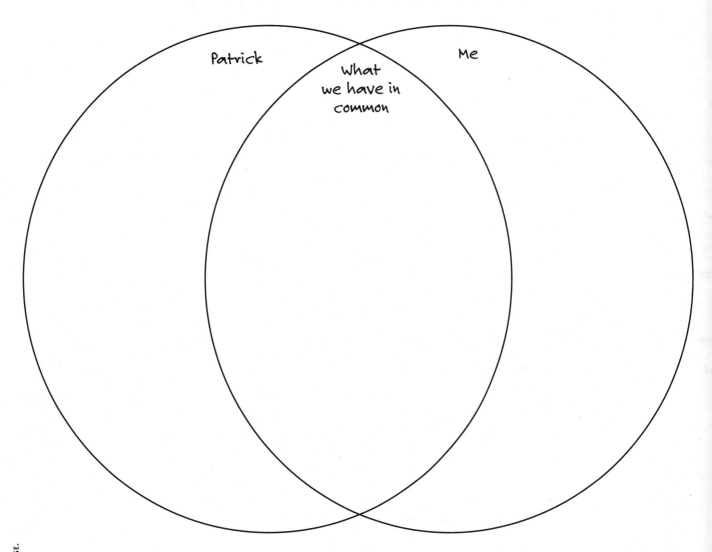

Patrick

What we have in common

Me

Name _____

PREWRITING
Writing a Descriptive Paragraph

DIRECTIONS A descriptive paragraph contains words that appeal to the five senses. Follow these steps to write a descriptive paragraph.

STEP 1. CHOOSE AN EXPERIENCE. Decide what experience you would like to describe.

My choice: _____

_____

_____

_____

STEP 2. WRITE TEN DESCRIPTIVE WORDS THAT RELATE TO YOUR TOPIC. Try to write words that appeal to the senses of sight, hearing, touch, taste, and smell.

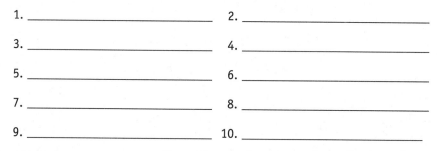

1. _____   2. _____

3. _____   4. _____

5. _____   6. _____

7. _____   8. _____

9. _____   10. _____

STEP 3. WRITE A TOPIC SENTENCE. Now write a topic sentence that tells about the experience.

_____

_____

_____

_____

STEP 4. WRITE A CONCLUDING SENTENCE. Write a sentence that tells what you learned from your experience.

_____

_____

_____

_____

Name _____

ASSESSMENT

Multiple-Choice Test

DIRECTIONS On the blanks provided, write the letter of the item that best completes each sentence or answers each question.

_____ 1. The Masai's tribal economy is based on . . .
    A. money.
    B. cattle herds.
    C. education.
    D. none of the above

_____ 2. Who led the 1993 Chicago tour to Kenya?
    A. Deloris Jordan
    B. Patrick Ntutu
    C. Michael Jordan
    D. Lerionka ole Ntutu

_____ 3. How did the sixth graders qualify to go to Kenya?
    A. They improved their grades.
    B. They improved their attitudes.
    C. They improved their attendance.
    D. all of the above

_____ 4. What did Deloris Jordan offer to Patrick Ntutu?
    A. a college scholarship
    B. money
    C. a new home
    D. a job in Chicago

_____ 5. Which material is NOT used in making a manyatta?
    A. mud
    B. leaves
    C. tree branches
    D. reeds

_____ 6. How did Patrick travel the six miles from his home to his school in Kenya?
    A. He took a school bus.
    B. He ran.
    C. He drove.
    D. He rode his bike.

_____ 7. On his way to school, Patrick worried about . . .
    A. bad weather.
    B. criminals.
    C. traffic.
    D. wild animals.

_____ 8. Patrick received his college degree in . . .
    A. hotel management.
    B. accounting.
    C. business administration.
    D. agriculture.

_____ 9. How does Patrick feel toward the Michael Jordan Foundation and Deloris Jordan?
    A. appreciative
    B. grateful
    C. fond
    D. all of the above

_____ 10. Where do you expect to find Patrick after he finishes his MBA?
    A. Chicago
    B. traveling the world
    C. Kenya
    D. none of the above

Short-Essay Test

How does Patrick feel about the Masai culture?

Apartheid

Unit Background   APARTHEID (pages 33–50)

The authors in this unit write of the violence and hardship of life under apartheid in South Africa from 1948 to 1991. Have students read the definition of apartheid on page 33.

Mark Mathabane (mah ta BON ee) was born in 1960 in the black township of Alexandra, South Africa, outside of Johannesburg. *Kaffir Boy: The True Story of a Black Youth's Coming of Age in Apartheid South Africa* was written and published after Mathabane emigrated to the United States. He was able to emigrate because he won a tennis scholarship. He taught himself to play tennis with a wooden racket his grandmother was given by a white family for whom she worked. He received coaching later and became a top player in South Africa.

A Kaffir is a member of a Bantu people in central and southern Africa. Kaffir also refers to any of the languages of this large group of people. The Bantu languages are spoken by more than 80 million people; the following words are of Bantu or West African origin: *banana, banjo, gumbo, okra, safari,* and *yam.*

Afrikaans is a language developed from the Dutch colonists who settled in South Africa in the 1600s. Among the words that entered English from Afrikaans, in addition to *apartheid,* are *aardvark, eland, veld, springbok,* and *wildebeest.*

Teaching the Introduction

The images on page 33 provide background for the selections. They show the poverty of non-whites, the location of South Africa, the prevalence of soldiers who enforced apartheid laws, and Nelson Mandela (born 1918), the black political leader who was imprisoned for thirty years for his anti-apartheid activities. Mandela shared the 1993 Nobel Prize for peace.

Apartheid

Apartheid means "separateness" in Afrikaans, one of South Africa's official languages. It refers to the period between 1948 and 1991, when South Africa's white-controlled government separated blacks, Asians, and other people of color from the white population. There was segregation in housing, education, jobs, and even transportation.

3.

1.

SOUTH AFRICA

2.

Nelson Mandela

33

1. Some students may have knowledge of life under apartheid or recognize the names Nelson Mandela and Desmond Tutu. If so, ask them to tell what they know.

2. Tell students that since the apartheid government was controlled by people who were in the minority (whites), they should be able to make some speculations about the political and social consequences of life under such a system. Students might suggest that violence, imprisonment of black political leaders, and curtailment of basic human rights were some of the consequences.

3. Ask students to discuss whether they think the rest of the world has responsibilities to stop a system like apartheid.

Opening Activity

Freedom of speech is a basic right that Americans take for granted. Ask students to list on the board other freedoms that Americans accept as their right. Where are these freedoms guaranteed? Why aren't such freedoms guaranteed in some other countries?

It's Quiet Now

Skills and Strategies Overview

THEME	Apartheid
READING LEVEL	average

VOCABULARY

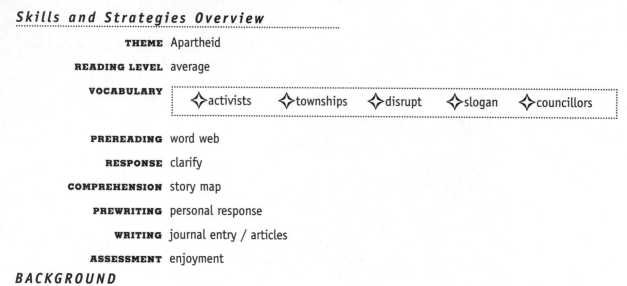

◆ activists   ◆ townships   ◆ disrupt   ◆ slogan   ◆ councillors

PREREADING	word web
RESPONSE	clarify
COMPREHENSION	story map
PREWRITING	personal response
WRITING	journal entry / articles
ASSESSMENT	enjoyment

BACKGROUND

"It's Quiet Now" is an eyewitness account of the street violence that was so common in South Africa during the time of apartheid. This essay was originally published in the book *Sometimes When It Rains,* an anthology of essays by South-African women.

Students might find Mhlope's story shocking for two reasons: one, because the scene she describes is so brutal; and two, because the witnesses to the scene seem so inured to the violence around them that they barely glance at the carnage in the streets. Mhlope uses sensory language to help readers see, hear, smell, and feel the violence she witnesses on a day-to-day basis. This language makes it easy for readers to understand and embrace her message of "Siyayinyova"—"We will destroy or disrupt."

UNIT THEME Gcina Mhlope presents readers with a disturbing look at the fight against apartheid.

GRAPHIC ORGANIZER The word web students are asked to create on page 34 might contain some of the following words.

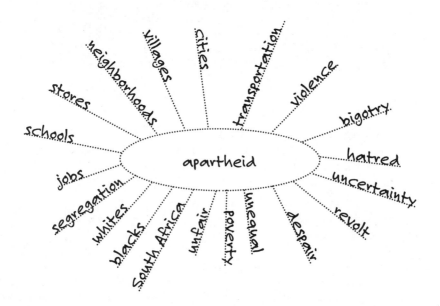

BEFORE YOU READ

After students have read the introduction to the theme on page 33, ask them to tell what they know about South African apartheid. What have they heard about it? What have they seen on TV or at the movies? Then ask students to read the introduction to the lesson on page 34. Tell them they can get ready to read the selection by continuing their discussion of apartheid. When you feel students are ready, ask them to complete the prereading activity, the **word web**, on page 34. (Refer to the **Strategy Handbook** on page 40 for more help with word webs.)

Motivation Strategy

ENGAGING STUDENTS To help students become interested in the topic of "It's Quiet Now," ask them to think of a time they've been discriminated against or treated unfairly. Have them explain what happened and how they felt. Listening to classmates' comments may help students better understand life under apartheid.

Vocabulary Building

Put these vocabulary words on the board: *activists, townships, slogan, disrupt,* and *councillors*. Point out that *disrupt* comes from the Latin root *rumpere,* meaning "to break," and ask students what they think the word means in this context. Other words with this root are *erupt, interrupt, corrupt,* and *rupture*. Tell students to read the footnotes that define the other vocabulary words. For additional practice with these words, see page 84.

STRATEGY LESSON: CONTEXT CLUES Help students use context clues as they read to figure out the meanings of difficult words. Many of these words are footnoted at the bottom of student pages, but there are bound to be more words in the selection that students are unfamiliar with. Show students how to use context clues to figure out the meanings of these words. Ask students to look for context clues for the word *informer* on page 35.

For additional practice on this strategy, see the **Vocabulary** blackline master on page 84.

Prereading Strategies

The purpose of a **word web** is to activate students' prior knowledge about a topic. Encourage students to write words that explore the denotative and connotative meaning of *apartheid*. Remind them to write the emotions they associate with the word: *anger, sadness, rage, confusion,* and so on. To extend the activity and further prepare students for the reading, consider doing a class web that incorporates the words students listed on their smaller webs. You might be surprised at the number of words that students are able to come up with.

QUICKWRITE As an alternate prereading strategy, have students do a one-minute quickwrite in which they explore what they know about apartheid. This activity will help them think actively about the topic of the article and also allow students to begin connecting the theme and topic to their own lives.

Spanish-speaking Students

En esta selección Gcina Mhlope describe el caos que estallaba en Sud África durante la época de segregación racial—el período cuando la gente negra fue oprimida por el gobierno blanco. Pinta un retrato vívido del terror y tumulto que contaminaba el ambiente. Muchos estudiantes, negros, y defensores de los derechos humanos exegían justicia. Pero como Mhlope señala, los soldados del gobierno frecuentemente quietaron las demandas para libertad e igualdad con fuerza brutal.

II. READ

As students begin to read, walk through the process of responding to literature. Explain that it is particularly important when reading nonfiction to stop along the way and **clarify** the point the author is trying to make. Students should write their notes of clarification in the **Response Notes**, along with any questions that come up during the reading.

Response Strategy

VISUALIZE As an alternate response strategy, students might visualize and then sketch the people and scenes that Mhlope describes. Their sketches will help them better understand the violence that is a natural offshoot of apartheid. In addition, their sketches might be useful when it comes time to write their journal entries responding to Mhlope's essay.

Comprehension Strategies

Story maps can help students keep track of the basic elements of a narrative. On the story map on page 38, students can list the characters, problem, major events, and outcome of "It's Quiet Now." You might have them add two boxes to the page—one for setting and one for goal. Help students see that no two story maps will be exactly alike. In general, however, students should be able to agree that the problem Mhlope describes is violence generated by apartheid, and that her goal (and the goal of her fellow South Africans) is freedom from discrimination.

For more help, see the **Comprehension** blackline master on page 85.

Discussion Questions

COMPREHENSION 1. What is apartheid? *(In Afrikaans, the word means "separateness." It refers to the period between 1948 and 1991 when South Africa's white government separated blacks, Asians, and other people of color from the white population.)*

2. Why do the people of South Africa throw bombs and light fires in the street? *(They intend to wreak havoc until apartheid is abolished forever.)*

3. What does the slogan "Siyayinyova" mean? *("We will destroy or disrupt.")*

CRITICAL THINKING 4. How does Gcina Mhlope feel about apartheid? *(She despises it.)*

5. Why do the people returning from work hurry past the violence in the streets? *(Answers will vary. Accept reasonable responses that are supportable with evidence from the selection.)*

Literary Skill

POINT OF VIEW To introduce a literary skill with this lesson, explain to students that a story changes when the point of view (or vantage point) changes. "It's Quiet Now" is told from Mhlope's point of view. She offers her perspective on the events and remains present throughout the entire narrative. She tells readers only what she saw and felt and cannot offer information about what other participants saw and felt. Ask students to imagine how Mhlope's story would be different if it were told from the perspective of one of the children screaming "Siyayinyova" or from that of one of the policemen whose van was damaged in the street. Would the tone change? Would the message change? How?

III. GATHER YOUR THOUGHTS

As a prewriting activity, students are asked to explore their **personal responses** to Mhlope's story. The two sentence starters at the bottom of page 38 will help students overcome their initial reluctance to write. Sentence starters are enormously helpful for inexperienced writers because the first sentence often requires the most effort. Once a writer has the first sentence down, however, the creative juices begin flowing and the writing becomes easier.

Prewriting Strategies

GROUP DISCUSSION As an alternate prewriting activity, ask students to get together in small groups and discuss their responses to "It's Quiet Now." Students should share their reactions and help each other with any points that need clarifying. Ask one group member to take notes on the group's discussion and then report to the rest of the class what was said. Students will benefit from hearing several different perspectives on the essay and may be able to incorporate some of their classmates' ideas into their own writing.

Have students use the **Prewriting** blackline master on page 86.

IV. WRITE

Before they begin, remind students that they are writing a **journal entry** that is a reaction to Mhlope's essay. Also remind them to use one of the sentence starters they wrote on page 38. When students have finished writing, explain that it would be a good idea for them to edit their work using the **Writers' Checklist** as a guide.

WRITING RUBRIC When students have finished editing their work, you can use the writing rubric for help with a quick assessment of their writing. You might also ask students to check their own work using the questions on the rubric.

Do students' journal entries

- begin with one of the starter sentences from the prewriting section?

- contain three or more details to support the starter sentence?

- fully explore their personal reactions to Mhlope's essay?

- stay focused on their own reactions and avoid discussing the reactions of others?

Grammar, Usage, and Mechanics

You might take this opportunity to remind the class that *an* is used before a word that begins with a vowel or vowel sound and that *a* is used before a word that begins with a consonant sound. Also explain the third item on the checklist: *the* is typically not used with nouns that refer to *all* or *in general*. Example:

Incorrect: We are used to the democracy.

Correct: We are used to democracy.

V. WRAP-UP

At the end of the lesson, ask students what they **enjoyed** and did not enjoy about the article. Take note of what students thought was interesting or dull. You can use their comments to help you plan strategies for future lessons, including the lesson that follows this one in the student book. It too explores the theme of apartheid.

Assessment

To test students' comprehension, use the **Assessment** blackline master on page 87.

Name _____

VOCABULARY
Words from the Selection

DIRECTIONS Answer these questions that use words from the selection. Explain your answers.

1. Would <u>activists</u> be more inclined to riot in the streets or to take no part in protests?

_____

2. Are <u>townships</u> geographical places or a type of government?

_____

3. Is a <u>slogan</u> a brief sentence or speech?

_____

4. If you <u>disrupt</u> class, are you likely to be talking or thinking?

_____

5. Are <u>councillors</u> government officials or teachers?

_____

Strategy Lesson: Context Clues

DIRECTIONS Use context clues to figure out the meaning of the underlined words. On the blanks, write your best guess about what you think each word means.

6. Although he was arrested as an <u>informer</u>, the man said he had never told anyone any government secrets. An <u>informer</u> is probably someone who

_____

7. She stood <u>transfixed</u> at the window, unable to turn away from the scene. <u>Transfixed</u> probably means

_____

8. The passengers were <u>grumbling</u> because the bus was stopped in traffic. <u>Grumbling</u> probably means

_____

9. When it began to <u>drizzle</u>, umbrellas popped up everywhere. <u>Drizzle</u> probably means

_____

10. The <u>authorities</u> ordered everyone off the streets. The <u>authorities</u> are probably

_____

Name _____

COMPREHENSION
Retelling

DIRECTIONS Answer these questions about "It's Quiet Now."

1. What problem is Mhlope's township facing?

_____

_____

_____

2. What do the schoolchildren do after they pour out of their school and into the streets?

_____

_____

_____

3. Why do the children behave the way they do?

_____

_____

_____

4. What happens when it starts to rain?

_____

_____

_____

5. How does Mhlope feel about apartheid? Support your answer with evidence from the selection.

_____

_____

_____

Name _____

PREWRITING
Storyboard

DIRECTIONS Use this storyboard to show the events Gcina Mhlope describes in her essay. Draw a picture of each event and then write a sentence describing it. Refer to your book if you need to.

"It's Quiet Now"

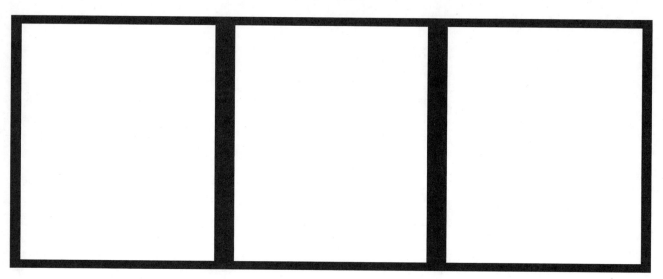

Name _____

ASSESSMENT

Multiple-Choice Test

DIRECTIONS On the blanks provided, write the letter of the item that best answers each question or completes each sentence.

_____ 1. What is the mood of the essay?
   A. happy
   B. defiant
   C. humorous
   D. depressed

_____ 2. At the beginning of the essay, Mhlope stands and watches . . .
   A. the rain.
   B. the television.
   C. a fight.
   D. a rally.

_____ 3. If someone is "necklaced," it means they've been . . .
   A. tortured.
   B. given a gift.
   C. shot.
   D. none of the above

_____ 4. Why do the company delivery vans stop making deliveries in the townships?
   A. The roads are blocked.
   B. Students have burned many vans.
   C. The drivers are on strike.
   D. They are not allowed.

_____ 5. Whose house was burned down?
   A. the author's
   B. the author's neighbor's
   C. the President's
   D. the Mayor's

_____ 6. Which type of legislation causes the black people of this country great suffering?
   A. taxation
   B. civil rights
   C. apartheid
   D. all of the above

_____ 7. The slogan "Siyayinyova" means the people will . . .
   A. destroy.
   B. deny.
   C. disrupt.
   D. A. and C.

_____ 8. Mhlope hears singing from the . . .
   A. school.
   B. church.
   C. television.
   D. police station.

_____ 9. What do the schoolchildren do?
   A. throw bricks and rocks
   B. chant
   C. run away
   D. all of the above

_____ 10. What ends the riots in the streets?
   A. the police
   B. tear gas
   C. rain
   D. a fire bomb

Short-Essay Test

Why do you think the people coming home from work ignore what's going on in the streets?

Skills and Strategies Overview

THEME	Apartheid
READING LEVEL	average
VOCABULARY	✧soliciting ✧eviction ✧malnutrition ✧perishables ✧expectantly
PREREADING	skim
RESPONSE	question
COMPREHENSION	reciprocal reading
PREWRITING	summarize
WRITING	letter / commas
ASSESSMENT	ease

BACKGROUND

Mark Mathabane and his six siblings were raised in terrible poverty in one of South Africa's many black ghettos. Mathabane's parents earned a mere ten dollars a week—not nearly enough to pay rent on their tiny shack and put food on the table for a family of nine. As a result, Mathabane's childhood was marred by devastating poverty. In addition, he and his siblings were forced to endure one brutal police raid after another to their own home and the homes of their neighbors. The Mathabane children lived in terror of stepping outside the walls of their home.

Although there was violence all around, Mr. and Mrs. Mathabane insisted that their children attend school. Mathabane's mother, who never learned to read, knew that education was the only way out of the ghetto. She also knew it would be the only way to keep her children from a dead-end life of street gangs and crime.

In 1978, with the help of Wimbledon champion Stan Smith, Mathabane (who had shown promise as a tennis player) left South Africa to attend a university in the United States. While in college, he realized that writing—not tennis—was his passion. His autobiography, *Kaffir Boy,* was published in 1986. Today it is used in classrooms across the United States.

UNIT THEME Mark Mathabane shows how truly devastating apartheid was for the children of South Africa.

GRAPHIC ORGANIZER A web like the one below can help students summarize what they learn about the author.

experienced the humiliation of having his
father imprisoned by an apartheid
government

writing is his passion

explores the subject of apartheid

attended college in the
United States

Mark Mathabane

endured severe poverty and
deprivation as a child

wrote about his experiences
in Kaffir Boy

helped his mother find food
for the family

BEFORE YOU READ

Read the introduction on page 41 aloud to students. Remind the class that the theme for this unit is apartheid, and that they should look for words and ideas that relate to this theme when they do their prereading activity, a **skim** of the selection.

Motivation Strategy

Before they **skim**, have students review what they know about apartheid. Even a quick review of the tenets of apartheid will help students better understand the Mathabane family's desperation.

ENGAGING STUDENTS Ask students: "Have you ever been really, truly hungry? What happened?" Help students see that the kind of hunger Mathabane describes in *Kaffir Boy* is not the routine "I-missed-my-breakfast" hunger that most American children feel from time to time. Ask students to imagine a type of hunger that would force them to go with their parents to look for food in the town dump. This gives students the opportunity to visualize the plight of the Mathabane family even before they begin reading.

Vocabulary Building

You might teach a short lesson on suffixes using four of the five key vocabulary words: *soliciting, eviction, perishables,* and *expectantly*. The *-ing* suffix in *soliciting* forms the present participle of the verb *solicit*. The *–ion* suffix in *eviction* forms a noun from the word *evict*. The *–able* suffix forms adjectives from verbs and nouns. For example, something *perishable* is likely to perish or decay. (The word *perishables* is a noun, however, meaning "something perishable.") Also point out the prefix in *malnutrition. Mal-* means "bad or badly, poor or poorly." Tell students to circle the five vocabulary words in the text. For additional practice with these words, see page 92.

STRATEGY LESSON: CONTEXT Tell students that authors sometimes define words they think may be unfamiliar to readers. Students should be on the alert for such instances. For example, in the last line on page 43, the author uses the word *kaya* and then defines it. On page 47, he uses the word *musadi* and again defines it.

For additional practice, see the **Vocabulary** blackline master, page 92.

Prereading Strategies

Skimming is an extremely helpful prereading strategy that most students don't use on their own. Skimming gives the reader a quick preview of the topic and theme of a selection, in addition to a "heads-up" about difficult vocabulary and confusing concepts. Encourage students to get into the habit of skimming first. If possible, have them skim with a few questions in mind, such as "What names, dates, and places did you notice?" and "What questions or vocabulary words are likely to cause you problems as you read?"

PREVIEW As an alternate prereading strategy, ask students to do a preview of the selection. In some ways, a preview is similar to a skim, although during a preview, the reader does a close reading of the first and perhaps the last paragraph of the selection. In addition, readers should glance at the art and captions during their previews and use what they've seen to make some thoughtful predictions about the text. You'll find that previewing is a good strategy to use with all types of nonfiction texts, including narrative nonfiction forms such as autobiography and biography.

Spanish-speaking Students

"Sobrevivencia" pinta otro retrato vívido de las condiciones terribles bajo las cuales la población negra en Sud África tenía que soportar durante los años de segregación racial. Mark Mathabane se enfoca en la vida de una familia que lucha para sobrevivir cada día. Como el padre está en la cárcel, la madre y los hijos han recurrido a buscar comida en la basura. El descubrimiento de unas sobras lleva mucha alegría que les satisfarán por lo menos hasta el próximo día, cuando tendrán que forrajear de nuevo.

II. READ

When students are ready to read, remind them once again how important it is to make comments in the **Response Notes** as they read. In particular, students should jot down any **questions** they'd like to ask the author, another reader, or even you. These questions can be used to initiate a whole-class or small-group discussion after everyone has finished reading.

Response Strategy

REACT AND CONNECT Many students will want to share their family experiences, just as Mathabane shares his. As an alternate response strategy, have students make react and connect comments, such as "I saw something like that once!" or "I know exactly what that feels like." Their observations will help them stay interested in and involved with the selection.

Comprehension Strategies

Students will do a **reciprocal reading** of "Survival." This means that they take turns reading the selection aloud with a partner, switching readers after every page. As students read, they will answer questions that help them 1. clarify the problem, characters, and setting of Mathabane's story; 2. predict what will happen next; 3. summarize the events; and 4. raise questions about the literature. Encourage students to stop as often as they like during their oral readings to make comments or ask questions of each other.

PREDICTION Another comprehension strategy that will work well with "Survival" is predicting. Making predictions as they read can help students stay interested and alert. At the bottom of each page, students can stop and decide what they think will happen next. If you like, write out some prediction questions beforehand and ask students to use these during their reading. Even the most general prediction questions, such as "What do you think will happen next?" can elicit insightful responses. When they've finished reading, students can review their predictions to see which came true.

For more help, see the **Comprehension** blackline master on page 93.

Discussion Questions

COMPREHENSION 1. Where does the family in this story live? *(South Africa)*

2. What are some of the challenges this family faces? *(The father is in jail. Because of this, the family is hungry and close to homeless.)*

3. Why do they go to the dump? *(to look for food)*

CRITICAL THINKING 4. Is the narrator ashamed to go to the dump? *(Answers will vary. Remind students to support what they say with evidence from the story.)*

5. Why doesn't the family share their food with the others at the dump? *(Answers to this question will also vary. Have students support their ideas with quotations from the story.)*

Literary Skill

AUTOBIOGRAPHY If you like, take this opportunity to discuss autobiography with students. Remind the class that an autobiography is a record of a life, written by the subject himself or herself. Autobiographies come in many different forms, including letters, memoirs, diaries, and journals. The advantage of reading an autobiography is that it can offer an unparalleled glimpse into the life and thoughts of a person. The disadvantage is that it is a highly subjective form of writing. The writer offers only the information that he or she wants the reader to know. Remind students that when they are studying historical events, it is important to use a variety of sources that include both narrative and expository nonfiction.

III. GATHER YOUR THOUGHTS

The goal of these prewriting activities is to help students pull together what they've learned from their reading. After they've made a critical-thinking response to the selection, students will be ready to do some writing of their own. At the top of page 48, students are asked to **summarize** what life was like for blacks under apartheid. At the bottom of the page, students will describe two specific aspects of life under apartheid. Remind the class to refer to their Response Notes for details about their topics.

Prewriting Strategies

GROUP DISCUSSION As an alternate activity, ask students to discuss their responses in small groups.

Have students use the **Prewriting** blackline master on page 94.

IV. WRITE

The writing activity on page 49 has two important purposes. First, students will show they understand what life was like for blacks under apartheid. They'll need to be clear and specific in their descriptions and should be encouraged to draw details from both "It's Quiet Now" and "Survival." The second purpose of the writing activity is to sharpen students' letter-writing abilities. Remind the class to follow proper letter-writing form in their **letters.** The **Writers' Checklist** can help students who are struggling with correct placement and punctuation of the date, salutation, and closing.

WRITING RUBRIC Refer to this writing rubric when students have finished their letters.

Do students' letters

- describe two aspects of life under apartheid?
- contain vivid details so that a reader can visualize the things described?
- make specific reference to "It's Quiet Now" and "Survival"?
- follow correct letter-writing form?

Grammar, Usage, and Mechanics

If you feel students need the help, teach a brief mini-lesson on writing friendly letters. Remind the class that the date belongs at the top right-hand side of the page and that the closing should be slightly to the left of the center of the page. A comma follows the last word of the salutation and the closing. Only the first word of the closing is capitalized, while each word in the salutation should begin with a capital letter.

Incorrect: dear Saundra

Correct: Dear Saundra,

V. WRAP-UP

Take a moment at the end of the lesson for students to think about what they've read. Point out the **Readers' Checklist** and ask students to decide whether "Survival" was **easy** or difficult to read. If they felt it was hard, have them explain why. Their comments about reading strategies can help you plan future lessons.

Assessment

To test students' comprehension, use the **Assessment** blackline master on page 95.

Name_____

VOCABULARY
Words from the Selection

DIRECTIONS Choose the word from the list at the right that correctly fits in each sentence, and write that word on the blank.

1. We were so poor, we were afraid we would be out _____ money before the weekend.

2. Since we could not pay the rent, we faced _____ from our home.

3. Thank goodness we had plenty of food, and none of us was suffering from _____.

4. Fortunately, we had put the _____ in the refrigerator.

5. We waited _____ for a check to arrive.

expectantly

evict

expectant

eviction

perishables

solicit

soliciting

nutrition

malnutrition

perish

Strategy Lesson: Context

DIRECTIONS Use clues in the sentences to find the meaning of the underlined words. Underline the correct answer.

6. Many people looked through the heap of ash and <u>refuse</u> in the dump.
   (a) trash; (b) say "no" to; (c) food; (d) mud

7. Some people found things at the dump deep in the <u>debris</u>.
   (a) papers; (b) piles; (c) earth; (d) rubbish

8. Her fingers were <u>gnarled</u>, just like the rough and knotted hands of my grandmother.
   (a) blue; (b) twisted; (c) short; (d) cold

9. We were poor and hungry, and we wrote a letter describing our <u>plight</u>.
   (a) angry boss; (b) rainy weather; (c) bad situation; (d) enemies

10. There was a <u>throng</u> of people—40 or 50 men, women, and children—scattered around.
    (a) carful; (b) large crowd; (c) long line; (d) dangerous mob

Name_____

COMPREHENSION
Graphic Organizer

DIRECTIONS Use this plot line to show the events of "Survival." Check your book for specific details.

Climax (the crisis or turning point—usually the most important moment in the narrative)

_____

_____

Rising action (problem or conflict)

_____

_____

_____

_____

Falling action (what the characters do and say to resolve the conflict)

_____

_____

_____

Exposition (background and opening events)

_____

_____

_____

_____

Resolution (denouement or outcome—final events of the narrative)

_____

_____

_____

Name_____

PREWRITING
Using Sensory Details

Sensory details can make your writing more interesting. Sensory details are details that come to you through the five senses *(smell, touch, taste, hearing,* and *sight)*. These kind of details give the reader a "you are there" feeling.

Example: *I could smell the smoke from the burning van and feel the heat of the fire upon my face.*

DIRECTIONS Imagine you are the narrator of "Survival." What do you smell, touch, taste, hear, and see as you are hunting for food to feed your family?

1. Write two or more details for each sense.

2. Then write one or two sentences describing the setting (where you are). Use some of your sensory words in the description.

Sensory Words	
I see ⟶	
I feel ⟶	
I taste ⟶	
I hear ⟶	
I smell ⟶	

Where am I? (the setting) _____

_____

_____

ASSESSMENT

Multiple-Choice Test

DIRECTIONS On the blanks provided, write the letter of the item that best answers each question or completes each sentence.

_____ 1. Who gives the family money at the beginning of the story?

    A. the dad   C. the storekeeper

    B. George   D. the grandmother

_____ 2. George and Florah are sick with . . .

    A. malnutrition.   C. measles.

    B. chicken pox.   D. A and B

_____ 3. Their father is . . .

    A. in prison.   C. living in another township.

    B. away on a job.   D. none of the above

_____ 4. The word *kaya* means . . .

    A. food.   C. house.

    B. money.   D. car.

_____ 5. Why does the storekeeper refuse to open the family's account?

    A. There is no man of the house to settle it.   C. The storekeeper doesn't open accounts for women.

    B. They owe money on their last account.   D. all of the above

_____ 6. The mother agrees to clean the storekeeper's house and wash his clothes in exchange for . . .

    A. food.   C. supplies.

    B. rent money.   D. clothes.

_____ 7. Where does the family go to search for food?

    A. restaurants   C. their neighbors

    B. grocery stores   D. the dump

_____ 8. Which item does the family NOT find at the Mlothi?

    A. clothes   C. furniture

    B. food   D. radios

_____ 9. When the boy thinks he has found food, he feels . . .

    A. embarrassed.   C. confused.

    B. excited.   D. disgusted.

_____ 10. Why does the family go to the Mlothi?

    A. They are starving.   C. They are proud.

    B. They are greedy.   D. They are nosy.

Short-Essay Test

Do you think the family was wrong to search for food in the Mlothi? Explain your opinion.

Zora Neale Hurston

Unit Background **ZORA NEALE HURSTON** (pages 51–72)

Zora Neale Hurston's mother died when Zora was a child, and when her father, a preacher and mayor of Eatonville, Florida, remarried, Hurston went to live with relatives. Soon, however, she got a job as a wardrobe girl in a traveling drama troupe. She left the troupe by 1918 and until 1924, she occasionally took courses at Howard University.

She moved to New York City and in 1928 graduated from Barnard College. Impressed with a paper she wrote, one of her professors sent it to anthropologist Franz Boas. Boas helped her begin graduate work in anthropology at Columbia University, and she returned to the South for her field work. In 1936 she was awarded a Guggenheim Fellowship for traveling and collecting folklore in Haiti and the West Indies. *Mules and Men* (1935) and *Tell My Horse* (1938) were based on her research in the South and in the Caribbean.

She was involved in the brilliant literary world of the Harlem Renaissance and began collaboration with Langston Hughes on a play, *Mule Bone*, which was largely written in 1930. They quarreled, however, and the play was not produced until 1991, when it had its premiere at Lincoln Center in New York. She published her autobiography, *Dust Tracks on a Road*, in 1942. In addition to the works mentioned, she published four novels and more than fifty shorter works. *The Complete Stories of Zora Neale Hurston* was published by HarperCollins in 1995 and contains more vignettes from *The Eatonville Anthology*.

In her later life, she was variously employed as a cleaning woman, journalist, and substitute teacher. She died in poverty in 1960.

Teaching the Introduction

The photographs on page 51 depict Hurston, the cover of her autobiography, and scenes of rural and urban life. The building at the upper right, a post office when the photo was taken but originally a house, is constructed in a typically Southern style, with an upper porch designed to catch cool breezes.

Zora Neale Hurston

Zora Neale Hurston (1891–1960) was born in the all-black town of Eatonville, Florida. After college, she moved to New York City, where she gained instant fame as a writer and became known for wearing outrageous clothing and big hats. Hurston's writing celebrates African-American culture.

ZORA NEALE HURSTON
Edited and with an Introduction by Robert E. Hemenway
Dust Tracks on a Road
An Autobiography
Second Edition — With a Foreword by Maya Angelou

51

1. Ask students to tell about times when they have met or seen people, young or old, they would like to know more about. What makes these people seem interesting?

2. Tell students that Zora Neale Hurston wrote about her life and about interesting people in her hometown in Florida. Ask why students think some people write an autobiography.

3. In the part of her autobiography included here, Hurston wrote about times when she felt most "colored," or African American. Ask students whether they have ever had the common experience of feeling alone in a crowd. Why did they feel that way? What advice could they give to someone who feels alone in a crowd?

Opening Activity

Students will be familiar with capsule interviews of entertainment figures in newspapers or magazines. Tell them they are going to do similar interviews with class members. Assign each student to a partner, preferably someone they don't know well, and ask them to interview each other, one at a time, for from five to eight minutes. Each interviewer should take notes. Give students time to prepare a few questions ahead of time. Questions about favorite foods, school subjects, leisure-time activities, music, movies, and books might be appropriate. "Celebrity" interviews might be posted on the class bulletin board, perhaps with a photo of the subject.

How It Feels to Be Colored Me

Skills and Strategies Overview

THEME	Zora Neale Hurston
READING LEVEL	challenging

VOCABULARY

◆venturesome   ◆compliments   ◆deplored   ◆emerges   ◆miscellany

PREREADING	preview
RESPONSE	mark
COMPREHENSION	word attack
PREWRITING	topic sentence and details
WRITING	personal narrative / fragments
ASSESSMENT	depth

BACKGROUND

Zora Neale Hurston (1891–1960) is recognized today as one of the true literary geniuses of the twentieth century. During her lifetime, however, she found it impossible to make a living as a writer and was forced to support herself as a ladies' maid and field hand.

As a young girl growing up in the South, Hurston loved to sit on the front porch of her house and listen while the adults gossiped and told stories. Although she was not allowed to join in the talk, young Zora occasionally performed songs or skits for the adults and other children. These little performances gave Zora the idea that she might one day be a stage performer.

Although her dream of becoming a star gradually faded, Zora maintained the poise and self-confidence she learned on the front porch of her parents' house. Her positive self-esteem is evident in "How It Feels to Be Colored Me," an excerpt from her autobiography.

UNIT THEME Zora Neale Hurston celebrates the theme of identity. She tells readers that if they feel good about themselves—if they feel that they are beautiful, smart, and talented—the world can't help but share the same opinion.

GRAPHIC ORGANIZER In the final paragraph of "How It Feels to Be Colored Me," Hurston compares herself to a "brown bag of miscellany" (student book page 59). Invite students to picture themselves as bags of "miscellany." What are the contents of their bags?

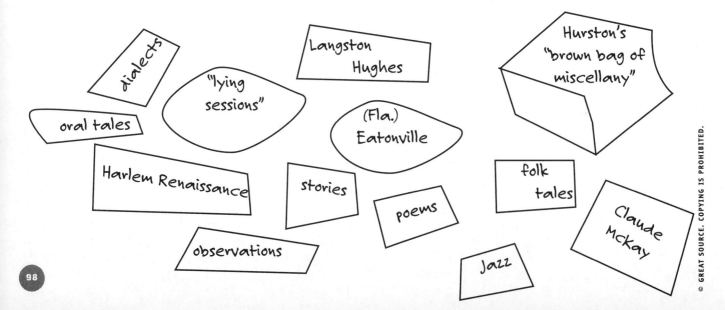

BEFORE YOU READ

Read the introduction to Zora Neale Hurston on page 51 and the lesson opener on page 52. If you think it will be helpful, supplement what's in the book with some additional biographical information about Hurston. Tell students that very often it is the *tone* of Hurston's writing that makes her books and stories so memorable.

Motivation Strategy

As a warm-up, and to help connect the topic of Hurston's writing to their own lives, ask students to rewrite the title of the selection so that it reflects their own feelings about themselves. Model this for students by explaining that your autobiography might be called "How It Feels to Be Teacher Me" or "How It Feels to Be Exhausted Me." Help students choose funny or serious nouns and adjectives that reflect their own identities.

ENGAGING STUDENTS Ask students to think of autobiographies they've read in the past. Which did they enjoy? Which didn't they enjoy and why? In their opinion, what makes for a good autobiography?

Vocabulary Building

Help students use **context clues** as they read to figure out the meanings of difficult words, especially the key vocabulary words for this lesson: *venturesome, compliments, deplored, emerges,* and *miscellany.* Although the footnotes define these words, students will want to get into the habit of searching for clues as they are reading because it's faster and easier than checking a footnote or a dictionary definition. Have students circle these words in the text. For additional practice with these words, see page 102.

Strategy Lesson: Latin Prefix

Write the word *circumlocution* (from page 57) on the board. Tell students that the prefix *circum–* means "in a circle, around" and that *locution* means "a style of speech, manner of expression." Thus, a circumlocution is a roundabout expression. For example, "The daughter of your mother's sister" is a circumlocution for "your cousin." Then ask students to tell what they think *circumnavigate* means.

For additional practice, see the **Vocabulary** blackline master, page 102.

Prereading Strategies

A **preview** is a sort of mini-introduction to the topic and theme of the reading. During a preview, students read the first and last paragraphs of the selection and then glance through the rest. They watch for words, phrases, and ideas that pop out and art that catches their attention. Although it's not mandatory that they record what they noticed in the preview, most readers find it helpful to jot down a few impressions before they actually begin reading. As always, the act of writing can help focus their attention and encourage them to read more carefully. In addition, a **preview chart** like the one on page 52 can give them a specific purpose for reading—to see if the quick observations they made during the preview are in fact correct.

Spanish-speaking Students

Zora Neale Hurston es una de las escritoras más celebradas del mundo literario. En esta selección famosa, ella habla francamente de la raza, y específicamente, de cómo ella misma se ha sentido como una negra. Describe su juventud en Florida y su experiencia viviendo en Nueva York, donde veía unas divisiones y diferencias muy claras entre la gente blanca y negra. Al final, rehusa ser clasificada solo como una persona negra. Insiste en ser hecha de mucho más de un sólo color.

READ

Before they begin, remind students that you expect them to write their comments and **questions** in the **Response Notes**. Point out the sample question in the Response Notes. Explain that the reader might find an answer to the question later on in the reading. If not, he or she may decide to share it with the whole group after the reading is finished.

Response Strategy

CLARIFY Since some of the vocabulary in "How It Feels to Be Colored Me" can be challenging, you also might want to ask students to clarify difficult words or ideas in the **Response Notes**. If a part of the selection seems too difficult, have them make a note in the margin so that they can ask you about it after the whole class has finished.

Comprehension Strategies

There are many different types of **word-attack** strategies. The most helpful strategy to use with low-level readers is context clues. As they read Hurston's essay, students should highlight words they don't know. If the word is essential to the meaning of the sentence, they should stop there and look for context clues in surrounding sentences. If the word is not essential, students can return to it later and once again look for context clues that can help them decide on the word's meaning. They should note unfamiliar words and context clues on the chart on page 60.

DOUBLE-ENTRY JOURNAL As an alternate comprehension strategy, suggest that students write their thoughts and feelings about two or three quotations that you've chosen beforehand. Doing a double-entry journal gives students the opportunity to react to bits and pieces of a text, which is less intimidating than reacting to the text as a whole. (Of course, their "small" reactions now will probably come in handy, when it is time to respond to the entire text.) Here are three quotations that will work well in a double-entry journal activity:

- "But I am not tragically colored. There is no great sorrow dammed up in my soul, nor lurking behind my eyes." (page 55)

- "The terrible struggle that made me an American out of a potential slave said 'On the line!' The Reconstruction said 'Get set!'; and the generation before said 'Go!'" (page 56)

- "At certain times I have no race, I am *me*." (page 58)

For more help, see the **Comprehension** blackline master on page 103.

Discussion Questions

COMPREHENSION 1. Who is Zora Neale Hurston? *(author, folklorist, narrator of the essay)*

2. Where did she grow up? *(Eatonville, Florida)*

3. Why did she enjoy hanging around the front porch when she was a child? *(She liked meeting the folks who were traveling down the street in front of her house.)*

CRITICAL THINKING 4. What does Hurston mean when she says, "I remember the very day that I became colored"? *(Refer students to the quote on page 53, paragraph 2, and have them explain what they think it means.)*

5. How does Hurston feel about herself? *(Remind students to support what they say with specific quotations from the text.)*

Literary Skill

METAPHOR Tell students that a metaphor is a figurative comparison of two things that does not use the words *like* or *as*. For example, Hurston writes on page 57 that "among the thousand white persons, I am a dark rock surged upon, and overswept, but through it all, I remain myself." (Had Hurston said "I am like a rock," she would have written a simile, another kind of figurative comparison.) Ask students why Hurston might compare herself to a rock. What does this comparison tell the reader about her?

III. GATHER YOUR THOUGHTS

The prewriting activities on page 61 will help students plan a **personal narrative** of their own. The activities take them step by step through the writing process. First they'll brainstorm possible topics. Then they'll narrow their focus, gather details, and write a closing sentence. Separating the process into manageable steps makes writing seem less intimidating to students.

Prewriting Strategies

GATHER DETAILS You can help students improve the details they use for their narratives by asking them to practice writing sensory details. Remind the class that sensory details are details that appeal to one or more of the five senses: sight, smell, taste, touch, hearing. (For an example of sensory language, have students turn to Hurston's description of her night in the jazz club on pages 57–58.) Ask students to say what they heard, saw, tasted, touched, and smelled during their memorable experience.

For more help, see the **Prewriting** blackline master on page 104.

IV. WRITE

Set aside some class time for students to write their **personal narratives**. Explain that, for the next 15 minutes, students will write about their memorable event or experience on page 61. Remind them to stay focused on just this one event. Also remind them to use plenty of sensory details when describing the experience.

WRITING RUBRIC When students have finished their narratives, you might use this writing rubric for help with a quick assessment of their writing.

Do students' paragraphs

- begin with a topic sentence?

- use specific, sensory details that give readers a "you are there" feeling?

- stay focused on just one event or experience?

Grammar, Usage, and Mechanics

When students have finished their first drafts, have them revise their writing using the **Writers' Checklist** as a reference. At this point, you may want to introduce a mini-lesson on sentence fragments. Inexperienced writers often confuse short sentences with fragments. Help students realize that fragments can be long and complicated, such as this one:

My next-door neighbor, who is really kind of strange and always kind of nosy.

Fragments can be fixed by adding a subject or a verb or combining the fragment with another sentence.

V. WRAP-UP

Take a moment at the end of the lesson for students to reflect on the **depth** of their understanding using the **Readers' Checklist**. Ask them to explain what Hurston's writing made them think about and the connections they found themselves making to their own lives.

Assessment

To test students' comprehension, use the **Assessment** blackline master on page 105.

Name _____

VOCABULARY

Words from the Selection

DIRECTIONS To help build your vocabulary, answer these questions about words from the selection.

1. Does a <u>venturesome</u> person like to take risks or play it safe?

_____

2. If you receive <u>compliments</u> on your clothes, are you happy or angry?

_____

3. If your actions are <u>deplored</u>, are they admired or disapproved of?

_____

4. If a car <u>emerges</u> through the mist, is it appearing or disappearing?

_____

5. Does <u>miscellany</u> refer to various things or to something specific?

_____

Strategy Lesson: Latin Prefix

DIRECTIONS The Latin term *circum-* means "in a circle, around." Study the words and their definitions in the box. Then write the word that correctly fits in each blank.

> circumnavigate—sail around
>
> circumscribe—to draw a line around
>
> circumference—the distance around
>
> circumvent—go around; outwit
>
> circumlocution—wordy language

6. What is the _____ of the earth?

7. Who was the first person to _____ the world?

8. Is it wise to try to _____ the law?

9. Can you _____ a square?

10. Can you speak without _____?

Name _____

COMPREHENSION
Reciprocal Reading
....

DIRECTIONS With a partner, work through the answers to these questions.

1. CLARIFY. What three words would you use to describe Zora Neale Hurston? Explain your choices.

_____

_____

_____

_____

2. SUMMARIZE. What is Hurston's main idea in "How It Feels to Be Colored Me"?

_____

_____

_____

_____

3. PREDICT. Based on what you've read, what do you think Hurston would want to tell people living in today's society?

_____

_____

_____

_____

4. QUESTION. If you had the chance, what question or questions would you like to ask Zora Neale Hurston?

_____

_____

_____

_____

Name _____

PREWRITING
Writing a Personal Narrative

A **personal narrative** tells a story of one kind or another. It should have a clear progression—a beginning, a middle, and an end. In a personal narrative, you need to give your readers an "I was there" feeling.

DIRECTIONS Write a narrative paragraph about an important event or experience in your life.

STEP 1. GET ORGANIZED. Figure out what experience you want to describe and how you want to describe it. Answering questions like the ones below can help.

When did the experience or event occur?
Where were you?
Who else was there?
What happened?
Why did it happen?
How did things turn out?
How did you feel afterward?

STEP 2. GATHER DETAILS. Now think of sensory details that can help your reader see, hear, smell, taste, and feel the experience you are describing. Use this chart to make notes.

Event or experience I am describing: _____

I saw _____

I felt _____

I smelled _____

I tasted _____

I heard _____

Name _____

ASSESSMENT

Multiple-Choice Test

DIRECTIONS On the blanks provided, write the letter of the item that best answers each question or completes each statement.

_____ 1. What type of writing is "How It Feels to Be Colored Me"?
    A. fiction
    B. autobiography
    C. historical fiction
    D. informational piece

_____ 2. Where did Hurston grow up?
    A. in the North
    B. on the West Coast
    C. in the South
    D. in the Midwest

_____ 3. What did Hurston do when Northerners passed through her town?
    A. She hid.
    B. She ignored them.
    C. She spoke to them.
    D. She peeked at them from behind the curtains.

_____ 4. People sometimes paid Hurston to . . .
    A. sing songs.
    B. "speak pieces."
    C. dance the parse-me-la.
    D. all of the above

_____ 5. How old was Hurston when she left town?
    A. 13
    B. 10
    C. 21
    D. 18

_____ 6. How did Hurston feel about her identity?
    A. bitter
    B. proud
    C. ashamed
    D. sad

_____ 7. When did Hurston feel "most colored"?
    A. in her home town
    B. at her school, Barnard
    C. at the New World Cabaret
    D. when she traveled

_____ 8. When walking down Seventh Avenue in Harlem, Hurston compares herself to . . .
    A. a jazz performer.
    B. a war drum.
    C. the Forty-Second Street Library lions.
    D. a dark rock.

_____ 9. Hurston says, "At certain times I have no race, I am *me*." At those times she feels . . .
    A. happy.
    B. confused.
    C. sad.
    D. uneasy.

_____ 10. How does Hurston feel when she is discriminated against?
    A. giddy
    B. tearful
    C. violent
    D. astonished

Short-Essay Test

What does Zora mean when she says she feels like "a brown bag of miscellany propped against a wall"?

The Eatonville Anthology

Skills and Strategies Overview

THEME	Zora Neale Hurston
READING LEVEL	average
VOCABULARY	◇foundation ◇commences ◇victuals ◇ridicule ◇spouting
PREREADING	think-pair-and-share
RESPONSE	react
COMPREHENSION	directed reading
PREWRITING	compare and contrast
WRITING	dialogue / punctuation and indents
ASSESSMENT	style

BACKGROUND

In *The Eatonville Anthology*, Zora Neale Hurston gives readers a taste of the tales she listened to as a child growing up in Eatonville, Florida. Even though the three selections here—"The Pleading Woman," "Turpentine Love," and "The Way of a Man with a Train"—follow the traditional form of a story (each has a beginning, a middle, and an end), in some ways they seem more like snapshots taken from a family photo album than stories one might put together in an anthology. As snapshots, they are brilliantly detailed and remarkably clear. Eccentric characters like Mrs. Tony Roberts and Jim Merchant come to life and seem like people we might have met once, one town over.

Encourage students to connect the people they read about in these selections to the people they know in their own lives. Encourage them to move beyond comments like "She's strange" and take the time to make careful, evaluative responses such as, "She's strange, but I know someone who's sort of like her, and this is what makes her strange. . . ."

UNIT THEME Zora Neale Hurston celebrates the quirkiness of human beings. We are all a little odd, she says, which is what makes us so interesting.

GRAPHIC ORGANIZER Students' diagrams on page 70 might look something like this one.

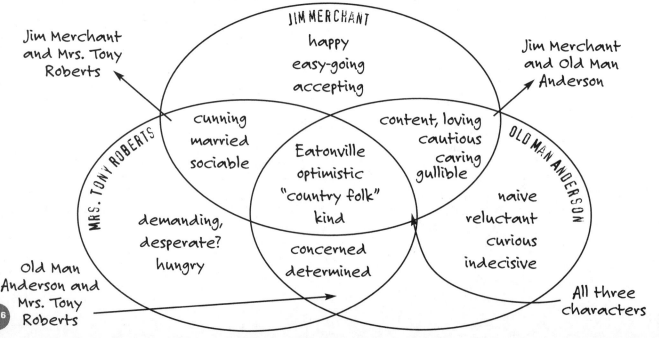

BEFORE YOU READ

Before you begin, remind students of what they know about Zora Neale Hurston and her writing style. Then turn to the introduction on page 64. The purpose of the introduction is to explain to students that they are about to read three "home folks" stories. Encourage readers to pay careful attention to characters and character motivation (as opposed to the plot) as they are reading.

Motivation Strategy

ENGAGING STUDENTS In these excerpts from *The Eatonville Anthology*, Hurston tells about three eccentric characters who are funny and strange at the same time. Ask students: "What does it mean to be eccentric? What eccentric people do you know? What makes these people different? What makes these people likable and fun to have around?"

Vocabulary Building

Help students use **context clues** as they read to figure out the meanings of difficult words, especially key vocabulary for this lesson: *foundation, commences, victuals, ridicule*, and *spouting*. The footnotes define these words, although students should look for clues about the words before checking the bottom of the page. Have students circle these words in the text. Model using context clues and then checking your ideas against the footnote: "I don't know the word *slab*. I see, though, that it follows a description of the butcher cutting off a piece of meat. Therefore, I can assume that *slab* means 'piece.'" For additional practice with these words, see the **Vocabulary** blackline master, page 110.

STRATEGY LESSON: HOMOPHONES A homophone is a word that has the same pronunciation as another word but a different spelling and meaning. For example, *ate* and *eight* are homophones. Tell students that the meaning of such words is usually made clear by context, but that their spelling is likely to cause trouble. It is helpful to visualize homophones in phrases that give a clue to their meanings: We *ate* dinner at *eight* o'clock.

For more help, see the **Vocabulary** blackline master, page 110.

Prereading Strategies

On page 64, students are asked to complete a **think-pair-and-share** activity that provides a thematic warm-up to Hurston's stories. In this case, they'll think about an unusual person they know and then list some of the qualities or traits they associate with this person. Encourage students to be creative in their responses. The more time they spend on this activity, the better prepared they will be to read about Mrs. Tony Roberts, Jim Merchant, and Old Man Anderson.

K-W-L Since this unit is devoted to just one author, you might have students complete a K-W-L that shows what they already know and want to find out about Zora Neale Hurston. For their K columns, students might focus on stylistic elements of Hurston's writing. For example, do they recall that she used a great deal of figurative language? Do they recall that she more often wrote about "country folks" than "city folks"? For their W columns, students might list questions they have that are left over from "How It Feels to Be Colored Me." Use their W comments to help you plan follow-up activities to this unit.

Spanish-speaking Students

En "La antología de Eatonville," Zora Neale Hurston da un ejemplar de la cultura de Eatonville, Florida, su pueblo natal. La primera selección muestra la manera única de hablar de algunas personas, mientras la segunda leyenda se trata de una pareja única que tiene rara suerte. La tercera selección da otro ejemplo de la cultura en Eatonville, contando la historia de un ciudadano que nunca ha visto un tren.

II. READ

Because there are three stories in this lesson, you'll have several natural stopping points that you can take advantage of if you feel students are lost. At the end of each story, you might ask students to summarize what happens and give a brief description of the main character.

Also remind the class that as they're reading, they should make comments in the **Response Notes** that show the ways they can **react and connect** to Hurston's stories. Remind them to make notes about characters or events that are similar to people or experiences in their own lives. These notes will help keep them actively involved in the writing, and may come in handy when they are asked to write a dialogue on page 71.

Response Strategy

VISUALIZE As an alternate or additional response strategy, have students visualize the people Hurston describes. Their mental pictures will help them understand the similarities and differences between the three major characters.

Comprehension Strategies

A **directed reading** strategy (**stop and think**) can help reluctant or low-level readers better comprehend what they are reading. In a directed reading, the teacher or volunteer reader guides the reading, adjusting the pace as necessary. Along the way, the reader poses comprehension questions that can help students think about character, setting, plot, or theme. Consider asking questions that allow students to make connections between stories, such as "How is Jim Merchant similar to Old Man Anderson"? Multi-selection questions will encourage students to do some higher-level thinking about the literature.

STORY FRAME As an alternate comprehension strategy, consider asking students to keep track of what happens in each story by filling in a story frame similar to the one on page 111 of this book. Story frames help organize the five essential elements of a story: setting, character, plot, conflict, and theme.

For more help with story frames, see the **Comprehension** blackline master on page 111.

Discussion Questions

COMPREHENSION 1. What does Mrs. Tony Roberts ask for? *(food)*

2. Why do people give it to her? *(She pleads with them until they can't stand it anymore.)*

3. Why does the mother give turpentine to Jim Merchant's wife? *(to stop her "fits")*

4. Why does Old Man Anderson go to see the train? *(The townspeople ridicule him until he feels he has no choice.)*

CRITICAL THINKING 5. Which character—Mrs. Tony Roberts, Jim Merchant, or Old Man Anderson—would you say is most naïve or unsophisticated? *(Remind students to support what they say with evidence from the selection.)*

6. Which character is the cleverest one? *(Accept reasonable responses.)*

Literary Skill

CHARACTERIZATION The technique a writer uses to create and reveal the personalities of characters is called *characterization*. Although Hurston does not describe her characters' physical appearance, she does reveal their personalities through their actions, the reactions of others, and, in "The Pleading Woman," through a character's words. Dialogue, which students are asked to write in Part IV, is also a common way of characterizing someone.

III. GATHER YOUR THOUGHTS

The prewriting activities on page 70 are designed to help students make inferences about character traits and character motivation. In the three-circle Venn diagram, students will list traits and qualities of the three main characters from the selection. To do this, they'll need to look for similarities among the three, which might require a bit of rereading. Remind them that their **Response Notes** will come in handy when working on the Venn.

Prewriting Strategies

BRAINSTORM The second activity on page 70 asks students to decide which character they'd like to write about. The goal here is to help prepare the class to write a dialogue between themselves and a character of their choice. Although the book asks them to think of only three questions they'd like to ask the character, you might consider having them write five or more. This way they'll have plenty to choose from when it comes time to write their conversations.

Have students use the **Prewriting** blackline master on page 112.

IV. WRITE

You might have pairs of students write a **dialogue**. One student can write in the voice of the character, while the other student writes in the voice of the "interviewer." Remind students to stay in character as they write. Before they begin, they should check to be sure they understand how the character speaks or might speak and what he or she likes to talk about. Students will have to make some inferences about Jim Merchant and Old Man Anderson.

WRITING RUBRIC Use this writing rubric to help students focus on the assignment requirements and for help with a quick assessment of their writing.

Do students' conversations

- focus on one character?

- sound like real people talking?

- include at least three questions and three responses?

Grammar, Usage, and Mechanics

After students have finished a first draft, ask them to revise their writing using the **Writers' Checklist**. At this point you might teach a mini-lesson on writing dialogue. Remind them that commas are used to set off quotations from the rest of the sentence. If the quote falls at the end of the sentence, the end punctuation belongs inside the quotation marks. Inexperienced writers often have trouble remembering this rule. For example:

Incorrect: She said "Stop jumping up and down"!

Correct: She said, "Stop jumping up and down!"

V. WRAP-UP

Point out the **Readers' Checklist** on page 72 and ask students to reflect on the **style** of Hurston's writing. See if they're able to discuss Hurston's style with some confidence. Also ask them to comment on whether or not they liked her writing style.

Assessment

To test students' comprehension, use the **Assessment** blackline master on page 113.

Name _____

VOCABULARY

Words from the Selection

DIRECTIONS Use these vocabulary words in sentences that show you understand their meaning.

> ✦foundation   ✦commences   ✦victuals   ✦ridicule   ✦spouting

1. _____

_____

2. _____

_____

3. _____

_____

4. _____

_____

5. _____

_____

Strategy Lesson: Homophones

DIRECTIONS A homophone is a word that has the same pronunciation as another word but a different spelling and meaning. For example, *bored* and *board* are homophones. Choose the word in parentheses that correctly fits in each sentence, and write it on the blank.

6. Mrs. Roberts asks for a little (peace-piece) of salt pork. _____

7. She cries out in (pain-pane) when she doesn't get enough. _____

8. She leaves the store carrying her (meet-meat). _____

9. Only two trains a day (past-passed) through the town. _____

10. Old Man Anderson was afraid his horse would run (aweigh-away). _____

Name _____

COMPREHENSION
Story Frame

DIRECTIONS Fill in one story frame for each of the three stories from *The Eatonville Anthology*.

Story Frame: "The Pleading Woman"

The story takes place _____.
_____ **is a character in the story who**
_____. _____**and**_____ **are other**
characters in the story who _____. **A problem occurs when**
_____. **The problem is**
solved when _____. **The story ends with** _____
_____.

Story Frame: "Turpentine Love"

The story takes place _____.
_____ **is a character in the story who**
_____. _____ **is**
another character in the story who _____. **A problem occurs**
when _____. **The problem**
is solved when _____. **The story ends with**
_____.

Story Frame: "The Way of a Man with a Train"

The story takes place _____.
_____ **is a character in the story who**
_____. _____**and**_____ **are**
other characters in the story who _____. **A problem occurs**
when _____. **After that,** _____. **The problem is**
solved when _____. **The story ends with**
_____.

Name _____

PREWRITING

Gather Details

DIRECTIONS   Before you can write in the voice of a character, you need to be sure you really understand who the character is.

First decide what character you want to focus on.

Then fill in this character diagram. Use specific details from the story.

How the character acts	How the character talks
How I feel about the character	How others feel about the character

Character
_____

Become a Character

DIRECTIONS   On page 71 of your book, you are asked to write an imaginary dialogue with a character. To help you get ready, try writing a journal entry from the point of view of one character.

1. First decide which character you want to become.

2. Then write a one-paragraph journal entry in which you tell about your day. (Use facts from the story.)

3. Try to write exactly how you think your character would write.

Date _____

Name _____

ASSESSMENT

Multiple-Choice Test

DIRECTIONS On the blanks provided, write the letter of the item that best answers each question or completes each statement.

_____ 1. What word would you use to describe Mrs. Roberts?
A. kind   C. greedy
B. mean   D. calm

_____ 2. Why is Mrs. Roberts upset with Mr. Clarke?
A. He gave her just a small piece of meat.   C. He wouldn't give her anything.
B. He charged her for the food.   D. He yelled at her.

_____ 3. What does Mrs. Roberts want from Mrs. Pierson?
A. salted meat   C. potatoes
B. collard greens   D. bread

_____ 4. What word would you use to describe Jim Merchant?
A. irritable   C. cheerful
B. shy   D. depressed

_____ 5. What stops Jim Merchant's wife from having "fits"?
A. falling in love   C. having her teeth pulled
B. getting married   D. turpentine in her eye

_____ 6. What kind of ending does "Turpentine Love" have?
A. happy   C. tragic
B. violent   D. none of the above

_____ 7. Old Man Anderson has never seen a . . .
A. city.   C. lake.
B. train.   D. car.

_____ 8. On Sundays, where do the kids go to see the train?
A. Tampa   C. Jacksonville
B. Eatonville   D. Maitland

_____ 9. Why does Old Man Anderson run away when he sees the train?
A. He is frightened by the noise.   C. He has to chase his horse.
B. The smoke gets in his eyes.   D. His wagon catches fire.

_____ 10. In which story is the main character influenced by ridicule?
A. "The Pleading Woman"   C. "The Way of a Man with a Train"
B. "Turpentine Love"   D. all of the above

Short-Essay Test

Which of the three main characters—Mrs. Roberts, Jim Merchant, or Old Man Anderson—is the happiest and why?

Family Ties

Unit Background   FAMILY TIES (pages 73–86)

In a time when families come in many configurations, the concept of what a family is may have changed, but family ties remain strong for most people. In his book *The Mountain of Names,* Alex Shoumatoff writes that the family "still provides the most intense, intimate, and permanent relationships most of us will ever have." This unit contains an excerpt from Maya Angelou's book *All God's Children Need Traveling Shoes* and two poems by Carolina Hospital. Angelou deals with the anguish she felt when her son was critically injured in an automobile accident (he recovered), and Hospital writes of ancestors.

Teaching the Introduction

The photographs and words on page 73 convey positive ideas about family relationships.

1. Students may know that many people are involved in researching their family history. Ask them to speculate about why this is such a popular hobby.

2. Ask students what they know about genetic influences on individuals. How big a part do genetics play in one's life?

3. Ask: "If you were a parent, what is the most important thing you could give to your children?"

Opening Activity

Give students time to write down the name of a relative followed by two adjectives describing the person's appearance, three adjectives describing the person's personality, and a sentence telling how they feel about that person. Then have them put the words into a free-verse poem with punctuation.

Visit to Africa

Skills and Strategies Overview

THEME	Family Ties
READING LEVEL	average
VOCABULARY	

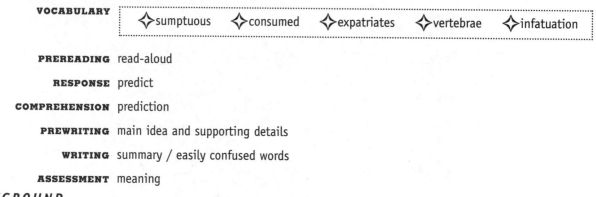

◇ sumptuous   ◇ consumed   ◇ expatriates   ◇ vertebrae   ◇ infatuation

PREREADING	read-aloud
RESPONSE	predict
COMPREHENSION	prediction
PREWRITING	main idea and supporting details
WRITING	summary / easily confused words
ASSESSMENT	meaning

BACKGROUND

Maya Angelou, one of the most gifted writers of the twentieth century, continues to have a long and varied career. She is a poet, historian, author, playwright, and civil-rights activist who supported herself early on as a singer and dancer. As a young woman, she married a South-African freedom fighter and lived in Cairo where she was editor of *The Arab Observer*, an English-language newspaper in the Middle East.

In the 1960s, at the request of Dr. Martin Luther King, Jr., Angelou became the northern coordinator for the Southern Christian Leadership Conference. She has written about her life experiences with King and others in a brilliant multivolume autobiography, the first of which is entitled *I Know Why the Caged Bird Sings*. "Visit to Africa" is an excerpt from the fifth volume of her autobiography, *All God's Children Need Traveling Shoes* (1986).

UNIT THEME Maya Angelou explores the importance of family and asks the thematic question: "How strong are the ties that bind family members?"

GRAPHIC ORGANIZER Students might benefit from seeing this bio-poem on the board.

Bio-Poem: Maya Angelou

Maya,

Poet.

Singer, writer, thinker, fighter;

Lover of words, music, and conversation;

Who believes in family;

Who wants equality, justice, and peace;

Who keeps her son as her rudder, his dreams as her vision,

　　　his words as her treasures;

Who gives her poetry to a nation, her ideas to a world;

　　　her understanding to all;

Who said, "You are my child."

Mother.

BIBLIOGRAPHY Maya Angelou's works include these: *I Know Why the Caged Bird Sings* (autobiography, 1970) *Just Give Me a Cool Drink of Water 'Fore I Diiie* (poetry, 1971); *Gather Together in My Name* (autobiography, 1974); *Singin' and Swingin' and Gettin' Merry Like Christmas* (autobiography, 1976); *And Still I Rise* (poetry, 1978); *The Heart of a Woman* (autobiography, 1981).

BEFORE YOU READ

Read through the introduction to the lesson on page 74 with students. Remind the class that as they read Maya Angelou's story, they should keep the unit theme—family ties—in mind. They can ask themselves: "What family ties does Angelou describe? How are these ties different than the ones that bind my family?"

Motivation Strategy

Ask students to think of a time someone in their family was in trouble. What happened? What did the family do? What did they learn from the experience? Students may enjoy talking about their own experiences before reading about another family's crisis.

ENGAGING STUDENTS Explain that "Visit to Africa" is the story of a woman who is desperately worried about the health of her child. Ask students to complete this statement: "I think mother-child relationships are _____." Their ideas will help them begin thinking about Angelou's theme.

Vocabulary Building

The key vocabulary words for this lesson are *sumptuous, consumed, expatriates, vertebrae,* and *infatuation*. Since more than half the words in English come from Latin roots, it is important for students to know something about them. Tell students that the root of *expatriate* is *patria*, "fatherland." *Consume* and *sumptuous* come from the same root, *sumere*, "to take, spend, or buy." *Vertere*, "to turn" is the root of *vertebrae*. Ask students to turn to a dictionary to find the root of *infatuation*. Help them find where in a definition the origin of a word appears. Then have students circle the five vocabulary words in the text. For additional practice with these words, see page 120.

STRATEGY LESSON: SYNONYMS As students read, point out synonyms in footnotes. Explain that synonyms can sometimes function as memory shortcuts if there isn't the time to memorize the full definition of a word. Have them think carefully about synonyms for these words from the selection: *obscene, cavorting, copious, plump,* and *melodious*.

For additional practice with this strategy, see the **Vocabulary** blackline master on page 120.

Prereading Strategies

One of the purposes of a **read-aloud** is to make a long or challenging selection seem less intimidating to readers. Students will probably welcome the chance to sit back and listen as someone else reads the story. You may want to remind them, however, that listening is an active process, just as reading is. Good listeners follow along in the book, taking notes on whatever they think is interesting, important, confusing, or puzzling. After students have finished the selection, you may want to take a moment or two to review the notes they made while reading.

PICTURE WALK You might want to do some additional prereading work that can help introduce the topic and theme of "Visit to Africa" to students. Consider asking the class to do a picture walk through the selection. Have them look carefully at the pictures and captions and then make predictions about setting and plot.

Spanish-speaking Students

En "Visita a África" Maya Angelou comparte una historia privada de su propia vida. Describe un viaje que hizo con su hijo hace unos años a Ghana, un país en África. Ella describe la alegría y la gran emoción que se sentían al ver a las miles de caras semejantes a las suyas. Fue invigorizante estar rodeados por otra gente negra. Pero cuando su hijo se encuentra en peligro de morir después de un accidente grave, Angelou se da cuenta de la fragilidad de la vida y de su propia debilidad contra las fuerzas del azar.

READ

Tell students that they should begin making **predictions** as soon as they begin reading. For example, point out the contrast Angelou sets up between the "intimate" African breezes and the "utter blackness" of the night. Something is coming, she seems to be saying. It's up to the reader to predict the trouble that lies ahead.

Response Strategy

REACT AND CONNECT As an alternate prereading strategy, have students react and connect to Angelou's narrative. Their responses to the topic of the piece can help them understand the author's message. Ask them to make notes about how parts of the author's story make them feel. Do they agree or disagree with Angelou's thoughts and ideas? Do they have a similar experience from their own lives that they'd like to share out loud or in writing?

Comprehension Strategies

At several points in the story, students are asked to **stop and predict** what they think will happen next. Making predictions can help readers feel more directly involved with what they're reading and involve them in the story's outcome. The reader keeps reading in order to see whether the prediction comes true. Predictions can also help readers make inferential-type responses to a text. To make a prediction, the reader needs to think inferentially about character, plot, and theme.

GRAPHIC ORGANIZER Another comprehension strategy that works well is a graphic organizer. You might create and photocopy an organizer that uses these time-sequence words: *first, next, then, after that,* and *finally.* Students can make notes on the organizer as they read.

For more help, see the **Comprehension** blackline master on page 121.

Discussion Questions

COMPREHENSION 1. Why are Guy and his mother in Ghana? *(She has taken Guy to enter the University of Ghana.)*

2. What kind of accident does Guy have? *(a car accident)*

3. What is Angelou's reaction to his accident? *(She becomes frantically worried about her son.)*

CRITICAL THINKING 4. What does Angelou want most for her son? *(Possible response: health and happiness)*

5. Is Angelou a good mother? Explain. *(Ask students to fully explain their responses and support what they say with evidence from the narrative.)*

Literary Skill

SETTING To introduce a literary skill with this lesson, explain to students how important setting is to Angelou's narrative. The story takes place in Ghana in 1962. In the opening paragraph and throughout the narrative, Angelou makes a point of describing the beauty and mystery of the land and its language. Her careful description of the setting makes the description of Guy's accident and injuries all the more dramatic. The reader is lulled by Angelou's descriptions, the same way she herself is lulled by Ghana—until Guy's life is suddenly at stake. The land she describes so lovingly becomes a prison from which she cannot escape.

III. GATHER YOUR THOUGHTS

After they finish reading, students will complete an organizer that explores the **main idea** and supporting **details** of Angelou's writing. If students are struggling to find Angelou's main idea, ask: "What do you think the author wants you to remember most from this selection? What point does she make?" Students might suggest that Angelou's main idea is that family, not place, makes a home.

Once they have Angelou's main idea, students will need to find supporting details. Explain to the class that details are the words an author uses to somehow support the central idea. Details can relate to character, setting, or plot.

Prewriting Strategies

GROUP DISCUSSION As an alternate prewriting strategy, hold a group discussion about the main idea and details of the selection. Students can listen to each other's thoughts and build upon individual ideas until they reach the point that they feel they understand Angelou's message. Remember that during a discussion, consensus is not essential. What is important is that each group member can support his or her ideas and interpretations with evidence from the text.

Have students use the **Prewriting** blackline master on page 122.

IV. WRITE

Remind students that their assignment is to write a **summary** of Angelou's narrative. Their summaries should begin with a statement of the main idea and contain details from the chart on page 79.

WRITING RUBRIC When they've finished their first drafts, show students the questions on this writing rubric. Students should keep these points in mind during the rewrite stage.

Do students' summaries

- open with Angelou's main idea?

- include a discussion of three or more details that help support the main idea?

- show that students understand the concept of summarizing—as opposed to quoting or reviewing?

Grammar, Usage, and Mechanics

Also consider using the revision time to introduce a brief mini-lesson on easily confused words. Remind the class of the correct way to use words that sound the same but mean different things. The box on page 80 discusses these problem words: *their, they're,* and *there; its* and *it's;* and *set* and *sit.* You might expand this lesson to include *to, too,* and *two.*

V. WRAP-UP

Take a moment at the end of the lesson for the class to reflect on "Visit to Africa." Encourage students to use the **Readers' Checklist** on page 81 to help focus on the **meaning** of the selection. Ask students to explain the effect Angelou's words and ideas had on them.

Assessment

To test students' comprehension, use the **Assessment** blackline master on page 123.

Name _____

VOCABULARY

Words from the Selection

DIRECTIONS The words in the word box are the Latin roots of the words in the two columns below. Draw a line from the word in Column A that has the same root as the word in Column B.

fatuus: foolish	*sumere*: to take, spend, buy
patria: fatherland	*vertere*: to turn

Column A

1. fatuous
2. invert
3. sumptuous
4. patriot

Column B

consumed

expatriate

vertebrae

infatuation

5. Use one of the words from Column B in a sentence that shows you know the meaning of the word.

_____

_____

Strategy Lesson: Synonyms

A **synonym** is a word that means the same thing as another word. For example, *start* is a synonym for *begin*.

DIRECTIONS Find the word in Column B that means the same thing as a word in Column A. Then draw a line between the two words. If there's a word you don't know, skip it and come back to it when you've finished the whole column.

Column A

6. obscene
7. cavorting
8. copious
9. plump
10. melodious

Column B

prancing

chubby

harmonious

abundant

indecent

Name _____

COMPREHENSION
Retelling

DIRECTIONS Answer these questions about "Visit to Africa." Consult your book if you need help remembering some of the details.

1. Where are Guy and his mother in 1962?

_____

_____

_____

2. What happens to Guy and his mother during July and August of 1962?

_____

_____

_____

3. How does Guy feel after his accident?

_____

_____

_____

4. How does his mother feel?

_____

_____

_____

5. What does Angelou mean when she says, "Had I been less timid, I would have cursed God"? (page 77)?

_____

_____

_____

Name _____

PREWRITING
Brainstorm Words

DIRECTIONS Remember that when you write a summary, you need to use your own words, not the author's words. Use this page to plan how you will summarize Angelou's narrative.

A. BRAINSTORM DESCRIPTIVE WORDS. Think of words that describe what happens to Maya Angelou and Guy in Ghana. Don't look at your book. Come up with your own descriptive words.

Descriptive words: Maya Angelou and Guy in Ghana

happiness
fear
isolation

B. WRITE AN INTRODUCTION. Next write an introduction for your summary. Use words from your word box. In your introduction, tell

→ some information about the selection (where Guy and his mother are; why they are there, and so on).

→Angelou's main idea.

→details that support the main idea.

_____

_____

_____

C. WRITE A CONCLUSION. On these lines, write a conclusion for your summary. In your conclusion, you should

→ restate your topic sentence.

→ explain how Angelou's narrative affected you. What did it make you think about?

_____

_____

Name _____

ASSESSMENT

Multiple-Choice Test

DIRECTIONS On the blanks provided, write the letter of the item that best answers each question or completes each statement.

_____ 1. Why does Guy go to Ghana?
   A. to see friends
   B. to go to the University of Ghana
   C. for a job
   D. for a vacation

_____ 2. Where is Guy's mother headed after he settles into his dormitory?
   A. Liberia
   B. Cairo
   C. Egypt
   D. Accra

_____ 3. Where did Guy finish high school?
   A. Ghana
   B. New York
   C. Egypt
   D. Liberia

_____ 4. What do Guy and his mother do for two days as they travel around the Ghanaian streets?
   A. eat
   B. see a show
   C. shop
   D. laugh

_____ 5. What type of accident causes Guy's injuries?
   A. bike
   B. bus
   C. boat
   D. car

_____ 6. How does the author feel in July and August?
   A. overwhelmed
   B. excited
   C. ashamed
   D. jealous

_____ 7. The doctors and nurses taking care of Guy were . . .
   A. American.
   B. African.
   C. Hispanic.
   D. Asian.

_____ 8. A very hard sneeze could cause Guy to . . .
   A. die.
   B. be paralyzed.
   C. slip into a coma.
   D. A. and B.

_____ 9. What is Guy's attitude toward his condition?
   A. He is optimistic.
   B. He is discouraged.
   C. He is indifferent.
   D. none of the above

_____ 10. "Visit to Africa" is . . .
   A. a short story.
   B. part of an autobiography.
   C. part of a biography.
   D. part of a novel.

Short-Essay Test

What does Angelou mean when she says, "He could die if he wanted to and go off to wherever dead folks go, but I, I would be left without a home."

Skills and Strategies Overview

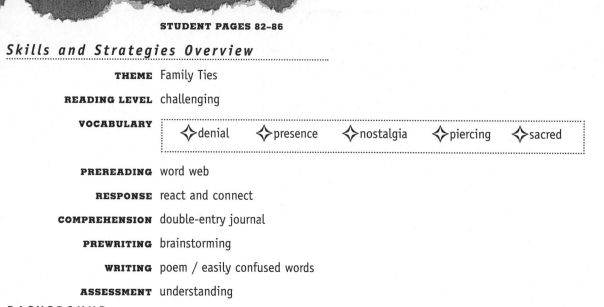

THEME	Family Ties
READING LEVEL	challenging
VOCABULARY	◇denial ◇presence ◇nostalgia ◇piercing ◇sacred
PREREADING	word web
RESPONSE	react and connect
COMPREHENSION	double-entry journal
PREWRITING	brainstorming
WRITING	poem / easily confused words
ASSESSMENT	understanding

BACKGROUND

Carolina Hospital's poems celebrate life, love, and family ties. Hospital seems to say that we are forever linked to family members, although these links can sometimes cause confusion and pain.

In "Dear Tía," the speaker reflects on an aunt who has died or disappeared. Although the speaker has the same name as her aunt and a photograph of her, she cannot remember the woman enough even to miss her voice, smile, skin, or laughter. She writes to establish a link with this departed relative.

The meaning of "Papa" is more difficult to decipher than the meaning of "Dear Tía." Specifically, who is the pair that sits on the beach while the children play? Siblings? Husband and wife? And who is the "Papa" of the title? Is he the sacred man who is "an outcast of our past"? Although obscure, the poem seems to say that no family is as perfect and simple as it first seems.

UNIT THEME Carolina Hospital considers the complexity of family relationships. Like Maya Angelou, she asks the thematic question: What are the ties that bind family members? How strong are they?

GRAPHIC ORGANIZER Students might create a cluster for the word *family*, which means different things to different people. Students' clusters might look something like this:

Word Cluster

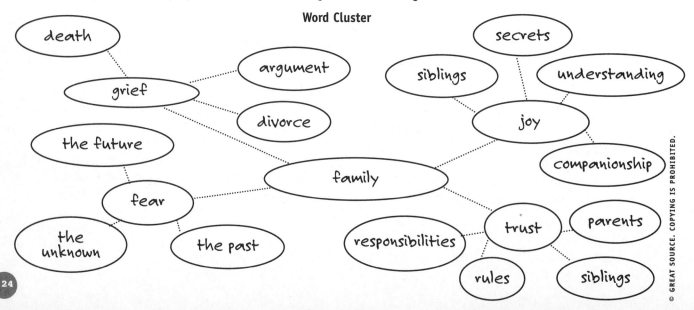

BEFORE YOU READ

Ask students to read the lesson opener on page 82. Explain again that good readers bring with them all the facts, opinions, and ideas that they've gathered over the years. Sometimes it's helpful to try and tally up some of these facts and ideas about a topic. The **word web** on page 82 can help students organize what they already know about the topic.

Motivation Strategy

In "Dear Tía" and "Papa," Carolina Hospital explores the relationship between love and loss. Some students may be able to tell about the loss of a loved one. What did they do—or what did others do—to help them through the grieving process? What advice can they offer to someone who is grieving?

ENGAGING STUDENTS Explain that "Dear Tía" is in some ways a celebration of the speaker's beloved aunt. Ask students to think of a family member that they could write a "Dear _____" poem about. Who would it be and why?

Vocabulary Building

Knowing the **pronunciation** of a new word is as important as knowing a definition. Write the following pronunciations on the board and ask students to practice pronouncing these five vocabulary words: *denial* (di NI l), *presence* (PREZ ns), *nostalgia* (nah STAL juh), *piercing* (PEERS ng), and *sacred* (SAY krid). Then have students circle the five vocabulary words in the text. For more practice with key vocabulary words, see page 128.

STRATEGY LESSON: MEXICAN SPANISH Remind students that *tía* means "aunt" in Spanish. Tell them that many English words come from the Spanish language or from Mexican Spanish. *Canyon, taco*, and *serape* are just a few such words.

For more practice, see the **Vocabulary** blackline master on page 128.

Prereading Strategies

Word webs are helpful exercises for three reasons. 1. They can improve a reader's vocabulary. 2. They can deepen a reader's understanding of the selection. 3. They can help forge a link between the reader's prior knowledge of a topic and the topic or theme of the work. When you create a word web for students, try to choose words that are thematically important. (For example, the web on page 82 asks students to write about "family ties," an important theme in both "Dear Tía" and "Papa.")

READ-ALOUD As an alternate prereading strategy, ask students to do a read-aloud of the first few lines of "Dear Tía." A read-aloud can help students who are reluctant to begin because they "hate poetry" or just don't understand it. If necessary, model for students how to express the meter or rhythm of the poems.

Spanish-speaking Students

En "Querida Tía," Carolina Hospital escribe a su tía muerta como si fuera escribiendole una carta. Lamenta que no pueda recordar todas sus características únicas. Pero por escrbir, espera recaptuar sus memorias nubladas. "Papa" también tiene que ver con las relaciones familiares y los efectos deteriorantes del tiempo. En este poema, una pareja se enfrenta con su vejez inevitable, viendo su futuro en los arrugos de otros.

II. READ

Since both poems in this section are fairly short, you'll be able to devote more class time to discussion and writing. Remind students that as they read, they should think about how individual words and lines make them feel. They can record their reactions in the **double-entry journals** on page 84.

Response Strategy

REACT AND CONNECT To help with comprehension, students should make comments in the **Response Notes** that show the ways they are reacting and connecting to what they are reading. Ask students to jot down their opinions about the speaker of each poem, and encourage them to make notes about people in their own lives who seem similar to the speaker or to the people written about. Do they see a little bit of themselves in either of the two poems?

Comprehension Strategies

In a **double-entry journal**, students note their individual responses to specific words, phrases, and lines from the selection. Have students comment on lines from the poems that they find interesting, confusing, or relevant to their own lives. A double-entry journal serves two purposes. 1. It gives students the chance to do a line-by-line analysis of the text. 2. It shows students that their own personal responses to a text can help them in their search for the author's meaning.

GRAPHIC ORGANIZER As an alternate strategy, have students work on a graphic organizer that is related to the poet's themes. More advanced readers can make a stylistic comparison of the two poems, focusing on language, rhythm, tone, and form. Other readers can compare and contrast the specific details in the two poems.

For more help, see the **Comprehension** blackline master on page 129.

Discussion Questions

COMPREHENSION 1. Who is "Dear Tía"? *(the speaker's aunt)*

2. Who or what are the two people on the beach focused on in "Papa"? *(each other)*

CRITICAL THINKING 3. What is it about Tía that causes the speaker so much pain? *(The speaker can't remember her.)*

4. Why might the people in "Papa" be "almost whispering" instead of talking out loud? *(Perhaps they don't want to be overheard.)*

5. Which of the two poems seems more optimistic? *(Encourage students to support their opinions with evidence from the text or from their own lives.)*

Literary Skill

FREE VERSE You might take this opportunity to introduce free verse to students. Free verse has rhythm and other poetic devices but has no fixed pattern of meter and rhyme. In free verse, sound is important, as is the way individual lines flow together. When they read free verse, students should look at the poem as a whole, rather than try to understand any one line by itself. They do, however, need to pay attention to punctuation. You might rewrite one of Hospital's poems as a paragraph on the board. Then ask: "What is the main idea of this paragraph?" Once they understand the message, students can begin thinking about how the poem is put together.

III. GATHER YOUR THOUGHTS

The goal of the prewriting activities on page 85 is to help prepare students to write a poem of their own. Because students are asked to model their poems on "Papa," you might spend an extra few minutes discussing the style of this poem with the class. Point out that the poem is written in free verse, that there is no rhyme scheme, and that the poem consists of three sentences.

Prewriting Strategies

To help them get started, students will do a **brainstorming** exercise in which they think of words that describe two of their own family members. Encourage students to choose words that show how the family members look, act, feel about themselves, and feel about others.

The second half of page 85 asks students to think of three different opening lines for their poems. If you like, reread the first few lines of "Papa" to the class and then brainstorm different ways of completing the line "The two sat."

Have students use the **Prewriting** blackline master on page 130.

IV. WRITE

On page 86, students are asked to write a **poem** that shows their feelings and ideas about two family members. Remind the class that their poems will begin with the line "The two sat" and should include descriptive words from the chart they completed on page 85. As always, the amount students write is not nearly as important as the quality of the writing. Use the writing rubric below to help you assess their work.

WRITING RUBRIC Do the students' poems

- begin with the opening line "The two sat"?

- tell what the two people are doing?

- contain descriptive details about each of the two people?

- follow the form of Hospital's "Papa"?

Grammar, Usage, and Mechanics

Before they write their final drafts, draw students' attention to the **Writer's Checklist** on the left side of page 86. If you like, take this opportunity to teach a mini-lesson on usage problems. Remind the class of the rules for using *good* and *well* and *bring* and *take*. People tend to misuse these words in writing and conversation both. For example:

Incorrect: The plane flew good.

Correct: The plane flew well.

Incorrect: Please bring me to the store, and be sure to take your wallet.

Correct: Please take me to the store, and be sure to bring your wallet.

V. WRAP-UP

Take a moment at the end of the lesson for students to talk about their understanding of "Dear Tía" and "Papa." Remind the class that many times a poet's message or theme is whatever the reader can take away from the reading. It is not important to reach consensus on what a literary work means.

Assessment

To test students' comprehension, use the **Assessment** blackline master on page 131.

Name _____

VOCABULARY

Words from the Selection

DIRECTIONS Draw lines between the vocabulary words in Column A and their correct pronunciations in Column B.

Column A	**Column B**
1. denial	PEERS ng
2. presence	SAY krid
3. nostalgia	PREZ ns
4. piercing	nah STAL juh
5. sacred	di NI l

Strategy Lesson: Mexican Spanish

DIRECTIONS The words in the right-hand column all come from Mexican Spanish. Use context clues to help you decide which words belong in the paragraph. Write the words on the blanks. You will not use one word.

(6) When the doors opened, there was a _____ toward the food line. (7) As we were standing in line in

the _____, we heard music coming from one end of the   burrito

room. (8) Maria said it sounded like a _____ band. (9) We   cafeteria

had to decide, however, what to order. Did we want tortilla wrapped around a

seasoned filling, called a _____? (10) Juan said we should save   chocolate

room for the _____ dessert.   mariachi

     canyon

     stampede

Name _____

COMPREHENSION

Sketch

DIRECTIONS Sometimes making a sketch of a piece of writing can help you understand an author's main idea or theme. Choose one of Hospital's poems to focus on. Sketch the scene in the poem.

```
┌─────────────────────────────────────────────────────────┐
│                                                           │
│                                                           │
│                                                           │
│                                                           │
│                                                           │
│                                                           │
│                                                           │
│                                                           │
│                                                           │
│                                                           │
└─────────────────────────────────────────────────────────┘
```

Reflect

DIRECTIONS Now answer these questions about your sketch. They can help you decide on the main idea of Hospital's poem.

Did I draw a sad scene or a happy scene?

_____

Who or what is the most important part of my scene?

_____

If a person from my sketch could talk, what would he or she say?

_____

I think Hospital's main idea has something to do with _____ and

_____ .

Name _____

PREWRITING
Writing a Free-Verse Poem

DIRECTIONS Follow these steps to write a free-verse poem. Remember that free verse does not follow a specific form, and it usually does not rhyme.

STEP 1. SELECT A SUBJECT. Write about two people who are important to you. (Your book asks you to write about two family members.)

person #1: _____

person #2: _____

STEP 2. COLLECT YOUR THOUGHTS. Write freely for a few minutes about these two people. Try to write about experiences you've shared.

My free-write:

_____

_____

_____

_____

STEP 3. WRITE A FIRST DRAFT. Now take your free-write and insert some line breaks so that you end up with a poem of five or six lines. Try to put breaks where you hear natural pauses in the sentences.

My free-write with line breaks:

_____

_____

_____

_____

STEP 4. SHAPE YOUR POEM. Pay special attention to your first line. It should give your readers an idea of the subject of the poem. (Your book asks you to begin with Carolina Hospital's first line, "The two sat . . .")

My first line: The two sat

Name _____

ASSESSMENT
Multiple-Choice Test

DIRECTIONS On the blanks provided, write the letter of the item that best answers each question or completes each statement.

_____ 1. What does the author have in common with "Dear Tía"?
   A. her smile
   B. her name
   C. life
   D. the weather

_____ 2. The poem is about . . .
   A. a friend.
   B. a cousin.
   C. a sister.
   D. an aunt.

_____ 3. What does the speaker hold on to as a reminder of Tía?
   A. a photograph
   B. a book
   C. a gift
   D. a ring

_____ 4. The speaker says she does not miss Tía's . . .
   A. urging voice.
   B. smiles.
   C. pride.
   D. all of the above

_____ 5. The speaker writes because she cannot . . .
   A. fall asleep.
   B. make a phone call.
   C. remember Tía.
   D. return to her native country.

_____ 6. What is the setting of the poem "Papa"?
   A. a field
   B. the beach
   C. a park
   D. a playground

_____ 7. The children in this poem want the adults to . . .
   A. take them to the beach.
   B. buy them a present.
   C. tell them a story.
   D. come and play.

_____ 8. The two adults are . . .
   A. arguing.
   B. sleeping.
   C. whispering.
   D. giggling.

_____ 9. When the children call to the adults, the adults . . .
   A. ignore them.
   B. make a joke.
   C. tell them to be quiet.
   D. offer advice.

_____ 10. "Papa" is a poem about . . .
   A. grandmothers and grandfathers.
   B. waves on the beach.
   C. adults and children.
   D. strangers.

Short-Essay Test

Which poem reminds you most of your own family? Why? Which character reminds you most of yourself?

Stories of the Arab World

Unit Background   STORIES OF THE ARAB WORLD (pages 87–104)

Writer and translator Inea Bushnaq was born in Jerusalem and educated there and in Damascus and London. She has a degree from Cambridge University. In her book of folktales, she writes that Djuha is a well-known comic character in Arab folklore and that "in North Africa Djuha's identity merges with that of Si' Djeha." In fact, there is a street named for Si' Djeha in Fez, Morocco.

The Bedouins (the Arabic word for "dwellers in the desert") are nomadic Arabs who live in the deserts of the Middle East and northern Africa. They subsist mostly on meat, milk, and dairy products, all of which are provided by their herds. In a traditional Bedouin society, families live in tents that are made from strips of cloth woven from goat or camel hair and vegetable fibers.

In some tales of the Arab world, the Bedouin is the wisest character. In others, he is gullible and is easily taken advantage of by tricksters from "the outside." In the following two stories, Bushnaq provides examples of both types.

Teaching the Introduction

The map on page 87 shows the extent of the Arab world, while the photographs depict the traditional dress of an older Arab man and a common means of transportation in the desert. You may want to caution students against thinking that the Arab world is universally like that depicted in these folktales. In fact, many parts of the oil-rich Arab world are extremely cosmopolitan today.

Stories of the Arab World

More than 200 million Arabs live in the Arab World, which spreads across the Middle East, southwest Asia, and northern Africa. Despite this vast extent of land, Arabs are united by a shared history, culture, and literature.

87

1. Students have undoubtedly read or heard folktales, but unless they or their families are native to one of the Arab countries, they may not know much about Arab folktales. Tell them that all folktales reveal something of the civilization from which they come, often in details of housing, dress, animals, and food. Ask students to speculate about what details might be mentioned in a traditional Arab folktale. (*tents, camels, robes, markets, coffee*)

2. In the last story in this unit, a character invokes the name of Allah. If no one knows who Allah is, explain that Allah is the Islamic name for God.

3. Ask students to tell what they think the function of a trickster is in a folktale. (*A trickster plays a trick or a prank on someone, often through lies and deception. Thus, the person who is tricked is made to look a fool, sometimes because of his own faults, such as vanity, a love of money, pride, or selfishness.*)

Opening Activity

Since most folktales are meant to be told, you might ask one or more students to prepare to tell a folktale to the class, although you may have to provide the folktale. Alternatively, ask a student to retell or read aloud "The Guest Who Ran Away."

LESSON 9

The Guest Who Ran Away

STUDENT PAGES 88–93

Skills and Strategies Overview

THEME Stories of the Arab World

READING LEVEL easy

VOCABULARY ✧stew ✧nibble ✧savory ✧snatched ✧hitching

PREREADING preview

RESPONSE clarify / predict

COMPREHENSION reciprocal reading

PREWRITING character attribute map

WRITING story beginning / comma splices

ASSESSMENT enjoyment

BACKGROUND

"The Guest Who Ran Away" is a Tunisian folktale that has been passed down from one generation to another as an oral tale. In 1986, folklorist Inea Bushnaq retold this and other popular regional folktales and published them together in an anthology called *Arab Folktales.*

"The Guest Who Ran Away" contains all the elements traditionally associated with the literary genre of folktales. The story is simple, although the message is somewhat complex. Characterization is not nearly as important as plot, which is why there is very little information about the traveler, the Bedouin, or his wife. Although there is no real trickster in "The Guest Who Ran Away," there is a lesson to be learned from the foolish actions of the wife. As is the case with most folktales, the friends and relatives of the one who has done wrong learn what happened only after the reader has had a full explanation of the event. In other words, the reader or listener knows everything, while some of the characters remain in the dark. Because the reader or listener is privy to everything that goes on, he or she ends up playing an important role in the telling of the tale.

UNIT THEME Inea Bushnaq tells a traditional tale with a modern message about greed.

GRAPHIC ORGANIZER Below is a story map, which is a useful way of looking at simple tales.

Circular Story Map: "The Guest Who Ran Away"

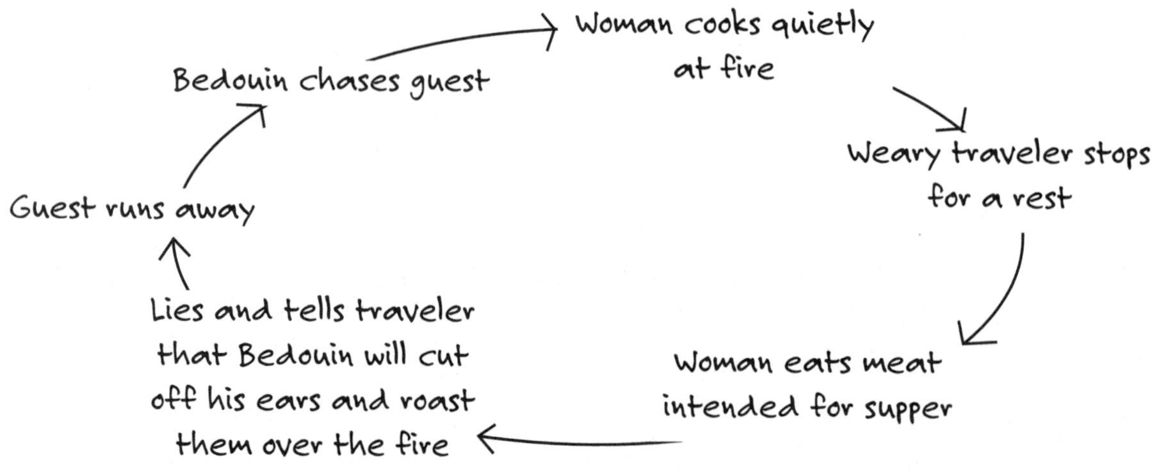

Woman cooks quietly at fire
Weary traveler stops for a rest
Woman eats meat intended for supper
Lies and tells traveler that Bedouin will cut off his ears and roast them over the fire
Guest runs away
Bedouin chases guest

BEFORE YOU READ

Together with students, take a look at the lesson introduction on page 88. If you like, begin the lesson by asking students what they know about folktales (or what they know about the broader genre, folklore, which includes myths, legends, fairy tales, and folktales). Make a list on the board of the characteristics students name. As they read "The Guest Who Ran Away," students can check to see which characteristics are evident in this tale.

Motivation Strategy

Ask students to tell you what their favorite folktales and fairy tales were as children. Then ask: "Why do kids like these kinds of stories so much? What kinds of lessons do they teach? Are these kinds of stories still worth reading once you get older? Why or why not?"

ENGAGING STUDENTS Explain that "The Guest Who Ran Away" is a story about greed. Ask students to complete this statement, which will help them begin thinking about theme: "Greedy people want _____."

Vocabulary Building

Help students use **context clues** as they read to figure out the meanings of difficult words, especially key vocabulary for this lesson: *stew, nibble, savory, snatched,* and *hitching.* Context clues can be found in the word's environment—that is, in surrounding words and phrases. Even though the footnotes define key vocabulary words for students, they still should try to define each word on their own. Once they understand how to search for clues, they'll get into the habit of doing it automatically. Tell students to circle the five vocabulary words in the text. For additional practice with these words, see page 138.

STRATEGY LESSON: IRREGULAR VERBS Most verbs are "regular." That is, the past tense is formed by adding *–ed.* But the past tense of some verbs is formed in other ways. The forms of these verbs sometimes cause trouble for speakers. For example, the word *fled,* the past tense of *flee,* appears on page 90. Other troublesome verbs include *run-ran, give-gave, leave-left,* and *teach-taught.* The past tenses of all of these verbs are in "The Guest Who Ran Away." the best way for non-native speakers to learn these troublesome verbs is to memorize at least some of them.

For additional practice, see the **Vocabulary** blackline master, page 138.

Prereading Strategies

Before they read, students are to do a **preview** of the tale. This preview helps students learn, for example, that they are to read a tale set in a tent and that hospitality is an important part of Bedouin culture.

QUICKWRITE As an alternate prereading strategy, have students do a quickwrite about the topic of greed. Tell students to spend just one minute writing whatever comes to mind about the topic. Later, you can ask students to read over their quickwrites, circling words, phrases, or sentences that they like. Some of these might come in handy when it comes time to respond to the Tunisian folk tale.

Spanish-speaking Students

"El huésped que huyó" es un chistoso cuento folclórico de Tunís. Cuando un viajero pide a unos beduínos que le den comida y alojamiento para la noche, es recibido cordialmente. La mujer prepara la cena que su marido ha conseguido, pero no puede resistir el sabor. Sigue probando la comida hasta que casi desaparece. Avergonzada, inventa una explicación asustante que le causa al viajero a huir.

II. READ

Explain to students that as they read, they should watch closely for names of people or places or ideas that they'd like to **clarify**. They should use the **Response Notes** section to make their comments of clarification. Have them write notes to themselves or make a list of questions that they can return to later.

Response Strategy

VISUALIZE As an alternate response strategy, ask students to try to visualize the people and places Bushnaq describes. Their mental pictures will help them realize the uniqueness of Bushnaq's tale. Because her language is so simple, students should have no trouble "seeing" the people, scenery, and action.

Comprehension Strategies

An excellent comprehension strategy to use with "The Guest Who Ran Away" is a **reciprocal reading**. Divide the class into pairs, and have students take turns reading aloud. As they are reading, students should 1. clarify the problem, characters, and setting; 2. predict outcomes; 3. summarize events; and 4. raise questions about the literature. Students' responses to the interrupter questions can help strengthen their understanding of and connection to the story. Tell the students to work together on each question. If they and their partner disagree about an answer, they should make a note of it and try to figure out why. Later, when everyone is finished, ask each group of two to report on their answers.

GRAPHIC ORGANIZER As an alternate comprehension strategy, have students create a sequence organizer or circular story map similar to the one on the first page of this lesson plan. These kinds of organizers can help low-level readers keep track of events of the story. When it comes time to think about the author's message, students can look at their organizers to refresh their memories on the events of the story.

For more help, see the **Comprehension** blackline master on page 139.

Discussion Questions

COMPREHENSION 1. Where does "The Guest Who Ran Away" take place? *(Tunisia)*

2. Who is the Bedouin? *(the father of the family, who kills the chicken for the stew.)*

3. What does the woman do with the meat? *(She eats it.)*

4. Why does the guest run away? *(He is afraid the Bedouin is going to chop off his ears.)*

CRITICAL THINKING 5. Who is the biggest fool in this story? *(Answers will vary. Remind students to support what they say with evidence from the selection.)*

6. Who is the smartest character? *(Invite students to compare and contrast the smartest to most foolish and support their ideas with lines from the text.)*

Literary Skill

FOLKTALE A folktale is a short narrative handed down verbally through many generations. Folktales reflect the culture from which they come. Not only do they reveal aspects of people's lives, they indicate what a culture considers important. Although the details of a folktale may change over the years, the basic narrative remains the same. Eventually, folktales are written down, as were the ones in this unit. These three tales are both instructive and amusing and rely on trickery for their effect.

III. GATHER YOUR THOUGHTS

The goal of the prewriting activities on page 91 is twofold. The activities will help students do a more careful analysis of the characters of "The Guest Who Ran Away" and they will help them plan a folktale of their own. First, students will need to think carefully about the woman in Bushnaq's story. They'll identify four qualities or character traits and then support their ideas with evidence from the selection.

Once students have a deeper understanding of the protagonist of Bushnaq's folktale, they'll be ready to begin the process of building their own tale. Give students who are reluctant writers the option of using Bushnaq's characters and story line in their own tale. Others might want create their own characters, setting, plot, and moral or lesson.

Prewriting Strategies

BRAINSTORM Once students have an idea of what their folktale will be about, they can begin thinking about how the story will begin. Encourage them to model their story openings on Bushnaq's. Or, as a group, brainstorm several different story openings from which student writers can choose.

For additional practice, have students use the **Prewriting** blackline master on page 140.

IV. WRITE

Set aside plenty of time for students to write their **story beginnings**. If they seem interested, have them continue their work at home, and then devote the next class period to editing and proofreading. At that point you might want to draw students' attention to the **Writers' Checklist** on page 92. Use the checklist to help you introduce a mini-lesson on comma splices.

Grammar, Usage, and Mechanics

Remind the class that a comma splice occurs when two simple sentences are connected ("spliced" together) with only a comma. A comma is not strong enough to hold together two independent statements; a period, semicolon, or conjunction is needed. For example:

Incorrect: The Bedouin ran fast, the guest ran faster.

Correct: The Bedouin ran fast, but the guest ran faster.

WRITING RUBRIC Use the writing rubric to help students focus on the assignment requirements and for help with a quick assessment of their writing.

Do students' story beginnings

- include information about setting?
- establish the characters?
- set up the conflict or problem that the characters will have to resolve?

V. WRAP-UP

Take time at the end of the lesson to talk to students about whether or not they **enjoyed** the tale. If they didn't like it, ask them to explain why. It's possible that they found it too difficult and might benefit from a second reading done aloud. Ask students who liked the story to explain their opinions. Their comments will help you in planning future lessons.

Assessment

To test students' comprehension, use the **Assessment** blackline master on page 141.

Name _____

VOCABULARY

Words from the Selection

DIRECTIONS Use the vocabulary words in a paragraph about the Bedouin, his wife, his son, and the traveler. Write the paragraph on the following lines.

◇ stew   ◇ nibble   ◇ savory   ◇ snatched   ◇ hitching

_____

_____

_____

_____

_____

_____

_____

Strategy Lesson: Irregular Verbs

The past tense of most verbs is formed by adding *–ed*. "They *walk* every morning." "They *walked* yesterday." But the past tense of some verbs is formed in other ways.

DIRECTIONS The verbs in Column A are in the present tense. The words that form the past tense of these verbs are in Column B. Draw a line between the verb in Column A and its past tense in Column B. The first one is done for you.

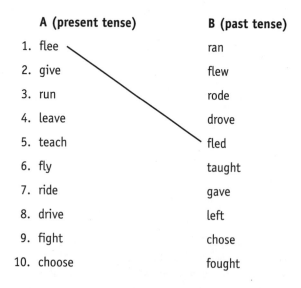

A (present tense)	B (past tense)
1. flee	ran
2. give	flew
3. run	rode
4. leave	drove
5. teach	fled
6. fly	taught
7. ride	gave
8. drive	left
9. fight	chose
10. choose	fought

Name _____

COMPREHENSION
Graphic Organizer

DIRECTIONS Show the sequence of events that Inea Bushnaq describes. Refer to the story as needed.

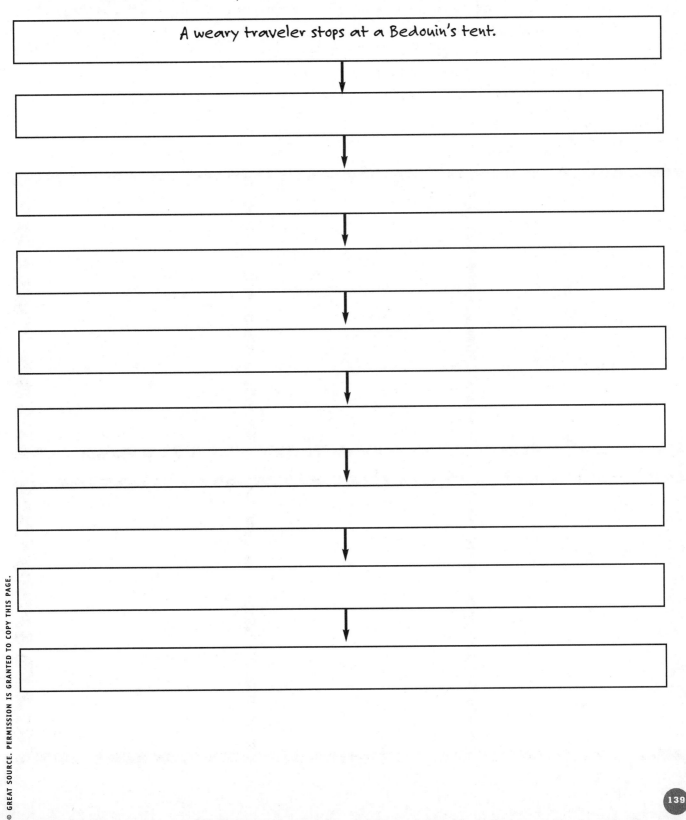

A weary traveler stops at a Bedouin's tent.

Name _____

PREWRITING
Storyboard

Good writers make a plan for their stories. (Sometimes they make a plan on paper, and sometimes they keep the plan in mind and then review or refine it as they go along.)

DIRECTIONS Make a plan for your folktale. Focus on the plot. What will happen first? What will happen next? How will things turn out in the end?

Sketch the events of your story.

Underneath each sketch, write a one- or two-sentence explanation of the event.

Storyboard for (story title) _____

Name _____

ASSESSMENT

Multiple-Choice Test

DIRECTIONS On the blanks provided, write the letter of the best answer for each question.

_____ 1. What does the traveler want from the Bedouin?
    A. camels
    C. clothing
    B. shelter
    D. money

_____ 2. What does the wife do that causes trouble for the family?
    A. She eats all the stew.
    C. She kills the chickens.
    B. She burns the stew.
    D. She ignores the guest.

_____ 3. What does the boy ask his mother for?
    A. more to eat
    C. someone to play with
    B. the visitor's ear
    D. none of the above

_____ 4. What is left in the woman's copper pot?
    A. two chickens
    C. one neck
    B. one wing
    D. nothing

_____ 5. What does the visitor fear he will lose?
    A. his money
    C. his ears
    B. his life
    D. his clothes

_____ 6. Who is the most dishonest character?
    A. the visitor
    C. the Bedouin
    B. the son
    D. the wife

_____ 7. What does the visitor do after he talks to the wife?
    A. He stays for dinner.
    C. He flees the tent.
    B. He tells a story.
    D. He takes a nap.

_____ 8. Why does the Bedouin chase the visitor?
    A. He thinks the visitor took the chickens.
    C. The visitor has taken his son.
    B. He is angry that the man offended his wife.
    D. all of the above

_____ 9. Who is tricked in the story?
    A. the Bedouin
    C. the visitor
    B. the wife
    D. A. and C.

_____ 10. What word would you use to describe the Bedouin?
    A. greedy
    C. crazy
    B. unreasonable
    D. generous

Short-Essay Test

What lesson did this folktale teach you?

The Price of Pride and How Si' Djeha Staved Off Hunger

Skills and Strategies Overview

THEME Stories of the Arab World

READING LEVEL easy

VOCABULARY

◇ crier ◇ kidnapper ◇ dwindled ◇ captor ◇ parched

PREREADING predict

RESPONSE read-aloud / predict

COMPREHENSION retell

PREWRITING sequencing a plot

WRITING story ending / run-ons

ASSESSMENT ease

BACKGROUND

Students will notice that "The Price of Pride" and "How Si' Djeha Staved Off Hunger" are similar in many ways to "The Guest Who Ran Away." All three stories include a Bedouin, or desert wanderer, as a central character. Review with students the background on the people known as the Bedouins in the chapter introduction in this guide.

UNIT THEME In these stories, Inea Bushnaq encourages readers to think about the differences between tricksters and those who are tricked. The contrast between the two is a popular topic in folktales from all around the world.

Graphic Organizer: The Trickster vs. the Tricked

	Who is the trickster?	What does he/she want?	Where does the trick take place?	When does the trick occur?	How does the trick work?	Is the trick successful?
In "The Price of Pride"	a kidnapper	ransom (money) for a child	at a cattle market in the desert	over the course of three days	The kidnapper steals the Bedouin's boy and demands a large ransom.	No. The Bedouin, who is the father of the child, refuses to pay the large sum.
In "How Si' Djeha Staved Off Hunger"	Si' Djeha	food	somewhere in the desert	over the course of just a few minutes	Si' Djeha pretends to know terrible news about the traveler's family and town.	Yes. The traveler flees, and Si' Djeha is able to grab his meal.

BEFORE YOU READ

Read through the introduction to the lesson with students. If you like, review the characteristics of folktales that students listed for "The Guest Who Ran Away." Explain that there are two stories in this lesson. Students will make **predictions** about outcomes in each.

Motivation Strategy

ENGAGING STUDENTS To help students connect the topic of these two stories to their own worlds, ask: "What is a trickster?" What kinds of tricksters (or "con men") can students think of in today's society? Have them tell you about times they played tricks or times they were tricked. What happened? How did they feel? How did things turn out in the end?

Vocabulary Building

Help students use **context clues** as they read to figure out the meanings of difficult words, especially the key vocabulary for this lesson: *crier, kidnapped, dwindled, captor,* and *parched.* Ask students to circle these words in the text. Although the footnotes define these words, students should get into the habit of defining in context. This makes reading faster and more enjoyable. Model using context and then checking your ideas against the footnote: "I don't know the word *parched,* but I see that it appears in a sentence with *throat* and that the person who is parched is in the desert. I assume, then, that parched has something to do with being dry." For additional practice with these words, see page 146.

STRATEGY LESSON: SUFFIXES As students read, point out words with suffixes, such as kidnapper, humbly, and hopefully. Model for students how to separate the suffix from the root word (kidnap + er). Remind the class that when a suffix is added to a word, it changes the way the word is used in the sentence.

For additional practice on this strategy, see the **Vocabulary** blackline master on page 146.

Prereading Strategies

Prediction is an excellent prereading strategy to use with folktales. Because the plot of a folk tale is usually fairly straightforward, students should be able to make more than a few good predictions about outcomes. Each time they make a "correct" prediction, students feel validated. For many, the predictions themselves become the chief motivating factor for reading. Students read to see if their predictions turn out to be true.

PREVIEW If you think it will be useful, have students do an additional prereading activity before they begin. Review the work students did on "The Guest Who Ran Away" before you preview the stories to come. Have a student volunteer summarize the plot and message of the first story. Then ask students to look at the notes they made for the lesson, paying special attention to the story beginnings they wrote on pages 92–93. When you've finished your review, ask students to do a quick preview of "How Si' Djeha Staved Off Hunger" and "The Price of Pride." Ask students to read the first paragraph of each story and then take a look at the art and captions that accompany the text. Also have them glance at vocabulary words and any interrupter questions. When they've finished, have them make predictions about both stories. Which story do they think will have the happier ending? Why?

Spanish-Speaking Students

"El precio de orgullo" es un cuento folclórico de Arabia Saudita. Un hombre sigue disminuyendo el rescate que ofrece al captor de su hijo, revelando el valor inmenso del honor en la cultura árabe. El cuento folclórico, "Como Si' Djeha evitó el hambre" viene de otra parte del mundo árabe, Algeria. Muestra la agudeza de los beduínas que tienen que buscar la vida como puedan. En este cuento cómico, Si' Djeha inventa cuentos y miente para conseguir comida para la cena.

II. READ

Before students begin, remind them that they'll want to pay careful attention to the plot of both stories. They'll make **predictions** about characters and outcomes along the way and then fill out a storyboard for each tale.

Response Strategy

REACT AND CONNECT Invite students to react and connect to the two tales. Perhaps students will want to comment on how gullible the tricked person is, or how "tricky" the trickster is. Or maybe students will want to offer advice to one of the characters. Encourage students to make comments in the **Response Notes**. As always, their comments are for them alone, so they can feel free to write their most honest reactions.

Comprehension Strategies

Storyboards, which can be used with fiction and nonfiction alike, are excellent comprehension strategies because they help readers keep track of the action of the story. Rather than simply asking students to "tell what happens in the story" (which can be difficult), a storyboard helps readers divide the story into more manageable chunks. Encourage the class to add cells to their storyboards as needed, but leave it up to them to decide where the plot breaks and what the sketches should look like.

STORY FRAMES Story frames are similar to storyboards, although they provide even more structure. If students are struggling with Bushnaq's tales, have them create a story frame for each (see page 57 for help). When they are ready to write their own folktales, you might suggest that these students start with story frames so that the job is less intimidating.

For more help, see the **Comprehension** blackline master on page 147.

Discussion Questions

COMPREHENSION 1. How does the Bedouin lose his son in "The Price of Pride"? *(He loses sight of him in the cattle market.)*

2. What does the kidnapper want from the Bedouin? *(money)*

3. Why does the Bedouin keep lowering the price of the ransom for the boy? *(He feels the value of the child goes down each day that the boy is away.)*

4. Who is Si'Djeha? *(He is a tricky traveler in the desert.)*

5. What does he want from another traveler? *(food)*

6. What trick does he play on the traveler? *(He pretends to know of terrible disasters in the traveler's town, so the traveler runs off, leaving his dinner.)*

CRITICAL THINKING 7. Which character would you say is the wisest in these two stories? *(Answers will vary. Ask students to use quotations from the text to support what they say.)*

8. Which character would you say is most foolish? *(Answers will vary. Ask students to support their ideas with evidence from the text.)*

Literary Skill

CONFLICT Conflict is the struggle between two opposing forces. Usually the conflict is resolved in a story, which is then followed by the conclusion. Conflicts may be internal or external. In folktales, the conflict is chiefly external. That is, the main character struggles with some outside force. For more detail, see **III. Gather Your Thoughts** in this guide.

III. GATHER YOUR THOUGHTS

The prewriting activities on pages 101–102 encourage students to think critically about the two stories they've just read. Before they answer the questions on page 101, you might want to teach a brief lesson on conflict. There are five basic types of conflict in literature.

person vs. person One character in the story has a problem with one or more of the other characters.

person vs. society A character has a problem with some element of society: the school, the law, the justice system, and so on.

person vs. self A character has a problem deciding what to do in a particular situation.

person vs. nature A character has a problem with some natural happening: a blizzard, an avalanche, and so on.

person vs. fate (God) A character has to battle what seems to be an uncontrollable problem. Strange coincidences, inexplicable events, and so on are often seen as the "hand of fate."

Prewriting Strategies

GRAPHIC ORGANIZER After students have answered the questions on pages 101 and 102, they can use a sequence organizer to plan the ending of their own stories. Remind them that they'll need to resolve the conflict in their stories.

For additional practice, have students use the **Prewriting** blackline master, page 148.

IV. WRITE

Stay involved with students as they write their story endings. Some might get stuck halfway through and not know how to tie things up. When they've finished a draft, have them revise using the **Writers' Checklist**.

WRITING RUBRIC Use the writing rubric to help students focus on the assignment requirements and for help with a quick assessment of their writing.

Do students' stories

- have a beginning, middle, and end?
- have a fully developed conflict or problem?
- include a sensible resolution of that conflict?

Grammar, Usage, and Mechanics

Use this opportunity to introduce the mini-lesson on run-on sentences. Explain that a run-on is actually two sentences joined without adequate punctuation or a connecting word. For example:

Incorrect: Si' Djeha tells stories the traveler runs home.

Correct: Si' Djeha tells stories, and the traveler runs home.

V. WRAP-UP

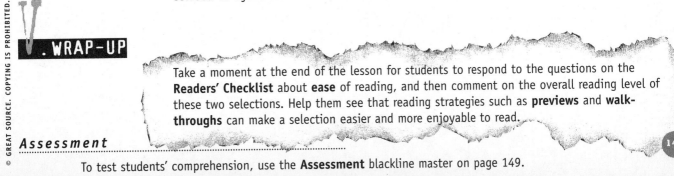

Take a moment at the end of the lesson for students to respond to the questions on the **Readers' Checklist** about **ease** of reading, and then comment on the overall reading level of these two selections. Help them see that reading strategies such as **previews** and **walk-throughs** can make a selection easier and more enjoyable to read.

Assessment

To test students' comprehension, use the **Assessment** blackline master on page 149.

Name _____

VOCABULARY

Words from the Selection

DIRECTIONS Using context clues, fill in each blank with the most appropriate word from the list.

> ✦crier ✦kidnapper ✦dwindled ✦captor ✦parched

1. Once a _____ stole a father's young son.

2. The father hired a _____ to shout through the streets and offer a reward.

3. The sum of money the father offered for his son's return _____ each day.

4. The boy's _____ continued to hold the boy prisoner.

5. At another time, a desert traveler was hungry, and his throat was _____.

Strategy Lesson: Suffixes

A suffix comes at the end of a word. A suffix can give you clues about the meaning of a word and how it should be used in a sentence. For example, if you add the suffix -er to the verb *hike,* you get *hiker,* a "person who hikes" or "someone who takes a long walk."

DIRECTIONS Three suffixes and their meanings are shown in the box. On the blanks below, write the root word and the suffix in each word. Then write what you think the whole word means.

> *-ful* = full of *or* showing   *-ate* = having *or* containing   *-er* = person or thing that does something

	root	+	suffix	=	meaning
EXAMPLE:	hike	+	er	=	person who hikes
6.	kidnap	+	_____	=	_____
7.	travel	+	_____	=	_____
8.	compassionate	+	_____	=	_____
9.	mercy	+	_____	=	_____

10. On the line below, write a sentence using the word *kidnapper.*

_____

Name _____

COMPREHENSION

Character Map

DIRECTIONS Use this character attribute map to explore the character of Si' Djeha. Support what you say with evidence from the story.

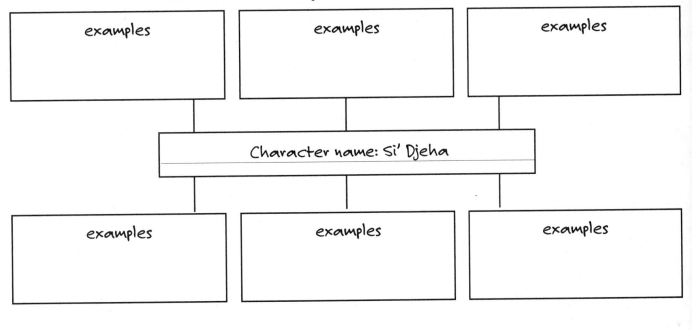

Story Map

DIRECTIONS Use this story map to show the plot of "The Price of Pride."

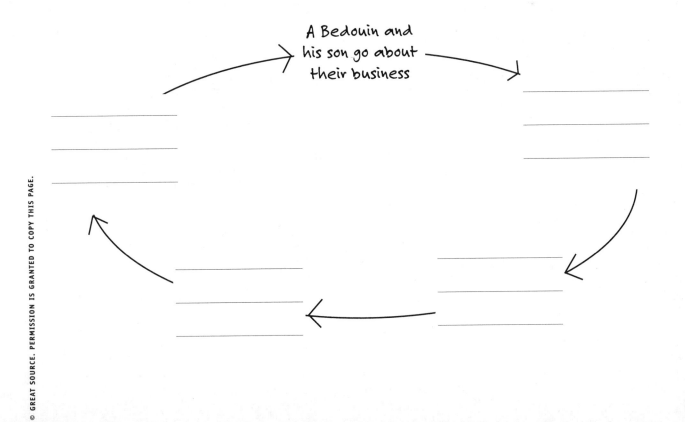

Name _____

PREWRITING

Brainstorm

As you know, the conflict in a story is resolved by the end. Sometimes it helps to brainstorm several different ways to solve the problem and then choose the one that you think is best.

DIRECTIONS Describe the conflict in your folktale in the left circle. Say which characters are involved and what the problem is. Then think of three possible solutions for the conflict. Write them in the three circles on the right.

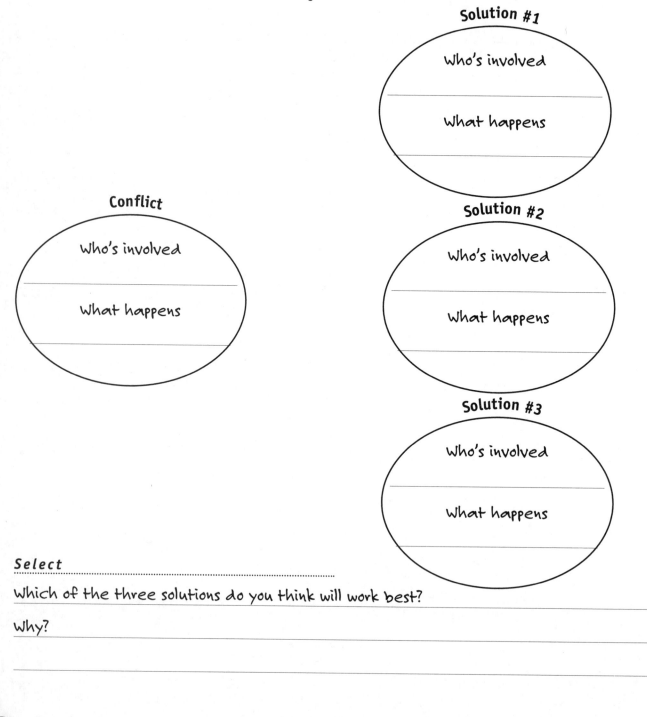

Select

Which of the three solutions do you think will work best? _____

Why? _____

_____

Name _____

ASSESSMENT

Multiple-Choice Test

DIRECTIONS On the blanks provided, write the letter of the item that best answers each question or completes each statement.

_____ 1. What type of story is "The Price of Pride"?
    A. fairy tale   C. folktale
    B. mystery   D. tall tale

_____ 2. What does the Bedouin lose at the cattle market?
    A. his son   C. his cows
    B. his money   D. his pride

_____ 3. Why does the kidnapper wait three days to return the boy?
    A. He doesn't hear the crier.   C. He likes the boy.
    B. He wants more money.   D. none of the above

_____ 4. How much does the father pay the kidnapper for his son?
    A. 10,000 piasters   C. 100 piasters
    B. 1,000 piasters   D. 0 piasters

_____ 5. Where does "How Si' Djeha Staved Off Hunger" take place?
    A. on a farm   C. in a city
    B. in a village   D. in the desert

_____ 6. Si' Djeha is very . . .
    A. kind.   C. tricky.
    B. smart.   D. B. and C.

_____ 7. Si' Djeha was hoping the traveler would . . .
    A. talk to him.   C. give him shelter.
    B. share his food.   D. tell him about his town.

_____ 8. Who was tricked in this story?
    A. the traveler   C. Umm Othman
    B. Si' Djeha   D. the son

_____ 9. The traveler runs home because he thinks his . . .
    A. wife is dead.   C. son is dead.
    B. dog is dead.   D. all of the above

_____ 10. How does Si' Djeha feel at the end of this story?
    A. satisfied   C. brave
    B. jealous   D. fearful

Short-Essay Test

How did the Bedouin in "The Price of Pride" and Si' Djeha use their cleverness to get what they wanted?

Piri Thomas

Unit Background   PIRI THOMAS (pages 105–122)

Piri Thomas was born in New York City, where he had a harsh childhood. During a time spent in prison, he began work as a volunteer in rehabilitation programs, work he continued upon his release. *Down These Mean Streets* is nonfiction and written in a Spanish Harlem dialect. At its publication in 1967, many critics objected to the violence in the book. Others were favorably impressed by its gritty realism, however, and by what they took to be an accurate portrait of life for the young Thomas and others in Spanish Harlem.

Puerto Rico, which Thomas's mother remembers fondly in the first excerpt, is an island between the Atlantic to the north and the Caribbean to the south. It is a self-governing Commonwealth but part of the United States. However, per capita income is much lower than that of the United States.

Tell students whose knowledge of Harlem is hazy that it is a section of New York City in northern Manhattan. A Dutch settlement called Nieuw Haarlem was founded there in the 1600s. Many African Americans began to settle there in the 1900s, and after World War II, many Hispanics settled in East (Spanish) Harlem.

Teaching the Introduction

The photos on page 105 show Piri Thomas and life in Spanish Harlem.

Piri Thomas (1928–) was born to Puerto Rican and Cuban parents. He grew up poor in New York City but overcame a troubled childhood. As a poet, writer, and storyteller, Thomas focuses on people's struggles for survival and recognition and the damaging effects of racism.

Piri Thomas

105

1. These excerpts contain descriptions of Thomas's family, their poverty, and gang life. Ask students what they know about gangs—why they are formed and their purpose. Do gangs benefit their members? If so, how? Are most gangs made up of criminals or potential criminals or not?

2. Some immigrants to the United States do not find life a great deal better, at least at first, than the life they left. Ask what some of the reasons for this might be.

Opening Activity

Ask students to imagine that they have moved to a city in a country where they know only a few words of the language. They have to find a place to live and a job, and have no real knowledge of the city they are going to live in. What would they do first?

STUDENT PAGES 106–114

Skills and Strategies Overview

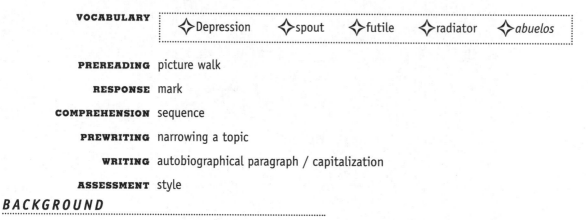

THEME	Piri Thomas
READING LEVEL	average
VOCABULARY	◇Depression ◇spout ◇futile ◇radiator ◇*abuelos*
PREREADING	picture walk
RESPONSE	mark
COMPREHENSION	sequence
PREWRITING	narrowing a topic
WRITING	autobiographical paragraph / capitalization
ASSESSMENT	style

BACKGROUND

"Puerto Rican Paradise" is an excerpt from *Down These Mean Streets,* Piri Thomas's lacerating memoir of his youth on the streets of Spanish Harlem. In the book, Thomas describes his troubled past, which included membership in a gang, experimentation with drugs, armed robbery, and a long imprisonment in Sing Sing for shooting a police officer.

In this portion of his autobiography, the author offers a glimpse of his home life. Ever since Thomas can remember, the Thomas family had been struggling—struggling to stay warm, struggling to find enough to eat, struggling to pay the rent. In this excerpt, Piri's mother, whom he calls "Moms," admits that she is dead tired of struggling, and longs to return to her homeland. The Thomas children listen with rapt attention as she recounts the "paradise" of her youth.

UNIT THEME Piri Thomas gives new meaning to the phrase "struggle for survival" in this excerpt from his autobiography.

GRAPHIC ORGANIZER Student time lines on page 111 might resemble this one.

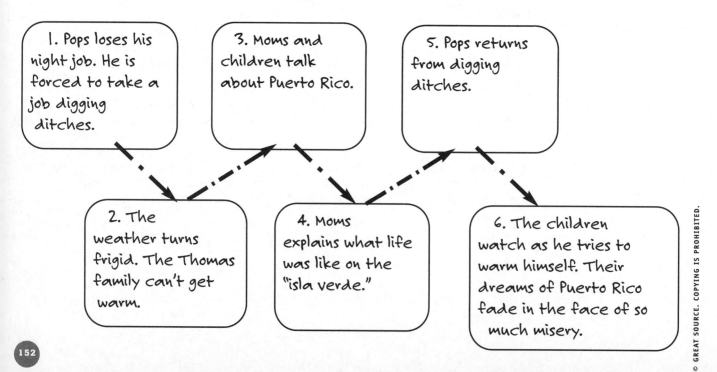

BEFORE YOU READ

Read through the introduction to the lesson with students, supplying additional information about Piri Thomas as you see fit. Be sure students understand how to do a **picture walk** of a text. They'll look at art and captions only, and avoid reading the selection. When you feel they are ready, ask students to turn to this prereading strategy for "Puerto Rican Paradise." (Refer to the **Strategy Handbook** on page 40 for more help.)

Motivation Strategy

ENGAGING STUDENTS In "Puerto Rican Paradise," Piri Thomas ponders his family's struggles. Ask students to discuss hardships their family has faced in the past. This will give them the chance to relate Thomas's theme to their own lives even before they begin reading the selection. Have students tell you what they know about the Depression of the 1930s. Who was affected and what happened? If you like, do a quick K-W-L on the board that students can refer to as they are reading.

Vocabulary Building

Context clues can be particularly helpful in reading a selection that includes words from a foreign language. Although many of the words in Thomas's memoir are footnoted at the bottom of the page, students should try to define in context so that there's no need to interrupt the rhythm of their reading. Have students watch for key vocabulary words for this lesson: *Depression, spout, futile, radiator,* and *abuelos*. Ask them to define these words in context if possible and then make a note of the definition of the word in the **Response Notes**. Have students circle the vocabulary words in the text. For additional practice, see page 156.

STRATEGY LESSON: ROOT WORDS A general knowledge of root words can help students learn new words. Ask students to think of words that contain these roots: *fac-, fact-* (do, make); *cred-* (believe); *leg-* (law); and *alter* (other). Words from the selection that use these roots include *factory, incredible, illegal,* and *alternative*. (Other words are *manufacture, legalize, credit,* and *alternate*.)

For additional practice on this strategy, see the **Vocabulary** blackline master, page 156.

Prereading Strategies

As a prereading warm-up, students are asked to take a **picture walk** through the selection. Remind them that during a picture walk, the reader looks only at the art, photographs, and captions, if any. These elements of a story can provide valuable clues about the topic and message. When they've finished their picture walks, students should explain how the pictures made them feel and then make predictions about the selection's topic. Later, after they've read the memoir, you might ask students to return to the pictures and explain the connections they see between the photographs and the narrative.

Spanish-speaking Students

"El paraíso puertorriqueño" es parte de la autobiografía de Piri Thomas, *Down These Mean Streets*. En esta selección, Thomas escribe sobre la pena que padecía viviendo en Harlem durante la Depresión. Describe en detalle vívido el frío y las otras dificultades inmensas que acompañan la pobreza. Pero con el amor de su padres y los cuentos de Puerto Rico, donde ellos vivían antes, Thomas mantiene un corazón cariñoso.

READ

Remind students to read slowly and carefully. Tell them that good readers **mark** or **highlight** a text as they are reading. They note everything they find interesting, important, confusing, or puzzling. Making notes helps the reader pay better attention to the author's words and ideas and can be tremendously useful when it comes time to respond critically to the text.

Response Strategy

PREDICT As an alternative response strategy, students could make predictions in the **Response Notes** columns.

Comprehension Strategies

GRAPHIC ORGANIZER **Sequence organizers** or **time lines** can help readers keep track of the events of the plot. They allow the reader to see the author's slow build toward the climax and resolution and can help isolate and clarify the details the author uses to support his or her theme. As they are reading "Puerto Rican Paradise," students will stop at two different points in order to make notes about the sequence of events. When they've finished the selection, they're asked to pull their notes together and create a large time line that represents Thomas's plot. Before they begin reading the memoir, you might point out the organizer on page 111. Show students that they'll need to pay special attention to the events of the story and will need to note at least six different events on this time line.

For more help, see the **Comprehension** blackline master on page 157.

Discussion Questions

COMPREHENSION 1. What are some of the troubles that the Thomas family faces? *(They have no heat; the father has lost his job; the United States is a cold place.)*

2. How does Moms feel about Puerto Rico? *(She misses it and longs to go back.)*

3. Why do the children ask her to tell stories about Puerto Rico? *(They like hearing about the warmth of the climate and the people.)*

CRITICAL THINKING 4. Does Piri share his mother's love of Puerto Rico? *(Answers will vary. He seems more reluctant than his mother to embrace these memories, but perhaps that's because they're not his own.)*

5. What is the tone of Thomas's memoir? *(Answers will vary. If needed, review the characteristics of tone with students.)*

Literary Skill

TONE Piri Thomas's writing provides an excellent opportunity to discuss tone with students. Tone is the author's attitude or feeling about his or her subject matter. Through his tone, Thomas makes it clear that although he wants to reveal the extent of his family's suffering, he doesn't want the reader to feel pity. In his descriptions of the family's hunger and discomfort, he inserts unexpected bits of humor that lighten the mood of the narrative. For example, he pretends to feel sorry for the suffering of the rats and clearly enjoys the ruckus caused by people banging on their radiators. Because of these bits of humor, the reader never feels sorry for Thomas. Instead it is easy for us to admire him for his ability to interject a little levity into a humorless situation.

III. GATHER YOUR THOUGHTS

The goal of the prewriting activities on page 112 is to help students write an autobiographical paragraph about their families. First they'll narrow the topic for their paragraph using the techniques that they learned on page 30 of their books.

Prewriting Strategies

STORYBOARD On the bottom of page 112, students are asked to complete a sequence organizer that shows the experience they plan to describe in their autobiographical paragraphs. They could also make a storyboard with four to six cells; in each cell they could draw a picture and then write a one-sentence description of the drawing. Storyboards are useful for students who have trouble thinking of what they want to say. These students often jump at the chance to draw first and describe later.

Have students use the **Prewriting** blackline master on page 158.

IV. WRITE

Make sure you give students plenty of time to plan and then write their **autobiographical paragraphs**. Remind them that they need to describe an experience from their own lives. They may want to tell what they actually learned from their experience.

WRITING RUBRIC If you like, show students this writing rubric to help them focus on the specifics of the assignment. Later, you can use it for help with a quick assessment of their writing.

Do students' paragraphs

- begin with a topic sentence?
- contain plenty of details about the experience they want to describe?
- use transition words?

Grammar, Usage, and Mechanics

When students have finished their rough drafts, have them revise their work using the **Writers' Checklist**. At this point you might want to teach a mini-lesson on capitalization. Remind the class that titles used before a name, place names, specific regions, bodies of water, and topographic regions are always capitalized. Also remind students that words like *grandfather* and *mother* are capitalized only when they are used with a person's name (Grandfather Smith) or as a substitute for a person's name unless it's preceded by *my, their,* and so on.

V. WRAP-UP

Take time at the end of the lesson to discuss Piri Thomas's writing **style**. Ask students how they felt about his use of slang ("copped a plea"). Encourage students to move beyond the mundane: "I liked it" or "I didn't like it." The questions on the **Readers' Checklist** can help them think more critically about his word choices, sentence structure, and tone.

Assessment

To test students' comprehension, use the **Assessment** blackline master on page 159.

Name _____

VOCABULARY

Words from the Selection

DIRECTIONS Answer these questions that use words from the selection. Explain your answers.

1. Was the <u>Depression</u> in the 1930's a time of great hardship or wealth?

_____

2. If fire hydrants <u>spout</u> water, is the water leaking or gushing?

_____

3. If something is <u>futile</u>, is it useful or useless?

_____

4. Do you use a <u>radiator</u> for warmth or cooling?

_____

5. Are your <u>*abuelos*</u> older than you are?

_____

Strategy Lesson: Root Words

DIRECTIONS Read this list of common roots and their definitions. Then use what you've learned to write the meaning of the underlined words on the blanks.

Roots

fac-, fact- = do, make
cred = believe
leg- = law
alter = other

6. Papa had no <u>alternative</u> but to go back on welfare.

_____

7. Papa tried to get a job in the shoe <u>factory</u>. _____

8. We all thought it was <u>incredible</u> that an apartment that was so hot in the summer could be so cold in the winter. _____

9. There was nothing <u>illegal</u> about the landlord's policies, but they sure were unfair.

_____

10. Write another word that contains one of the roots in the box.

_____

Name _____

COMPREHENSION
Directed Reading

DIRECTIONS Answer these questions about "Puerto Rican Paradise." Your answers can help you understand Piri Thomas's message.

1. Why is Piri worried about his father?

_____

_____

2. What has caused the Thomas family's difficulties?

_____

_____

3. According to Moms, what are some of the differences between life in Puerto Rico and life in New York?

_____

_____

4. Why is she so desperate to return to Puerto Rico?

_____

_____

5. Do you think Thomas wants you to feel sorry for his family? Explain your answer.

_____

_____

Name _____

PREWRITING
Writing an Autobiographical Paragraph

DIRECTIONS **A. CHOOSE A TOPIC.** Before you can write a paragraph about yourself, you need to decide what you want to say. First think of a topic. Tell about an event or experience that happened in your family.

My topic: _____

B. GATHER DETAILS. Gather details about the experience. These questions can help you consider the most important details.

What happened? _____

_____

Where were you? _____

Who else was there? _____

When did it happen? _____

Why did it happen? _____

How did it end? _____

_____

How did you feel once the whole thing was over? _____

_____

What did you learn? _____

_____

_____

C. WRITE A TOPIC SENTENCE. Write a topic sentence that tells about the experience and what you learned. Use this formula:

What happened + What I learned = my topic sentence.

My topic sentence: _____

_____

Name _____

ASSESSMENT

Multiple-Choice Test

DIRECTIONS On the blanks provided, write the letter of the item that best answers each question or completes each statement.

_____ 1. Why doesn't Poppa talk much to anyone?
- A. He is tired of all the kids.
- B. He is upset about his job.
- C. He is angry with his wife.
- D. He is bored with the family.

_____ 2. After he loses his job in the factory, Poppa goes to work for . . .
- A. the Depression.
- B. Puerto Rico.
- C. the government.
- D. the railroad.

_____ 3. Why is Momma upset with the landlord?
- A. There are holes in the floor.
- B. They have only cold water.
- C. The window is broken.
- D. There is not enough heat.

_____ 4. Momma's memories of Puerto Rico are . . .
- A. pleasant.
- B. sad.
- C. terrifying.
- D. forgotten.

_____ 5. What could they always eat in Puerto Rico no matter how poor they were?
- A. They could eat bananas.
- B. They could eat steak.
- C. They could eat cereal.
- D. all of the above

_____ 6. When Momma was a girl, she got water from . . .
- A. the well.
- B. the lake.
- C. the sink.
- D. the river.

_____ 7. When Momma talks about Puerto Rico, she refers to it as . . .
- A. my island.
- B. Moses' land of milk and honey.
- C. *isla verde*.
- D. all of the above

_____ 8. Why was Momma happier in Puerto Rico?
- A. It's warm there.
- B. She had family there.
- C. They were able to share their poverty with those around them.
- D. all of the above

_____ 9. What happened to her parents' land?
- A. They ruined it with bad farming methods.
- B. They lost it because they had no contract.
- C. They lost it in a gambling game.
- D. They gave it to their children.

_____ 10. What does Poppa use to warm up his ears and hands?
- A. warm water
- B. a towel
- C. a water bottle
- D. a snowball

Short-Essay Test

What does Momma mean when she says the United States is a cold place "because of the snow in the hearts of people"?

If You Ain't Got Heart, You Ain't Got Nada

Skills and Strategies Overview

THEME	Piri Thomas
READING LEVEL	average
VOCABULARY	◆reassemble ◆stoop ◆expression ◆prestige ◆overtures
PREREADING	quickwrite
RESPONSE	react and connect
COMPREHENSION	graphic organizer
PREWRITING	group discussion
WRITING	narrative paragraph / consistency
ASSESSMENT	depth

BACKGROUND

"If You Ain't Got Heart, You Ain't Got Nada," is another excerpt from Piri Thomas's *Down These Mean Streets*. In this selection, Piri is a little older and a little tougher. He and his family have moved to a new part of Spanish Harlem, which forces Piri to "prove himself" once again to a new set of boys. Rather than rush headlong into a fight, however, Piri uses a little psychology to separate the gang leader from his gang. His goal is to get the leader to agree to a fair fight.

Thomas's memoir is as gritty as the streets he grew up in. He is unflinching in his descriptions of boyhood activities and is so graphic in his descriptions that the reader can't help but cringe each time another bloody punch is thrown. Through it all, though, you can sense Thomas's *corazón*—the same *corazón* that helps keep the Thomas family smiling even when they are tired, hungry, and freezing in their little apartment.

UNIT THEME Piri Thomas, a boy of the streets, struggles for survival when his family moves to a new neighborhood.

GRAPHIC ORGANIZER Students might benefit from working on a story pyramid.

Story Pyramid: "If You Ain't Got Heart, You Ain't Got Nada"

1. __Piri__
Name of main character

2. __tough__ __smart__
Two words describing main character

3. __poor__ __grim__ __mean__
Three words describing setting

4. __new__ __street,__ __new__ __fights__
Four words stating problem

5. __Waneko__ __challenges__ __Piri__ __to__ __fight__
Five words describing one event

6. __Fight__ __between__ __two__ __is__ __a__ __draw__
Six words describing second event

7. __Piri__ __shows__ __Waneko's__ __gang__ __he__ __has__ __heart__
Seven words describing solution

I. BEFORE YOU READ

Before beginning this lesson, you might have a volunteer summarize what happened in "Puerto Rican Paradise." Then have students read the introduction on page 115. When they're ready, they can begin the prereading activity, a one-minute **quickwrite**. Ask someone to define *nada* in the title.

Motivation Strategy

In this part of his autobiography, Piri Thomas describes a gang tussle that frightens him, yet at the same time gives him a feeling of exhilaration. Ask students to tell about a time they were scared and excited at the same time. What happened? What did they do? This short discussion will help introduce the topic of "If You Ain't Got Heart" to students.

ENGAGING STUDENTS You might also take this opportunity to ask students to discuss street gang problems where they live. Does the problem exist? Why or why not? If gangs are a problem, what are local authorities trying to do about it? Have their techniques been effective? Why do people join gangs?

Vocabulary Building

Help students use **context clues** to figure out the meaning of unfamiliar words, especially key vocabulary words for the lesson: *reassemble, stoop, expression, prestige,* and *overtures*. If necessary, model the process of using context clues. For example, explain that you can figure out what the word *expression* (page 119) means by looking at surrounding sentences. It's clear from what Piri says that he is examining Waneko's face for clues. We can assume that *expression* has to do with the emotions displayed on a person's face. Since two words are not footnoted, ask students to find the meaning of *prestige* (page 119) and *overtures* (page 120) in a dictionary. Ask students to circle the vocabulary words in the text. For more practice with context clues, see page 164.

STRATEGY LESSON: WORD ANALYSIS By now students have learned a number of strategies for defining new words, analyzing word parts, and understanding word origins. To help students review some of these strategies, assign the **Vocabulary** blackline master, page 164.

Prereading Strategies

The purpose of a **quickwrite** is to have students start writing about a topic before they've hardly begun to think about it. Stress that during their quickwrites, students should write whatever comes to mind that relates to the topic. In this case, students will read the first few paragraphs of the selection and then respond to what Thomas has said. They may want to connect the topic to their own lives or express approval or disapproval of Thomas's ideas. When they've finished, have them read over their quickwrites and circle words, phrases, or sentences that they particularly like. Tell the class that they may be able to use some of these to help with a later writing assignment.

Spanish-speaking Students

"Si no tienes corazón, no tienes nada" cuenta otra parte de la vida de Piri Thomas. En esta selección, describe sus experiencias fuera de su casa, donde tenía que navegar el mundo de bandas y violencia callejera. Es un mundo donde los adolescentes luchan para mostrar su fuerza y probar su prestigio. A lo largo, Thomas sabe que tiene que mantener su "corazón," y esperar que sus adversarios también lo mantengan.

II. READ

As students read, they will make comments in the **Response Notes** that show their willingness to **react and connect** to the people, places, and situations Thomas describes. Encourage them to jot down their initial, off-the-cuff reactions to his writing. Sometimes these comments about a piece of literature end up being the most insightful ones of all.

Response Strategy

QUESTION Questions are bound to come up whenever students read, especially when they read a piece that is as provocative as this one is. As an alternate response strategy, have students make notes about their questions as they go along. You can use their questions to help lead an impromptu discussion of the literature once everyone has finished reading. For example, "Why does Thomas say he has two names?" (page 117) "What are brass knuckles? Did anyone win the fight?" (page 120).

Comprehension Strategies

Graphic organizers keep students organized and on task as they read. For this selection, students will complete two different cause-effect organizers that can help them do some critical thinking about plot. Remind them to consider the causes carefully. Whom do they think initiates the argument with the gang members? What is the outcome or effect of the fight? Students can use their notes on the organizers to help them in Part III, when it comes time to discuss character motivation.

For more help, see the **Comprehension** blackline master on page 165.

Discussion Questions

COMPREHENSION 1. Why is Piri nervous about the move to a new neighborhood? *(He knows he will have to prove himself to a new group of kids.)*

2. How do the other kids act toward Piri when they first see him? *(They are wary. They watch him, but say nothing.)*

CRITICAL THINKING 3. Why does Piri agree to fight Waneko? *(Answers will vary. Possibly, he wants to prove himself.)*

4. Do you think Piri and the other boys will eventually become friends? Explain. *(Accept reasonable predictions about the text.)*

5. Would you say Piri has earned the respect of the gang? Why or why not? *(Accept reasonable responses so long as they are supported with evidence from the selection.)*

6. What would you have done or said if you had been in Piri's shoes? *(Answers will vary, depending on students' experiences. Remind them to fully explain their responses.)*

Literary Skill

VERNACULAR To introduce a literary skill with this lesson, explain to students that some stories are more effective—and seem more real—if they are told in the vernacular, the everyday spoken language of the people in a particular place and time. Notice that Thomas switches back and forth between Spanish and English, street talk and standard English. Thomas's linguistic flip-flops allow him to tell his story quickly and graphically. The language he uses lends a kind of realism to his writing that he would not have been able to achieve had he written his autobiography in standard English.

III. GATHER YOUR THOUGHTS

At the top of the page, students are asked to think about what motivates Piri to fight. Encourage students to discuss what they might have done had they been in his shoes. Asking them to compare Piri's actions to their own ideas about how to act may help them better understand the decisions he makes.

Prewriting Strategies

CAUSE AND EFFECT   On the second half of page 121, students are asked to plan a **narrative paragraph** about a time they had to prove something. In order to do this activity, they'll first need to think about the experience and then think about the causes and effects. If students seem stumped, have them look at the cause and effect organizers they filled in as they were reading the selection.

Have students use the **Prewriting** blackline master on page 166.

IV. WRITE

When students are ready to write, you might want to take a moment to remind them of the characteristics of a narrative paragraph. A narrative paragraph should

- have a beginning, middle, and an end.
- include details that will pull readers into the story.
- keep readers wondering what will happen next.

WRITING RUBRIC   Consider using this writing rubric to help students focus on the assignment requirements or for help with a quick assessment of their writing.

Do students' narrative paragraphs

- have a first-person point of view?
- have a beginning, middle, and end?
- contain adequate details?
- explain what happened, where it happened, and the effects?
- end with a closing sentence that ties things together?

Grammar, Usage, and Mechanics

When they've finished their first drafts, have students revise using the **Writers' Checklist** as a guide. Introduce a mini-lesson on consistency. Explain to students that writers should keep their point of view and verb tense consistent throughout the piece. If they begin their paragraphs in the first person, then they should use the first person throughout. If they are writing in the past tense (which most students will do for this assignment), then they should continue using the past tense for the entire paragraph.

V. WRAP-UP

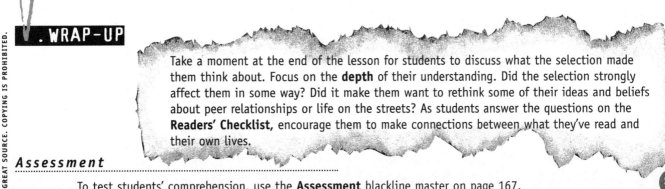

Take a moment at the end of the lesson for students to discuss what the selection made them think about. Focus on the **depth** of their understanding. Did the selection strongly affect them in some way? Did it make them want to rethink some of their ideas and beliefs about peer relationships or life on the streets? As students answer the questions on the **Readers' Checklist,** encourage them to make connections between what they've read and their own lives.

Assessment

To test students' comprehension, use the **Assessment** blackline master on page 167.

Name _____

VOCABULARY

Words from the Selection

DIRECTIONS To help you learn new words from the selection, answer each question. Then write the meaning of the underlined word on the line.

1. If a group is trying to <u>reassemble</u> itself, are they trying to meet for a first time or a second time?

_____

2. Why do people often hang out on a <u>stoop</u>?

_____

3. If you are happy, what is your <u>expression</u>?

_____

4. If you have <u>prestige</u> in your school, are you admired?

_____

5. If you make <u>overtures</u> of peace, are you proposing peace?

_____

Strategy Lesson: Word Analysis

DIRECTIONS Write the word from the list at the right that correctly answers each question.

6. Which word means both "a fruit drink" and "a quick blow"?

_____

7. Which word comes from the earlier English word *knokel*?

_____

8. *Terra* is Latin for "land." Which word has this Latin root?

_____

9. Which word has a prefix meaning "again"?

_____

10. Which word means both "bend forward" and "steps at a front door"?

_____

territory

reassemble

stoop

punch

knuckle

Name _____

COMPREHENSION
Group Discussion

DIRECTIONS Use these discussion questions to help you and your group understand Thomas's memoir. Refer to the book as needed.

DISCUSSION QUESTION #1

What three adjectives (descriptive words) would you use to describe Piri?

_____

_____

_____

DISCUSSION QUESTION #2

Is the match between Piri and Waneko fair? Explain.

_____

_____

_____

DISCUSSION QUESTION #3

Was Piri wrong to fight? Support your opinion.

_____

_____

_____

DISCUSSION QUESTION #4

What advice do you have for Piri? How should he act the next time he sees Waneko and his gang?

_____

_____

_____

_____

Name _____

PREWRITING

Writing About an Experience

....

DIRECTIONS How do you write about an experience? Follow these steps.

STEP 1. CHOOSE AN EXPERIENCE. Decide what experience you'd like to describe.

My choice: _____

STEP 2. GATHER DETAILS. Then gather details about the experience. List them here.

What I saw:
_____

What I heard:
_____

What I said:
_____

What others said to me:
_____

How I felt before the experience:
_____

How I felt during the experience:
_____

How I felt after the experience was over:
_____

STEP 3. WRITE A TOPIC SENTENCE. Now write a topic sentence that explains the experience and why it had an effect on you. Use this as the first sentence of your paragraph.

_____

_____

_____

STEP 4. WRITE A CONCLUDING SENTENCE. Write a sentence that tells what you learned from the experience. Make it clear and memorable.

_____

_____

_____

Name _____

ASSESSMENT

Multiple-Choice Test

DIRECTIONS On the blanks provided, write the letter of the item that best answers each question or completes each statement.

_____ 1. In the beginning of the selection, Piri is upset because . . .
- A. he got into a fight.
- B. he is threatened by a gang.
- C. he is moving to a new neighborhood.
- D. he got in trouble at school.

_____ 2. According to Piri, when you're a new kid, the other kids are like "some kind of . . . "
- A. friend.
- B. enemy.
- C. family.
- D. stranger.

_____ 3. When Piri looks at the faces of the neighborhood kids, he sees . . .
- A. distrust.
- B. hate.
- C. suspicion.
- D. all of the above

_____ 4. What name does Piri use when he is fighting?
- A. Johnny Gringo
- B. Waneko
- C. Panin
- D. Piri

_____ 5. When Piri refers to "stomping time," he is talking about . . .
- A. fighting.
- B. dancing.
- C. eating.
- D. sleeping.

_____ 6. When Piri goes to face Waneko and the other boys, he tries to act . . .
- A. annoyed.
- B. silly.
- C. brave.
- D. frightened.

_____ 7. Piri decides he wants to fight . . .
- A. no one.
- B. Waneko.
- C. Alfredo.
- D. all the boys.

_____ 8. According to Piri, what do you have to have to be a good leader?
- A. money
- B. heart
- C. power
- D. brains

_____ 9. How does Piri feel after the fight?
- A. defeated
- B. angry
- C. energetic
- D. satisfied

_____ 10. This story takes place . . .
- A. on a farm.
- B. in the suburbs.
- C. in the city.
- D. in the country.

Short-Essay Test

Why did Piri fight Waneko and what did it prove?

Unit Background   **DREAMS** (pages 123–142)

All people have dreams, but making them come true is more difficult for some people than for others. Columnist Bob Greene wrote his column in response to jokes about Helen Keller made by "dim-witted comics." Craig Kielburger wrote of his horrified response to child labor and how this response changed his life.

After reading about the murder of Iqbal Masih, a young Pakistani carpet weaver, Canadian Craig Kielburger (born 1982) traveled for seven weeks with Alam Rahman through the slums and sweatshops of Bangladesh, Thailand, India, Nepal, and Pakistan to talk with children and young people. He then formed Free the Children and received the Roosevelt Freedom Medal and the State of the World Forum Award. He was named a Global Leader of Tomorrow at the 1998 World Economic Forum in Davos, Switzerland and also received Canada's Governor General's Award for Meritorious Service.

Teaching the Introduction

The images on page 123 are of Helen Keller as a young woman (left), Craig Kielburger at the time he wrote his book, and two small street children.

1. Ask students to tell what they know, if anything, about Helen Keller, who could not see, hear, or speak as a child and only learned to speak later in life.

2. Students might know that the Americans with Disabilities Act signed into law in 1990 barred discrimination against people with disabilities. Ask students to mention some of the ways disabled people are helped in public places today in the United States.

3. Students may be aware of recent furor over the manufacture of U.S. products in overseas sweatshops, many of them employing child labor. If so, ask them what they have heard, read, or seen on television about such sweatshops and the controversy over whether they should be closed. What are the advantages to employers of having underage—even very small—children employed? What are the advantages to families of these children? What is the effect on the lives of the children?

Opening Activity

Divide the class into small groups and have them research more information about Helen Keller or recent information about sweatshops in foreign countries and in the United States and report to the class.

Some students might enjoy watching the movie version of the Broadway play *The Miracle Worker* about the childhood of Helen Keller. Anne Bancroft and Patty Duke star in the 1962 film. As an alternative, you might show parts of the film to the class.

Her Life Was Not a Joke

Skills and Strategies Overview

THEME	Dreams
READING LEVEL	easy
VOCABULARY	◇flailed ◇rampant ◇manual ◇prestigious ◇advocating
PREREADING	anticipation guide
RESPONSE	question
COMPREHENSION	prediction
PREWRITING	graphic organizer
WRITING	character sketch / verbs
ASSESSMENT	understanding

BACKGROUND

Bob Greene, an enormously popular syndicated columnist for the *Chicago Tribune,* began his newspaper career as a summer copy boy for the Columbus (Ohio) *Citizen-Journal.* On the very first day of his very first newspaper job, he fell in love with the hustle and bustle of the newsroom, and decided that this job—writing, researching, reporting, and printing news—was what he wanted to do for the rest of his life. It took a long time for Greene to work his way up to columnist for a newspaper as large as the *Tribune,* but he was determined to make a name for himself, so he persevered, accepting story assignments that no one else wanted, staying late to talk to veteran reporters, and writing whenever and whatever he could.

Unlike most of his colleagues, Greene avoids writing about hard news in his columns. Instead, he uses his column to present what are essentially snapshots of "the stage play of life that never ends."

UNIT THEME Our dreams motivate us and keep us centered. In his column, Bob Greene explains the simple dreams of an extraordinary woman.

GRAPHIC ORGANIZER Students might benefit by seeing the following organizer.

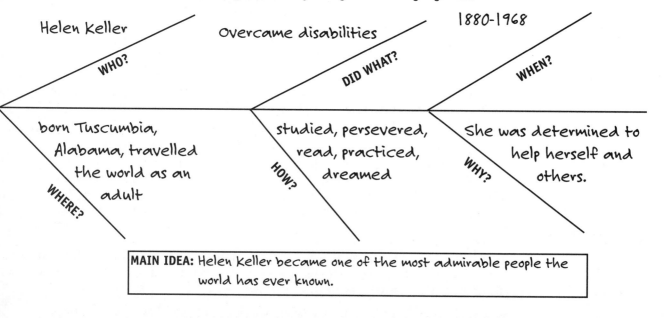

BIBLIOGRAPHY Other books by Bob Greene include these: *Be True to Your School* (1990); *Hang Time: Days and Dreams with Michael Jordan* (1993); *The Fifty Year Dash* (1998).

BEFORE YOU READ

Read through the introduction to the lesson with students. Remind them that this lesson, and the others in the book, will help sharpen their critical reading skills. When you feel they are ready to begin, ask them to turn to the prereading strategy: an **anticipation guide**. (Refer to the **Strategy Handbook** on page 40 for more help.)

Motivation Strategy

Tell the class that "Her Life Was Not a Joke" is about Helen Keller. Ask what students know about this famous woman. What have they read or seen on TV? Students' comments can help you assess their prior knowledge before reading.

ENGAGING STUDENTS Ask students to think about a time someone made fun of them. What happened? How did they feel? Were they able to defend themselves? Why or why not? Students should keep this experience in mind as they read Greene's column.

Vocabulary Building

Help students use context clues as they read to figure out the meanings of difficult words. Remind them to pay particular attention to key vocabulary words for the lesson: *flailed, rampant, manual, prestigious,* and *advocating.* Ask students to circle these words in the text. The footnotes define some of these words for students, although you'll want to encourage them to try to define on their own before checking the footnote. Help them get into the habit of using their own "built-in" dictionaries. It's faster, easier, and makes reading more enjoyable. For more practice defining in context, see page 174.

SUFFIXES Word games can improve students' vocabulary and make them feel more confident about their language skills. Show how easy it is to attach suffixes to words. Give students a group of common suffixes such as *-ed, -able, -ate, -ful,* and *-ology* and have them think of words that use the suffixes. Make a list on the board of the words and then ask for volunteers to define each one. You might incorporate these words from the selection: *guttural, partial, prestigious, contentment,* and *buffoonish.*

For additional practice on this strategy, see the **Vocabulary** blackline master, page 174.

Prereading Strategies

The **anticipation guide** on page 124 will help students begin thinking about Greene's message. Tell students that since no teacher will be examining their answers, they should be as honest as possible. After they've finished reading the selection, have students return to the anticipation guide to see if their attitudes have changed. This is an excellent way to show students that what they read really can change the way they view the world.

PICTURE WALK As an additional strategy, have students do a quick picture walk of the selection. This strategy will serve as another introduction to the topic—and message—of the selection. From the photos, students should be able to infer that "Her Life Was Not a Joke" has to do with Helen Keller and Anne Sullivan. Ask students to make a one-sentence prediction about Greene's main idea: "Bob Greene thinks that Helen Keller was _____."

Spanish-speaking Students

La leyenda de Helen Keller es poderosa. Ella nació sorda, ciega, y muta, pero lograba en comunicarse con otras personas, y también en enseñarles. En "Su vida no era una broma" Bob Greene exige respeto para esta mujer, que, debido a su menosvalidez, ha sido el sujeto de muchas bromas. Por describir sus logros, prueba que las limitaciones físicas no tienen nada que ver con el valor de un individuo.

II. READ

Response Strategy

REACT AND CONNECT As they read, students should react and connect to the author's words. Their reactions can help them understand Greene's main idea. Ask them to make notes about how the people and events he describes make them feel. Do they agree or disagree with his opinions? Do they have an experience from their own lives that they'd like to share out loud or in writing? They can use their responses later, when it is time to write their character sketches.

Comprehension Strategies

Students are asked to make a **prediction** on page 126. Making predictions can help readers make inferences about what the writer will say next.

DOUBLE-ENTRY JOURNAL A double-entry journal can also encourage active response to a text. For a double-entry journal, students find statements, quotations, ideas, or events in the selection, record them, and then make notes about their thoughts and feelings. To help students get started, you might ask them to respond to these two quotes from Bob Greene's column:

- "From an early childhood that had seemed destined to cage her forever inside a sightless and soundless despair, she had become one of the most admired people in the world." (page 128)

- "If only more people in this lazy, sloppy-thinking age of ours would show that courage and that intellect." (page 129)

For more help, see the **Comprehension** blackline master on page 175.

Discussion Questions

COMPREHENSION 1. How did Helen Keller become deaf and blind? *(She had a serious illness at the age of 19 months.)*

2. How did Helen break free of her "self-contained prison"? *(She learned to communicate with others through sign language.)*

CRITICAL THINKING 3. What was Helen Keller's mission in life? *(She wanted to spread her message of hope and perseverance all over the world.)*

4. Why does Bob Greene admire her so much? *(Have students support their opinions with evidence from his writing.)*

Literary Skill

AUTHOR'S PURPOSE Because Greene's purpose is very clear in this column, you might take this opportunity to discuss author's purpose as a literary technique. Remind students that most writers have one or more of the following purposes in mind when writing: 1. to entertain; 2. to enlighten or inform; 3. to persuade; and 4. to reveal some interesting truth. In his column, Greene clearly wants to inform and persuade. He tells readers about Helen Keller's life in the hopes that they will take her message of hope and her perseverance and apply it to their own lives.

III. GATHER YOUR THOUGHTS

After they've finished reading Greene's column, students will **reflect** on what they've learned about Helen Keller. Then they'll complete a character organizer that helps them consider her unique qualities. These activities will in turn prepare students to write about a person (of their choice) whom they think is interesting or important. On page 131, they'll name the person they want to write about and then create an organizer similar to the one they made for Helen Keller.

Prewriting Strategies

TOPIC SENTENCE AND DETAILS After students finish their organizers, you might want to help them create a topic sentence and details chart that they can refer to as they write the first paragraph of their **character sketches**. If students need additional practice with writing topic sentences and gathering details, have them complete the **Prewriting** blackline master on page 176.

IV. WRITE

Encourage students to discuss their writing ideas with a partner before they begin. Have them share with their partners their ideas and topic sentences. When students are ready to start writing, you might show them the writing rubric below. It will give them a strong understanding of the assignment requirements.

WRITING RUBRIC Use this writing rubric for help with a quick assessment of students' writing.

Do students' character sketches

- begin with a topic sentence that tells how they feel about their character?

- contain three or more vivid details that support the topic sentence?

- conclude with a closing sentence that ties things together?

- stay focused on the person they've chosen to describe?

Grammar, Usage, and Mechanics

After students have finished a rough draft of their character sketches, have them revise (either alone or with a writing partner), using the **Writers' Checklist** as a guide. You might use this opportunity to teach a **mini-lesson** on verbs and their correct form. Stress the proper use of difficult verbs, such as *lay, lie; rise, raise;* and *learn, teach*.

Incorrect: She was laying on the bed. I told her to raise up.

Correct: She was lying on the bed. I told her to rise up.

V. WRAP-UP

Take a moment at the end of the lesson for students to reflect on Bob Greene's writing. Point out the **Readers' Checklist** in the top right-hand corner of page 133. Ask students to answer these questions aloud so that you can get a sense of the level of their **understanding**.

ASSESSMENT To test students' comprehension, use the **Assessment** blackline master on page 177.

Name _____

VOCABULARY

Words from the Selection

DIRECTIONS Using context clues, fill in each blank with the most appropriate word from the list.

> ✧flailed ✧rampant ✧manual ✧prestigious ✧advocating

1. The coach gave _____ signals to the team before the halftime.

2. During time out, he _____ his arms about.

3. Apparently he was _____ better scoring.

4. The team played for a _____ and highly respected school.

5. There was _____ fan disapproval of the referee's decisions.

Strategy Lesson: Suffixes

Suffixes are word parts that come at the end of a root word. Suffixes can give you clues about the meaning of the word and how to use it in a sentence. For example, if you add the suffix *-ous* to the noun *nerve,* you get the adjective *nervous,* which means "full of nerves" or "anxious."

```
                    SUFFIXES

      -less = without

      -ous = full of, having much

      -ment = act of, state of, result

      -ish = resembling
```

DIRECTIONS Write the root word and then the suffix of each word. Then write what you think the word means.

6. sightless _____ + _____ = _____
     root   suffix   I think the word means

7. prestigious _____ + _____ = _____
     root   suffix   I think the word means

8. government _____ + _____ = _____
     root   suffix   I think the word means

9. buffoonish _____ + _____ = _____
     root   suffix   I think the word means

10. soundless _____ + _____ = _____
     root   suffix   I think the word means

Name _____

COMPREHENSION

Double-entry Journal

DIRECTION Read these quotations from the article. Say how each makes you feel.

Double-entry Journal

QUOTATIONS	MY THOUGHTS AND FEELINGS
She doesn't need defending; she's been dead for more than twenty-five years now, and no one can hurt her feelings. But the staying power of Helen Keller jokes is more than just another depressing testament to the rampant stupidity of our know-nothing age. . . . In these days especially, with so many people endlessly complaining that their birthright in society makes them "victims," with so many people telling the rest of society how "disadvantaged" they are, the life of Helen Keller is not a bad reminder of what one person with courage can overcome.	

Directed Reading

DIRECTIONS Work with a partner to answer these questions about the story.

1. What qualities did Helen Keller have that allowed her to triumph over her difficulties?

_____

_____

_____

2. What is the tone of Greene's column? Is he angry? Is he proud? Or is he something else? Explain your answer.

_____

_____

_____

3. Do you agree with Greene that Helen Keller is a woman worth admiring? Explain.

_____

_____

_____

_____

Name _____

PREWRITING

Writing a Topic Sentence and Details

DIRECTIONS Your character sketch must begin with a topic sentence. The topic sentence lets readers know what to expect.

STEP 1. Use this formula to help you write your topic sentence.

A specific person + a specific feeling about this person = a good topic sentence.

My topic sentence:

_____

STEP 2. Write three details that help support your topic sentence. Use your chart on page 131 for ideas.

detail #1:

_____

_____

detail #2:

_____

_____

_____

detail #3:

_____

STEP 3. Write a concluding sentence that explains how you feel about the person you've described.

My concluding sentence:

_____

_____

_____

Name _____

ASSESSMENT

Multiple-Choice Test

DIRECTIONS On the blanks provided, write the letter of the item that best answers each question or completes each statement.

_____ 1. Bob Greene worries that Helen Keller will always be known as . . .
   A. a great lecturer.
   B. someone to joke about.
   C. a woman who rose above hardship.
   D. the little girl who worked with Anne Sullivan.

_____ 2. What is Bob Greene's opinion of Helen Keller?
   A. She is a hero.
   B. She is a mystery.
   C. She is a joke.
   D. none of the above

_____ 3. How did Helen Keller lose her hearing and sight?
   A. She was in an accident.
   B. She was born that way.
   C. She had an illness.
   D. none of the above

_____ 4. Who was Anne Sullivan?
   A. Helen's married sister
   B. Helen's teacher
   C. Helen's mother-in-law
   D. none of the above

_____ 5. Helen learned to communicate with the rest of the world by . . .
   A. reading Braille.
   B. using a special typewriter.
   C. using the manual alphabet.
   D. all of the above

_____ 6. How did Helen understand the lectures at her schools?
   A. Anne translated them by touch.
   B. She didn't attend the lectures.
   C. They were typed out in Braille for her.
   D. both A. and C.

_____ 7. What did Helen do after college?
   A. She worked for her father.
   B. She taught at a local college.
   C. She went to medical school.
   D. She helped with blind and deaf causes.

_____ 8. What book did Helen Keller write first?
   A. *The Story of My Life*
   B. *My Religion*
   C. *Teacher*
   D. *The World I Live In*

_____ 9. Which word best describes how Bob Greene feels about Helen Keller?
   A. pity
   B. admiration
   C. anger
   D. sadness

_____ 10. What is the tone of the very beginning and the very end of this article?
   A. pity
   B. admiration
   C. anger
   D. sadness

Short-Essay Test

Do you agree with Bob Greene that this is a "sloppy-thinking" age?

Skills and Strategies Overview

THEME Dreams

READING LEVEL average

VOCABULARY
◇ jolt   ◇ loom   ◇ abolished   ◇ intrigued   ◇ imbedded

PREREADING think-pair-and-share

RESPONSE visualize

COMPREHENSION story board

PREWRITING research

WRITING article/ apostrophes

ASSESSMENT meaning

BACKGROUND

When he was 12 years old, in 1994, Canadian citizen Craig Kielburger had a wake-up call. Just by chance, he noticed a newspaper article about the forced slavery and subsequent murder of a Pakistani boy named Iqbal Masih. Outraged by what he read, Kielburger began researching the problem of child labor. What he found in his library deeply shocked him. Forced child labor under appalling conditions, he learned, was a problem in many parts of the world. Armed with disturbing facts about child-related injustices, he convinced his schoolmates at his Canadian elementary school to form a group that would advocate for children's rights. This group, called Free the Children, gathered information, wrote world leaders, and led conferences on child labor. In 1998 Kielburger published a searing account of a journey he took through the factories and farms of Southeast Asia. This book, entitled *Free the Children*, is Kielburger's definitive call to action. "One Morning" is an excerpt from the first chapter of that book.

UNIT THEME Kielburger's dream is an admirable one: to stop forced child labor around the world.

GRAPHIC ORGANIZER Students might devise an organizer like this one.

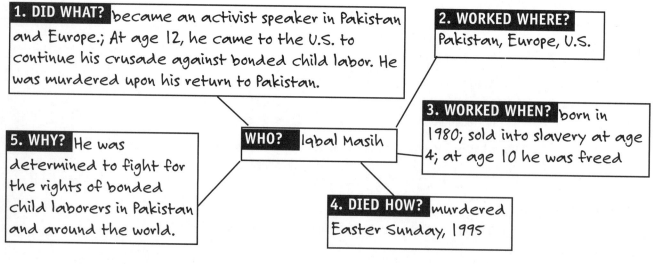

1. DID WHAT? became an activist speaker in Pakistan and Europe.; At age 12, he came to the U.S. to continue his crusade against bonded child labor. He was murdered upon his return to Pakistan.

2. WORKED WHERE? Pakistan, Europe, U.S.

3. WORKED WHEN? born in 1980; sold into slavery at age 4; at age 10 he was freed

5. WHY? He was determined to fight for the rights of bonded child laborers in Pakistan and around the world.

WHO? Iqbal Masih

4. DIED HOW? murdered Easter Sunday, 1995

BIBLIOGRAPHY Other works on the topic of child slavery include these: *Stolen Dreams: Portraits of Working Children* by David L. Parker (1997); *When I Was Chillun* by Belinda Hurmence (1997); *Kids at Work* by Russell Freedman (1998); *Iqbal Masih and the Crusaders Against Child Slavery* by Susan Kuklin (1998).

BEFORE YOU READ

Read through the introduction to the lesson with students. The purpose of the opening of the lesson is to motivate and focus students. Then introduce the prereading activity, a **think-pair-and-share**. Be sure students understand the directions for the activity before dividing them into pairs. (Refer to the **Strategy Handbook** on page 40 for more help.)

Motivation Strategy

In "One Morning," Craig Kielburger explains how horrified he was to learn that forced child labor is a deadly serious problem in the world today. Ask students what they know about child labor. Does the practice exist in the United States? Try to determine students' prior knowledge before beginning the lesson.

ENGAGING STUDENTS Have students tell you about an injustice they witnessed or heard about. How did it make them feel? Did they speak out? Why or why not? These questions will allow students to connect to Kielburger's topic on a more personal level.

Vocabulary Building

Help students use context clues as they read to figure out the meanings of difficult words, especially the key vocabulary for this lesson: *jolt, loom, abolished, intrigued,* and *imbedded.* Some of these words may be familiar to students, and some may be completely new. Demonstrate how to search for and apply context clues in order to define these and other challenging words in the selection. (*Jolt* and *loom* are not footnoted.) Ask students to circle the vocabulary words in the text. For additional practice with words from the selection, see page 182.

STRATEGY LESSON: SYNONYMS Learning the synonym of an unfamiliar word is a shortcut for those who don't have the time or memory skills to learn the full definition. (As an added advantage, learning synonyms is an especially helpful strategy for students preparing to take standardized tests.) Ask the class: "What are synonyms for these words from the selection: maimed, trek, hauled, defied, and crusade?" If they don't know, ask them to check a dictionary definition and then make a note of the synonym in their books. Once they've thought of a synonym for each word, you might have them turn to a thesaurus to discover additional words that mean the same thing.

For additional practice on this strategy, see the **Vocabulary** blackline master page 182.

Prereading Strategies

Students are asked to complete a **think-pair-and-share** before they begin reading "One Morning." A think-pair-and-share can help students become actively involved in a selection even before they begin reading. In addition, this activity can help refine students' ability to work cooperatively in a group. During the "pair" exercise, students should build upon others' ideas and help the group reach consensus on the ordering of the statements from the text.

QUICKWRITE As an alternate prereading strategy, ask students to do a quickwrite. Read the first paragraph of the article aloud while students follow along in their books. Then have them do a one-minute quickwrite about a topic you assign. For example, you might have them write about "child labor," "becoming an activist," or "fighting for what you believe in." Remind them that a quickwrite can't be right or wrong. Quickwrites are meant to help readers begin connecting their own thoughts and ideas to a piece of writing.

Spanish-speaking Students

"Una mañana" es parte de la autobiografía de Craig Kielburger, *Free the Children.* Un adolescente impresionante, Kielburger ha luchado contra el ejercicio del labor de niños. En esta selección, describe el momento en que se dio cuenta de la existencia del maltratamiento de niños, y su decisión rápida de hacer algo para salvarles. Kielburger sirve como un ejemplo a todos de lo que una persona, incluso un adolescente, puede lograr con dedicación y determinación.

II. READ

As students begin to read, explain once again how important it is to **visualize** the people, places, and events the author describes. These mental pictures will keep students actively involved in the reading and may help with comprehension problems as they come up.

Response Strategy

PREDICTION As an alternate or additional prereading strategy, have students stop at one or two different points in the reading and make predictions about outcomes. Have them pause at each **stop and think** interrupter and make a quick prediction about what they think Kielburger will do or say next. Remind them that they'll need to keep reading to find out if their predictions come true.

Comprehension Strategies

As they are reading, students will need to pause at three different points in order to retell the events of Kielburger's article on **storyboards**. Storyboards can help students understand the sequence of events the author describes. Rather than simply asking students to "tell what happens," storyboards give a framework for response that prods the reader into thinking carefully about elements of the plot. Encourage students to reread their storyboard notes once they've finished the selection. They may want to make some small revisions to their thoughts and ideas.

DIRECTED READING As an alternate comprehension strategy, try doing a directed reading of the selection. In a directed reading, you or a group leader reads the selection aloud, pausing every once in awhile to ask **stop and think** questions that can help students make factual and inferential responses. A directed reading allows you to see what (if anything) is causing problems in the selection. Using students' comments as a guide, you might want to speed up or slow down the pace of the reading. Adjusting the pace of the reading can give your low-level readers a chance to catch up to the rest of the class.

For more help, see the **Comprehension** blackline master on page 183.

Discussion Questions

COMPREHENSION 1. Who is Craig Kielburger? *(the narrator of the selection)*

2. Who was Iqbal Masih? *(a Pakistani boy who was brutally murdered after he spoke out against child labor)*

3. Why is Kielburger so disturbed by Masih's story? *(He can't believe that a child would be murdered over the issue of child labor. He also can't believe that child labor continues to be such a terrible problem around the world.)*

CRITICAL THINKING 4. What does Kielburger mean when he says, "And my own world seemed a shade darker"? *(Accept reasonable responses. Ask students to support what they say with evidence from the selection.)*

5. What makes child labor so unjust? *(Have students support their opinions using information from the article and what they know from their own reading.)*

6. Why might parents sell a child into slavery? *(Students might suggest that a desperately poor and large family might have had little choice.)*

Literary Skill

CHRONOLOGICAL ORDER You might use Kielburger's article to teach a brief lesson on chronological order. Tell students: "Kielburger uses chronological order to tell his story. This makes his narrative easy to read and follow." Remind students that when writers use chronological order, they usually use transitional words and phrases to help their narratives read smoothly. Words and phrases such as *first, last, later, after that, the next day, a week later,* and so on cue readers as to where they are in the story. You might want to keep a list of transitional words and phrases posted on the board. Students can refer to the list as they write their articles for Part IV.

III. GATHER YOUR THOUGHTS

At the top of page 140, students are asked to **retell** the events of "One Morning" to a partner. This exercise will further strengthen their understanding of Kielburger's narrative. After that, students will think of an injustice they can write about.

Prewriting Strategies

Remind the class that they should look in recent magazines or newspapers or do a topic search at an Internet Web site to find a story idea. The stories they write should have to do with injustice, although they may be totally unrelated to the idea of child labor.

NARROWING A TOPIC Once they have their story ideas, students will need to narrow the focus of their writing. (Refer students to page 30 of their books if they need help narrowing the focus.) After they've made their topic as specific as they can, students can get ready to research. Remind them that they'll be searching for answers to the questions on page 140. These questions will keep students focused during the research process, so that they don't become overwhelmed by the amount of information they find.

Have students use the **Prewriting** blackline master on page 184.

IV. WRITE

Allow plenty of time for students to conduct their research and write their **articles**. Tell the class that the lead (or opening paragraph) of their articles should include specific information about who, what, where, when, why, and how.

WRITING RUBRIC Use this writing rubric to help students focus on the assignment requirements and for help with a quick assessment of their writing.

Do students' articles

- open with information about the who, what, where, when, why, and how of the injustice?
- stay focused throughout on the injustice discussed in the lead?
- include examples or events culled from their research?

Grammar, Usage, and Mechanics

After they've finished their rough drafts, ask students to revise. Refer them to the **Writers' Checklist** on page 141 and teach a brief mini-lesson on using apostrophes. Remind the class that apostrophes are used to show possession and to replace the letters that have been removed in contractions.

Incorrect: Kielburgers attitude is that no child should be forced to work. Children arent strong enough or mature enough.

Correct: Kielburger's attitude is that no child should be forced to work. Children aren't strong enough or mature enough.

V. WRAP-UP

Take a moment at the end of the lesson for students to reflect on the **meaning** of the article using the **Readers' Checklist**. Its purpose is to help students ask the kinds of questions that good readers ask of themselves after they've finished a selection. Students should understand that every reader will have a different response to a selection.

Assessment

To test students' comprehension, use the **Assessment** blackline master on page 185.

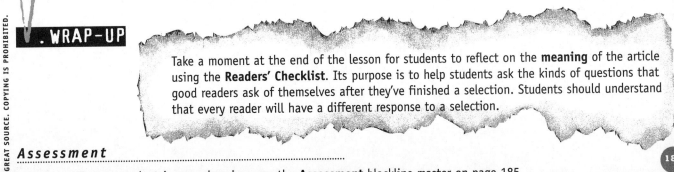

Name _____

VOCABULARY
Words from the Selection

DIRECTIONS To build your vocabulary, answer these questions about five words from the selection.

1. If you are <u>intrigued</u>, are you bored or curious? _____

2. If an object is <u>imbedded</u>, is it easy or hard to get out? _____

3. When you use a <u>loom</u>, are you weaving or cooking? _____

4. Is a <u>jolt</u> soothing or shocking? _____

5. If a law is <u>abolished</u>, do you have to follow it? _____

Strategy Lesson: Synonyms

A **synonym** is a word that has the same or almost the same meaning as another word. For example, *scared* is a synonym for *afraid*.

DIRECTIONS Find the word in Column B that most closely matches the meaning of the word in Column A. Then draw a line between the matching words. If there's a word that you don't know, skip it and come back to it when you've finished the whole column.

Column A	Column B
6. maimed	campaign
7. trek	journey
8. hauled	crippled
9. defied	dragged
10. crusade	disobeyed

Name _____

COMPREHENSION
Graphic Organizer ....

DIRECTIONS Use this chart to make notes about your research. An example has been done for you.

My topic: _____

Name of source (name of the book, newspaper, magazine, or Internet article)	Where I found it (be specific)	What I learned	Quotations I want to remember
"One Morning"	pp. 134–142 of <u>Reading and Writing Sourcebook: Gr. 10</u>	forced child labor is a terrible problem around the world	"I was angry at the world for letting these things happen to children. Why was nothing being done to stop such cruelty?"

Name _____

PREWRITING
Writing an Article
....

DIRECTIONS To write an article, follow these steps.

STEP 1. DECIDE ON A TOPIC. On the line below, write the topic for your article. (Your book asks you to write an article about injustice.)

_____

_____

STEP 2. MAKE NOTES. Next make notes about the who, what, why, where, when, and how of your topic. Use this organizer.

HOW

DID WHAT?

WHEN?

WHO?

WHY?

WHERE?

STEP 3. WRITE A LEAD. The lead of an article tells what the article is going to be about. In the lead, you explain who, what, where, when, why, and how. Write your lead here. It should be no more than three or four sentences.

_____

_____

_____

STEP 4. WRITE AN ARTICLE. Write your complete article in your book on pages 141–142.

Name _____

ASSESSMENT

Multiple-Choice Test

DIRECTIONS On the blanks provided, write the letter of the item that best answers each question or completes each statement.

_____ 1. When he first woke up, why was Craig Kielburger looking forward to the day?
  A. He had baseball tryouts.   C. He had cross-country tryouts.
  B. He had a band competition.   D. There was a play rehearsal.

_____ 2. What morning ritual did Craig perform each day?
  A. He took a shower.   C. He read the comics.
  B. He watched TV.   D. He called a friend.

_____ 3. Where does Craig live?
  A. in Pakistan   C. in Europe
  B. in the United States   D. in Canada

_____ 4. What country was Iqbal Masih from?
  A. Pakistan   C. Canada
  B. Iran   D. El Salvador

_____ 5. What did Iqbal Masih do for most of his life?
  A. He worked in a coal mine.   C. He worked on a coffee plantation.
  B. He worked in a carpet factory.   D. He led a fight against child labor.

_____ 6. Some people believe Iqbal Masih was murdered because . . .
  A. he tried to run away.   C. he brought attention to the horrors of child labor.
  B. he refused to work any longer.   D. none of the above

_____ 7. Craig was disturbed by Iqbal Masih's murder because . . .
  A. they were both the same age.   C. he thought slavery didn't exist anymore.
  B. Iqbal's parents had sold him   D. all of the above
     into slavery.

_____ 8. Where did Craig go to learn more about child labor?
  A. a school library   C. both A. and B.
  B. a public library   D. his computer

_____ 9. What was Craig's relationship to Iqbal Masih?
  A. They were distant cousins.   C. They never knew each other.
  B. They met once on a school trip.   D. They were pen pals.

_____ 10. Who is Craig angry at for letting bad things happen to children?
  A. the world   C. himself
  B. his parents   D. all of the above

Short-Essay Test

What questions would you like to ask Craig Kielburger?

Knights and Chivalry

Unit Background **KNIGHTS AND CHIVALRY** (pages 143–160)

John of Salisbury (1120–1180) wrote that the function of knighthood was "to protect the Church, to fight against treachery, to reverence the priesthood, to fend off injustice from the poor, to make peace in your own province, to shed blood for your brethren, and if needs must, to lay down your life." The humble peasant, if he was not massacred, had a different view, however. During skirmishes between rival noblemen, his cottage was usually burned, his fields and livestock destroyed, and his meager provisions stolen. The purpose of an attack on a rival nobleman, after all, was to destroy his source of income.

The two selections in this unit give a broad picture of feudalism and of the role and character of knights in the Middle Ages.

Teaching the Introduction

Page 143 shows a kneeling knight, a full set of armor, and a diagram showing the relationships in the feudal system. Kings or queens ruled by divine right, nobles and knights owed fealty to the monarchy and devotion to the Church and allowed servants or vassals to farm their estates.

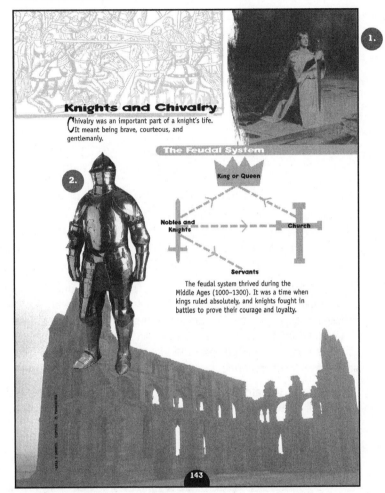

1. Some people think that it is the nature of humans, especially men, to fight. Do students agree?

2. Ask students what they know about the armor worn by knights. (You may want to tell them that a knight who fell from his horse was as good as dead since he could not get up unaided because of the weight of his armor.)

Opening Activity

Some students might like to investigate and then show or draw pictures of the weapons mentioned in "The Victorious Feudal Knight": the shortbow, lance, sword, axe, mace, and dagger. Many books show and label parts of medieval armor. Interested students might like to give a short illustrated talk on armor.

The Knight in Person

Skills and Strategies Overview

THEME	Knights and Chivalry
READING LEVEL	average
VOCABULARY	◆robust ◆vermin ◆tongs ◆shears ◆armor
PREREADING	K-W-L
RESPONSE	mark or highlight
COMPREHENSION	directed reading
PREWRITING	main idea and details
WRITING	summary / commas
ASSESSMENT	ease

BACKGROUND

Julek Heller's "The Knight in Person," an excerpt from the informational book *Knights,* should be interesting reading for students. Heller dispels many of the myths surrounding knights—that they were rough and tough and didn't care a bit what others thought of them—while at the same time reinforces information that students probably already have about men in armor.

In this excerpt, Heller focuses the reader's attention on the knight himself. What was he like? What did he wear? Where did he live? How did he endure the hardships of his job? These are all questions that Heller attempts to answer for readers. Heller's style is clear and unadorned, and admiration for these men shines through the writing, although the tone of the piece is even and unbiased. Heller leaves it up to readers to decide whether or not these men were worth admiring.

UNIT THEME "Knights and Chivalry" gives students the chance to hear the "real" story behind the legends. This theme can help reinforce the notion that one of the most important reasons for reading is to learn new facts and information.

GRAPHIC ORGANIZER Students' organizers on page 149 might look something like this.

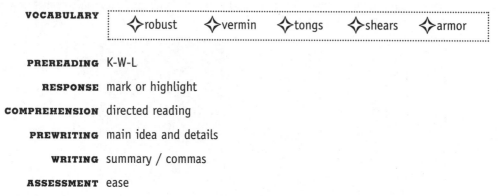

MAIN IDEA:
Knights were actually quite human.

DETAIL: They took baths often.

DETAIL: They worried about their appearance.

DETAIL: They fussed with their hair.

DETAIL: They suffered from the same illnesses and diseases as other people.

BEFORE YOU READ

Read through the introduction to the lesson on page 144. The purpose of the opening of the lesson is to motivate and focus students. In particular, you'll want to emphasize the factual nature of this article. When students are ready to begin, have them read the first paragraph and then fill in the **K-W-L** on page 145. (Refer to the **Strategy Handbook** on page 40 for more help.)

Motivation Strategy

Start by asking students what they know about knights of the Middle Ages. What kinds of people were they? Why did they dress up in all that armor? What was their reputation? After your discussion, students might record some of the information on the K-W-L.

ENGAGING STUDENTS Ask students: "What is bravery? Do you know a brave person? Was it easier to be brave back in the Middle Ages? Why or why not?" These questions will encourage students to ponder the topic of the selection before they begin reading.

Vocabulary Building

Help students use **context clues** as they read to figure out the meanings of difficult words, especially the key vocabulary for this lesson: *robust, vermin, tongs, shears,* and *armor.* Model using context and then checking your ideas against the footnote: "I don't know the word *tongs.* I see, though, that it appears in a sentence that describes how the knights curled their hair, and that the tongs they used could be heated in the fire. I also see the word *combed* is already used, so I know that *tongs* doesn't refer to combs or brushes. I can guess that tongs are a type of metal instrument that can somehow hold onto the hair so that it might be curled. I can check the footnote to see if my guess is correct." Ask students to circle the vocabulary words in the text. For additional practice with these words, see page 192.

STRATEGY LESSON: PRONUNCIATION Knowing the pronounciation of words is as important as knowing a definition. Write the following words and pronounciations on the board, and ask students to practice saying the words: *medieval* (mee dee EE vul); *physique* (feh ZEEK); *omens* (O muns); *cholera* (KOL er uh); *medallions* (muh DAL yuns).

For additional practice on this strategy, see **Vocabulary** page 192.

Prereading Strategies

The purpose of a **K-W-L** is to activate prior knowledge and allow students to take responsibility for their own gaps in knowledge. Students will tell you what they need to find out about knights, and whether or not the article provided the information they were looking for. A K-W-L can show students that ultimately they are the ones in charge of their own learning. For this reason, it is best to allow students to work on their own and to give them plenty of time to consider their answers.

PICTURE WALK As an alternate prereading strategy, ask students to do a picture walk of the selection. Some students might be interested in looking closely at the art that is included with this reading. Others can use the art to familiarize themselves with a topic that they haven't thought much about lately. When they've finished their picture walks, have them make predictions about the topic of the selection and whether or not they think it will be difficult to read.

Spanish-speaking Students

El caballero medieval ha sido el sujeto de mucho interés y especulación a lo largo de los años. Esta selección describe algunas características de los caballeros típicos y de la época en la cual vivían. Autor Julek Heller incluso expone las falsedades de unas creencias comunes que han sido asociadas con la vida de los caballeros.

II. READ

Response Strategy

When students are ready to begin reading, remind them how important it is to **mark** things they find interesting, important, confusing, or puzzling. Have them underline sentences and phrases, use a highlighter to draw attention to key words, and make extensive notes in the **Response Notes**. Teaching this response strategy is your first step in the process of helping your students become more active readers.

Comprehension Strategies

Directed reading (stop and think) can help reluctant or low-level readers better comprehend what they are reading. In a directed reading, the teacher or a student volunteer guides the reading by adjusting the pace as needed and by interrupting the narrative to pose comprehension and inferential questions about the text. You can set the stage for a directed reading by asking an open-ended question, such as "What were knights really like?"

GRAPHIC ORGANIZER As an alternate comprehension strategy, have students make an informational chart about knights that they can turn to at several different points in the article. Categories on their charts might include "appearance," "habits," "likes and dislikes," and so on. A chart such as this will be a useful reference tool when it is time for students to write their summaries in Part IV.

For more help, see the **Comprehension** blackline master on page 193.

Discussion Questions

COMPREHENSION 1. What time period does Julek Heller describe? (*the Middle Ages*)

2. How did most medieval knights feel about their appearance? (*Have students support their ideas with lines from the text.*)

3. Why were knights so superstitious? (*Because they tended to die young, knights did everything they could to protect themselves. This included listening to omens and predictions.*)

CRITICAL THINKING 4. What were medieval knights really like? (*Have students support their opinion.*)

5. What type of person do you think would want to become a knight? (*Accept reasonable responses. Encourage students to imagine who might have chosen the profession had it actually been a profession of choice.*)

6. Why do you think people today are so fascinated by knights? (*Give students the chance to explain their own attitudes toward knights and the Middle Ages. Are they interested or bored? Why?*)

Literary Skill

INFERENCE With this lesson, you might introduce the literary skill of making inferences. Explain that no writer will tell readers everything. The writer expects the reader to make inferences, or reasonable guesses, about the behavior of a character or the meaning of something that takes place. In this excerpt, for example, the reader is expected to make inferences about why childhood diseases were so common or why knights were not particular about their clothing. As critical readers, our job is to read the words the author gives us and then think carefully about what those words mean.

GATHER YOUR THOUGHTS

Students' first step in the prewriting section will be to return to their **K-W-L** charts so that they can fill in the L section. Then they'll use what they've learned to decide on the main idea and supporting details of the article. If students have trouble deciding on a main idea, ask: "What does Heller want readers to remember most about knights?" and "What information does Heller give to reinforce this message?"

Prewriting Strategies

TOPIC SENTENCES After students have decided on Heller's main idea, they'll need to write a topic sentence for a summary of the article. Remind the class that a topic sentence must clearly state the topic (or subject) of the selection. Students' topic sentences at the bottom of page 149 might read "'The Knights in Person' is a selection about medieval knights that describes their size, beliefs, grooming, and habits."

Have students use the **Prewriting** blackline master on page 194.

IV. WRITE

On page 150, students are asked to write a **summary** of Heller's article. Before they begin, you might offer these tips for writing a summary:

1. First decide on the main idea of the piece.

2. Then skim the selection looking for details that support the main idea.

3. Next describe, in your own words, these supporting details.

4. Arrange your ideas in the most logical order.

5. Finish with a concluding sentence that ties all your points together and brings the summary to an effective close.

WRITING RUBRIC Do students' summaries

- begin with a topic sentence?

- include a discussion of each of Heller's most important points?

- end with a closing sentence that ties things together?

Grammar, Usage, and Mechanics

After students have written a first draft of their summaries, have them consult the **Writers' Checklist** before they revise. At this point you might want to introduce a brief mini-lesson on comma usage. Ask students to pay particular attention to how they use commas in compound sentences.

Incorrect: Knights were brave but they were fussy too.

Correct: Knights were brave, but they were fussy too.

V. WRAP-UP

Before moving on to the next lesson, ask students to discuss what (if anything) they thought was **easy** or difficult about Heller's article. Remind them of the many reading strategies they can choose from if they find a selection hard to read. Encourage them to use these strategies with future selections.

Assessment

To test students' comprehension, use the **Assessment** blackline master on page 195.

Name _____

VOCABULARY

Words from the Selection

DIRECTIONS To build vocabulary, answer these questions about five words taken from the selection.

1. If a man is <u>robust</u>, is he healthy or sick?

_____

2. If you have <u>vermin</u> in your home, are you happy?

_____

3. What might <u>tongs</u> be used for?

_____

4. Are <u>shears</u> used by a barber or a musician?

_____

5. Why would you wear <u>armor</u>?

Strategy Lesson: Pronunciation

DIRECTIONS Each sentence below contains the pronunciation of a word in parentheses. From the list on the right, choose the word that matches pronunciation. Write that word on the blank. You will not use one word.

6. Knights of (mee dee EE vul)

_____ days often had missing

ears and teeth.

7. The (feh ZEEK) _____ of a

knight was probably the same as that of most modern

men.

8. A knight was lucky to have escaped childhood

diseases such as (KOL er uh)

_____.

9. Most knights were superstitious and believed in

(O muns) _____.

10. They often wore religious (muh DAL yuns)

_____.

omens

medieval

physique

physical

cholera

medallions

Name _____

COMPREHENSION
Graphic Organizer

Fill in this chart using details from Heller's selection. Refer to your book if you need to.

Medieval Knights

INFORMATION ABOUT . . .	WHERE I FOUND THIS INFORMATION
their appearance • They were short but robust. • •	paragraph 1, page 144
their habits	
their likes	
their dislikes	

Name _____

PREWRITING

Writing a Summary

DIRECTIONS To write a good summary, you must select the most important ideas and combine them into clear, easy-to-understand sentences. Follow these steps to write a summary for "The Knight in Person."

STEP 1. SKIM. Use a highlighter to mark key words and phrases.

STEP 2. LIST. Make a list of the most important ideas and opinions in the article.

Heller's important ideas: _____

• _____

• _____

• _____

STEP 3. CHOOSE. Select the most important idea or opinion from your list and make this the main idea of your summary. Write a topic sentence that states the main idea.

Heller's main idea in the article is: _____

my topic sentence: "The Knight in Person is an article about _____

_____ that describes _____ .

STEP 4. FIND DETAILS. Gather important details from the article. Names, dates, times, and places are examples of important details.

Heller's important details:

1. _____	6. _____
2. _____	7. _____
3. _____	8. _____
4. _____	9. _____
5. _____	10. _____

STEP 5. WRITE. Now write your summary on pages 150–151.

1. Begin with the topic sentence.

2. Then summarize Heller's most important details.

3. Start a new sentence for each new detail.

4. End with a concluding sentence that ties things together.

Name _____

ASSESSMENT

Multiple-Choice Test

DIRECTIONS On the blanks provided, write the letter of the best answer for each question.

_____ 1. Which phrase or phrases describe medieval knights?
   A. broad shoulders   C. a little vain
   B. not very tall   D. all of the above

_____ 2. Why was it hard for a knight to "survive his medieval childhood"?
   A. constant threat of diseases   C. lack of food
   B. lack of a good education   D. terrible living conditions

_____ 3. What was the average life expectancy for those who survived to adulthood?
   A. 15 to 20 years   C. 40 to 50 years
   B. 30 to 35 years   D. 60 to 70 years

_____ 4. What did knights do to protect themselves from bad omens?
   A. They wore religious medallions.   C. They wore heavy suits of armor.
   B. They refused to cut their hair.   D. all of the above

_____ 5. Why did some knights wear beards?
   A. Beards kept them warm during battle.   C. Beards were in style.
   B. They wanted to look wise.   D. They didn't have time to shave.

_____ 6. What did knights have that showed a lifetime of fighting?
   A. a collection of medals   C. battle scars
   B. a whole stable of horses D. none of the above

_____ 7. Why would a knight think twice about cutting his hair?
   A. He was superstitious.   C. Long hair was a sign of power.
   B. The cutting tools were primitive.   D. He didn't want to appear vain.

_____ 8. How often did knights take baths?
   A. never   C. occasionally
   B. daily   D. frequently

_____ 9. What was one way knights eased the discomfort of flea-bites?
   A. They used flea powder.   C. They used body lotion.
   B. They bathed.   D. They carried a holy relic.

_____ 10. Which of the following does the author describe about knights?
   A. their grooming habits   C. how they dressed for sleep
   B. their bathing habits   D. all of the above

Short-Essay Test

What were the positive aspects of being a medieval knight?

The Victorious Feudal Knight

STUDENT PAGES 152–160

Skills and Strategies Overview

THEME	Knights and Chivalry
READING LEVEL	average
VOCABULARY	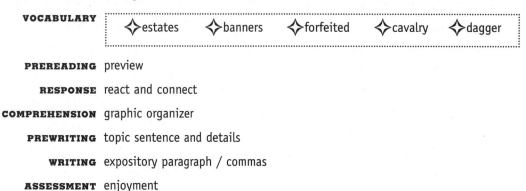

PREREADING	preview
RESPONSE	react and connect
COMPREHENSION	graphic organizer
PREWRITING	topic sentence and details
WRITING	expository paragraph / commas
ASSESSMENT	enjoyment

BACKGROUND

In this article about medieval knights, Jay Williams reveals what a difficult job it was to be a knight in the Middle Ages. Students might be surprised to learn that knights were forced into military service, very often against their will. The risk of injury was great, as was the risk of displeasing the Crown. As such, many knights rode into battle only with great reluctance. When the battle began, most knights fought with courage and continued to fight until the bloody end. In this they had no choice. If they failed to show courage or forfeited a battle, their land could very well be seized by the king.

Williams's article about feudal knights is full of information about the time period, the system of government, and the knights themselves. When paired with "The Knight in Person," these two selections offer readers a highly detailed view of the life of the medieval warrior.

UNIT THEME "Knights and Chivalry" gives students the chance to hear the "real" story behind legends of feudal times. Use this theme to reinforce students' realization that one of the most important reasons we read is to find out new information.

GRAPHIC ORGANIZER Better students might work on an organizer similar to this one before writing an expository paragraph.

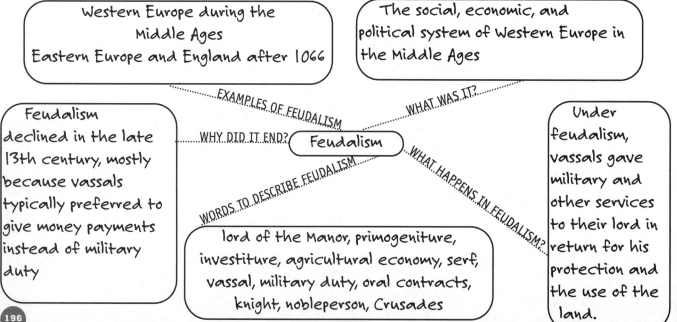

BEFORE YOU READ

Read through the introduction to the lesson with students. Be sure they understand the comparison between movie previews and **previewing** a text. Explain how helpful previewing can be when they're getting ready to read a nonfiction text such as an informational article or textbook chapter. You may want to tell them that William the Conqueror crossed the English Channel from Normandy (France) to defeat the English King Harold. Then ask students to begin the prereading activity on page 152.

Motivation Strategy

ENGAGING STUDENTS Ask students to tell you about movies, books, and even toys from their childhood that relate to knights, dames, and other people of the Middle Ages. Then have them finish these sentences: "Knights of the Middle Ages were _____." and "Women in the Middle Ages were _____."

Vocabulary Building

Show students that **synonyms** can function as context clues that can help in defining unfamiliar words. In several places in the article, Jay Williams provides synonyms for words that he anticipates might be difficult for readers. (For example, he gives a synonym for the unfamiliar word *vassal* in this sentence, "This tight-knit relationship between a lord and his tenant, or vassal, had already spread over most of Europe. . . .") Ask students to watch for unfamiliar words and synonyms as context clues. If the author doesn't provide a synonym, have students think one up themselves. They should pay particular attention to these key vocabulary words: *estates, banners, forfeited, cavalry,* and *dagger.* Have students circle these words in the text. For additional practice with these words, see page 200.

STRATEGY LESSON: CONTEXT CLUES As an additional or alternate vocabulary strategy, work with students to sharpen their ability to find context clues in the environment of an unknown or difficult word. This skill will be particularly useful when reading articles such as Williams's, in which there is a great deal of specialized vocabulary. For practice, ask students to find context clues for these words from the selection: *tenants, warriors, mailed, canter,* and *scoundrels.*

For additional practice on this strategy, see the **Vocabulary** blackline master, page 200.

Prereading Strategies

During a **preview**, the reader looks carefully at the first and perhaps last paragraph of the selection and then glances through the rest of the text, paying particular attention to headlines, questions, vocabulary words, art, and captions. A preview can familiarize the reader with the topic of the selection and often will provide valuable clues about the author's main idea. Encourage students to make notes after they finish their previews. The chart on page 152 is an example of how they might record their notes. Have them add to this chart any ideas or information they noticed on their previews that they think might be useful later on.

Spanish-speaking Students

Al igual que la selección anterior, esta relato detalle las vidas de los caballeros en los siglos medievales. El autor describe el sistema feudal bajo lo cual toda la sociedad vivía y obedecía. Los caballeros y hidalgos hicieron unos papeles muy importantes en esta sociedad porque su servicio a la corona significaba su propia sobrevivencia. Pero el autor tiene cuidado en no retratar la vida caballera idílicamente. De hecho, señala claramente las faltas de los miembros del sistema feudal.

II. READ

Mention again how important it is for students to **react** to what they're reading. Ask them to make notes about information that surprises them or conflicts with what they already know about feudalism and knights. Their reactions will help them stay focused on what they're learning while at the same time encourage them to utilize their prior knowledge about the topic.

Response Strategy

VISUALIZE As an alternate response strategy, have students visualize the armor, battles, and activities of the knights they're reading about. Although the art on the pages can help fill some of students' knowledge gaps, they'll probably still enjoy dreaming up a few pictures of their own. Ask them to put their sketches in the **Response Notes** so that they can share them with the class after everyone has finished reading.

Comprehension Strategies

Graphic organizers can help readers organize facts and details that they would be likely to forget as soon as they turn the page. The first organizer on page 155 asks students to make notes about feudalism. Have them stop and record their ideas on this organizer when they come to it, but they should feel free to add more information to the organizer as they go along. The second organizer, on page 157, asks students to draw conclusions about knights. Here they might want to use information from "The Knight in Person" in addition to information from Williams's article.

For more help, see the **Comprehension** blackline master on page 201.

Discussion Questions

COMPREHENSION 1. Under the feudal system, who owned the land? *(the kings)*

2. How many days a year did warriors have to serve their lords? *(forty)*

3. According to Williams, what are some of the qualities that distinguished knights from other men? *(For the most part, they were courageous, loyal, and dedicated servants of the Crown, although some were robbers.)*

4. Why did knights of olden times wear such heavy armor? *(for protection)*

5. What weapons did a knight carry with him into battle? *(a shield, a scabbard, a sword, a dagger, a lance, and perhaps an axe)*

CRITICAL THINKING 6. What made the job of being a knight so difficult? *(Answers will vary. Ask students to support their ideas with evidence from the article.)*

7. Why were horses important to a knight? *(They enabled a knight to travel farther and faster than he could on foot.)*

Literary Skill

DETAILS Because they will write an expository paragraph in Part IV, students might benefit from a quick lesson on details in a piece of writing. Most writers use either personal (sensory, memory, or reflective) details, details from other sources, or a combination of the two. Jay Williams relies mostly on details from other sources, as you might expect, since he could have no personal involvement with his topic. Details from other sources come from

- other people (people who have information about the topic);

- an expert (someone who is knowledgeable about the topic);

- written sources (books, magazines, library resources, and so on);

- the computer (Internet searches, information archives, and so on).

III. GATHER YOUR THOUGHTS

The purpose of the prewriting activities on page 158 is to prepare students to write about some aspect of feudalism. Students will choose a topic and then use a **web** to brainstorm descriptive words and facts about the topic. Their webs will help prepare them for the writing that's to come. Encourage students to keep their webs in front of them as they write.

Prewriting Strategies

DETAILS Once students have written their topic sentences, they'll need to find three or four details as support for the point they want to make. As often as possible, they should use direct quotations from the text. If necessary, review the rules for punctuating a quotation before they begin. A short lesson on quoting from the text can help them later on, when it is time to write a research paragraph or essay about a subject.

For additional practice, students should use the **Prewriting** blackline master on page 202.

IV. WRITE

On page 159, students are asked to write an **expository paragraph** about feudalism. Remind them to use the article they've just read to shape what they want to say. When they've finished their rough drafts, refer students to the **Writers' Checklist**. Ask them to keep this information about commas in mind as they are revising their work.

WRITING RUBRIC You might use this writing rubric to help students focus on the assignment requirements and for help with a quick assessment of their writing.

Do students' expository paragraphs

- begin with a topic sentence and contain three or more details to support the topic sentence?

- present information and not opinions?

- stay focused on the topic of feudalism?

Grammar, Usage, and Mechanics

At this point, you may want to teach a mini-lesson on punctuating dependent clauses. Many inexperienced writers have trouble knowing which clauses are dependent and which are independent. The result is sentences that are punctuated incorrectly.

Incorrect: Because knights were trained from childhood they became expert horsemen. (introductory dependent clause missing a comma)

Correct: Because knights were trained from childhood, they became expert horsemen.

Incorrect: A horse before he went into battle had to be taught to canter. (a dependent clause within a sentence that is missing a comma)

Correct: A horse, before he went into battle, had to be taught to canter.

V. WRAP-UP

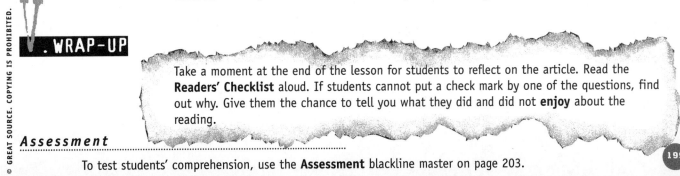

Take a moment at the end of the lesson for students to reflect on the article. Read the **Readers' Checklist** aloud. If students cannot put a check mark by one of the questions, find out why. Give them the chance to tell you what they did and did not **enjoy** about the reading.

Assessment

To test students' comprehension, use the **Assessment** blackline master on page 203.

Name _____

VOCABULARY

Words from the Selection

DIRECTIONS Substitute a synonym (a word that means the same thing) from the word box for the underlined word or words.

> ✦estates   ✦banners   ✦forfeited   ✦cavalry   ✦dagger

1. King William gave out <u>large pieces of land</u> if you showed loyalty to him.

_____

2. We chose to follow King William's <u>flags</u> against King Harold.

_____

3. You had to know how to ride a horse to be in the King's <u>troops</u>.

_____

4. The knight carried a sword and a <u>knife</u> on his belt.

_____

5. Knights seldom <u>gave up</u> their land.

_____

Strategy Lesson: Context Clues

DIRECTIONS Context clues can help you figure out the meaning of a word without looking in a dictionary. Use context clues to figure out what these words mean. Write the meaning of the word on the line.

6. Under feudalism, only the king owned land; all the other people were <u>tenants</u>.

_____

7. For <u>warriors</u>, feudalism meant military duty.

_____

8. The <u>mailed</u> cavalry of Europe wore suits of armor.

_____

9. A knight's horse was taught to <u>canter</u> and then how to gallop quickly.

_____

10. The records are full of complaints against knights who were "devils and <u>scoundrels</u>."

_____

Name _____

COMPREHENSION
Main Idea

DIRECTIONS Answer these questions. They will help you think about the main idea of "The Victorious Feudal Knight."

1. What adjectives (descriptive words) would you use to describe feudal knights?

_____

_____

_____

2. What does Jay Williams mean when he says of knights: "War was their trade, their livelihood, and they were generally good for nothing else"?

_____

_____

_____

3. What was feudalism?

_____

_____

_____

4. Would you say feudalism was a fair or unfair system? Why?

_____

_____

_____

Name _____

PREWRITING
Fact and Opinion

Sometimes it is hard to decide what's a fact and what's an opinion. An **opinion** is a view or belief held by a person. A **fact** is a statement that can be checked or proven to be true. For example:

Fact: Feudal knights were a special class of armed and mounted landowners.

Opinion: Feudal knights were the bravest men in all the world.

DIRECTIONS Look at these facts and opinions from the story. Write F next to the facts and O next to the opinions.

1. Under feudalism, only the king owned land. _____

2. Feudalism discriminated against the poor. _____

3. It was extremely difficult to be a knight in the Middle Ages. _____

4. Knights wore heavy armor. _____

5. Knights were underpaid for their work. _____

Sorting Details

DIRECTIONS Read the main idea statement in the box. Then read the five facts from the story. Decide which facts best support the main idea. Write them in the organizer.

Fact: Knights wore more than a third of their weight in armor into battle.

Fact: Knights protected the kingdom from invasion.

Fact: Many knights were vain about their looks.

Fact: Each time he went to battle, a knight would put his life on the line for the Crown.

Fact: Most knights were farmers.

Main idea statement: Feudal knights had a tough but important job.

FACT 1	FACT 2	FACT 3

Name _____

ASSESSMENT

Multiple-Choice Test

DIRECTIONS On the blanks provided, write the letter of the item that best answers each question or completes each statement.

_____ 1. What was King William the Conqueror's main goal?
A. to own all the land in England
B. to conquer North America
C. to make peace with neighboring countries
D. to install a democratic government

_____ 2. How did King William reward those who helped him in his fight against King Harold?
A. He gave his soldiers gold and jewels.
B. He gave his soldiers their freedom.
C. He gave out large pieces of land.
D. none of the above

_____ 3. What did King William get in return when he gave away land?
A. loyalty and part of the crop
B. loyalty and military service
C. gold
D. unrest

_____ 4. Under feudalism . . .
A. the people owned the land.
B. the knights owned their land.
C. only the king owned land.
D. the people elected their own government.

_____ 5. What was the relationship between a lord and a vassal?
A. Lord and vassal lived together.
B. Lord and vassal worked together.
C. Lord performed certain services in exchange for land.
D. Vassal performed certain services in exchange for land.

_____ 6. How many days each year was a knight required to fight when called upon?
A. 40
B. 80
C. 120
D. 160

_____ 7. A knight's horse had to be taught to . . .
A. canter.
B. trot.
C. sit.
D. kneel.

_____ 8. What weapons did knights of the eleventh century use?
A. guns and grenades
B. lances and swords
C. bombs and mines
D. none of the above

_____ 9. The author says that many knights were thought of as . . .
A. heroes.
B. robbers.
C. teachers.
D. slaves.

_____ 10. A knight's armor and weapons made him weigh more than . . . his normal weight.
A. three times
B. one fourth
C. one third
D. twice

Short-Essay Test

What three descriptive words would you use when talking about feudal knights? Why?

Naguib Mahfouz

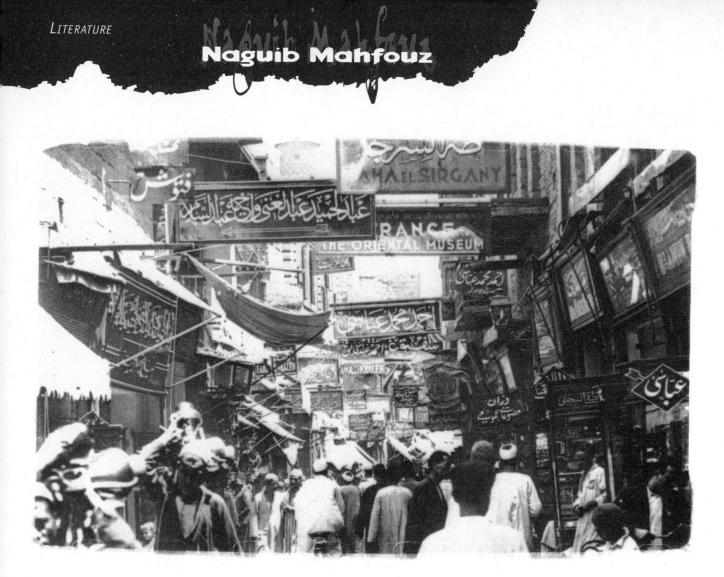

Unit Background   **NAGUIB MAHFOUZ** (pages 161–178)

Naguib Mahfouz was born in the Gamaliya quarter of Cairo, Egypt. The first Arab writer ever to win the Nobel Prize for literature (1988), he is best known for his Cairo Trilogy, which traces three generations of a middle-class Cairo family. He has more than 40 novels and short-story collections to his credit, most written while he was employed by the Egyptian civil service. Much of his work has been translated into French, Hebrew, and English, but some of his work has been banned in Arab countries. He was stabbed by an Islamic extremist in 1994 and has partly recovered.

Tell students that the excerpts from Mahfouz's autobiography that they are about to read seem like journal entries and that they should read them as such rather than as a connected narrative telling the story of his life. Nadine Gordimer, in the introduction to *Echoes of an Autobiography* from which the excerpts in this unit are taken, wrote that "these pieces are meditations which echo that which was, has been, and is the writer, Mahfouz."

Teaching the Introduction

The images on page 161 evoke some of the world native to Mahfouz and show the cover of the book from which the excerpts are taken.

Tell students that some writers choose to sum up their life in terms of their thoughts or beliefs rather than relating a narrative of events, which biographers would choose to do. Ask students to think about a happening in their life that confirmed their belief in something—perhaps the value of honesty, of family life, of fair play, or of life itself. If they would like to talk about this experience, encourage them to do so.

Opening Activity

Ask students to think about the word *justice* (the title of the last Mahfouz selection) and what it means. Then ask each student to write a definition of the word, perhaps resorting to a dictionary, and to give an example of when, in their experience or reading, justice was or was not done. Ask: "How, in the world, is justice administered? Is true justice ever obtainable in this world?"

Forgetfulness and An Unwritten Letter

Skills and Strategies Overview

THEME	Naguib Mahfouz
READING LEVEL	average
VOCABULARY	◇ sheik ◇ pavement ◇ quarter ◇ execution ◇ waned
PREREADING	read-aloud
RESPONSE	questions
COMPREHENSION	reader's log
PREWRITING	brainstorming
WRITING	anecdote / adjectives and adverbs
ASSESSMENT	style

BACKGROUND

"Forgetfulness" and "An Unwritten Letter" are excerpts from Naguib Mahfouz's 1997 work, *Echoes of an Autobiography,* which was published when the writer was 86 years old. In the early years of his career, Mahfouz tended to employ a straightforward narrative style. Later, he began to experiment with a stream-of-consciousness technique that he felt better captured his impressions of Egypt and its rich cultural history. (See the Literary Skill section on page 208 for a discussion of stream-of-consciousness.) Both "Forgetfulness" and "An Unwritten Letter" have stream-of-consciousness elements.

In the first story, Mahfouz offers readers a snapshot of a man he never names. The unnamed sheik can be seen as a symbol of all the men and women who once played important roles in society but have become, because of age, people who have "forgotten relatives and neighbors, students and the rules of grammar."

The second work in this lesson, "An Unwritten Letter," also explores the themes of aging and isolation. In this story, Mahfouz examines the effect the years can have on friendship with others and our own feelings about ourselves. Mahfouz seems to ask whether it is inevitable that as the years go by, our enthusiasm can "wane" to such a degree that we no longer have the energy to focus on people and places apart from ourselves.

UNIT THEME Introduce students to Naguib Mahfouz, an immensely popular and prolific writer whom they've probably never read before. Take this opportunity to remind the class that there is a whole world of literature waiting to be read and that some of the finest books they'll ever come across will be shelved outside of the American and European literature sections of their bookstores or libraries.

GRAPHIC ORGANIZER Students might benefit by seeing or working on the following organizer.

Growing old			Friendship		
THEME			THEME		
Physical exertion becomes difficult.	Memories are lost.	People look the other way.	We often lose touch with childhood friends.	We are hesitant to renew old aquaintances.	We question our friends' interest in earlier times.
SUPPORTING DETAIL	SUPPORTING DETAIL	SUPPORTING DETAIL	SUPPORTING DETAIL	SUPPORTING DETAIL	SUPPORTING DETAIL
Growing old can be painful.			As we grow older, our enthusiasm for friends can waver.		
MAIN IDEA			MAIN IDEA		

BEFORE YOU READ

Read through the opener on page 162 with students, offering additional biographical information on Mahfouz as you see fit. The purpose of this part of the lesson is to give students a general introduction to the author and the selections they'll be reading. When they seem ready, ask students to do the prereading activity, a **read-aloud** and **listener's guide**. (Refer to the **Strategy Handbook** on page 40 for more help.)

Motivation Strategy

Ask students to think about the theme of growing old. What movies, books, and stories about aging do they remember most? What makes these works so memorable? As they read Mahfouz's stories, students will be able to compare his writing to works they have read or seen before.

ENGAGING STUDENTS Explain that "Forgetfulness" and "An Unwritten Letter" are about growing old. Ask students to complete this sentence: "Growing old is _____ because _____ ." Have students explain what they mean by offering examples and anecdotes from their own lives.

Vocabulary Building

Help students use **context clues** as they read to figure out the meanings of difficult words, especially the key vocabulary for this lesson: *sheik, pavement, quarter, execution,* and *waned.* Model using context and then checking your ideas against the footnote: "I don't know the word *sheik.* I see, though, that it appears in a sentence with the pronoun *he,* so I know the word refers to a person and that the person is a man. In the surrounding sentences, I find clues that a sheik must be a person of some importance. Could *sheik* mean 'a man of importance'? I'll check the footnote to see if my guess is close. I'll use the footnote to help me refine my own definition." Ask students to circle the vocabulary words in the text. For additional practice with these words, see page 210.

STRATEGY LESSON: GREEK PREFIXES Remind students that an autobiography, from which these excerpts were taken, is the story of one's life written by oneself. The prefix *auto-* means "self" or "of or by oneself."

For more practice with this prefix, see the **Vocabulary** blackline master, page 210.

Prereading Strategies

Read-alouds show students that reading does not have to be a solitary activity. Critical readers know that sharing a book or story can make the reading process easier and more enjoyable. Reading partners can take turns reading aloud, stopping as often as necessary to ask each other questions or make comments about the text. Encourage students to share information, ideas, and interpretations of the two stories. Stress that every reader will have a slightly different take on a character or situation. What's most important here is a free exchange of ideas, with both readers contributing their own thoughts about the selection.

Spanish-speaking Students

"Olvido" y "Una carta no escrita" vienen de la autobiografía del autor árabe Naguib Mahfouz. Ambas selecciones muestran los efectos poderosos del olvido. En la primera leyenda, un pueblo entero ignora a un ex-líder respetado y honrado porque piensa que es demasiado viejo para saber quién es y qué ha hecho para la comunidad. En la segunda selección, el autor admite a su deseo de escribir a un amigo de su juventud. Pero cambia de opinión al concluir que su amigo no va a acordarse de su amistad.

II. READ

Response Strategy

Remind readers that they'll need to read with expression. Remind listeners that they should follow along as they are listening, writing their **questions** and comments in the **Response Notes.**

Comprehension Strategies

Reader's logs give students the opportunity to react to different parts of the literature. The aim here is for students to interpret what a particular line from the text means. Remind the class that when they interpret, there are no right or wrong answers. What they need to do is keep their focus on the text and forget for a moment how the words relate to their own experiences. The first reader's log on page 163 asks students to explain a quotation from "Forgetfulness." The following two reader's logs ask students to respond to lines from "An Unwritten Letter" and then choose quotations of their own that they'd like to write about.

DOUBLE-ENTRY JOURNAL For an additional comprehension strategy, ask students to set up a double-entry journal box and then respond to the quotations they wrote about in the reader's logs. In a double-entry journal, readers say how the quotation makes them feel, who or what it reminds them of, and the ways in which it applies to their own experiences. A double-entry journal prompts evaluative response, while a reading log elicits interpretive response. See page 22 of the student book for an example of the format of a double-entry journal.

For more help, see the **Comprehension** blackline master on page 211.

Discussion Questions

COMPREHENSION 1. Why is the sheik in "Forgetfulness" so forgetful? (*He has grown old and has lost his memory.*)

2. Why do most people ignore the sheik? (*They think he won't know them, so they decide not to bother saying anything. It's also possible that his age makes them remember that they too are growing older. This makes them uncomfortable.*)

3. Who was Sayyid al-Ghadban and what crime did he commit? (*He was a nightclub bouncer who was executed for killing a dancer.*)

4. What is his relationship to the narrator? (*He was a childhood friend.*)

CRITICAL THINKING 5. What is the tone of "Forgetfulness"? (*Accept reasonable responses with support.*)

6. What is the tone of "An Unwritten Letter"? (*Accept reasonable responses with support.*)

7. Why do you think the narrator is so shaken by the news of Sayyid al-Ghadban's execution? (*Accept reasonable responses with support.*)

Literary Skill

STREAM-OF-CONSCIOUSNESS You might take this opportunity to introduce the narrative technique of stream-of-consciousness. In stream-of-consciousness, the narrator attempts to envelop the reader in a flow of impressions—visual, auditory, physical, associative, and subliminal. In this type of writing, rational thought is less important than the entire workings of the narrator's mind. Point out to students the richness of the imagery in "Forgetfulness" and "An Unwritten Letter." A heavy use of imagery is a hallmark of the stream-of-consciousness style. Explain that Mahfouz's narrative technique allows readers a glimpse into the workings of his mind. Does this style help students better understand the author, or do they feel it is a distraction?

III. GATHER YOUR THOUGHTS

The prewriting activities on pages 166 and 167 are meant to help students examine the **sensory language** Mahfouz uses in the two stories and the kind of sensory language they might use if they were to write about loneliness. After they **brainstorm** their sensory words, students will try their hand at writing an anecdote.

Prewriting Strategies

ANECDOTES Explain to students how important it is to be able to write (and tell) a good anecdote. If necessary, supplement the book definition of *anecdote* by saying: "An anecdote is a short narrative of an interesting, amusing, or biographical incident. Anecdotes can be used to illustrate an author's message or emphasize the point that he or she is trying to make." On page 167, students are asked to write an anecdote about a time in their lives that they felt lonely. Tell your writers that the purpose of their anecdotes will be to capture one quick moment in time. To help them do this, ask that they keep a mental "snapshot" of the moment in front of them and then answer the who and what questions at the top of the page. Once they've described the snapshot, students will generate a list of sensory words that can help make the moment come alive for readers.

Have students use the **Prewriting** blackline master on page 212.

IV. WRITE

Most students will be able to write their anecdotes fairly quickly, although you'll want to be sure to allow plenty of time for struggling writers to get their thoughts down on paper. When the class is finished, explain that you'd like them to read what they've written and then revise using the **Writers' Checklist** as a guide.

WRITING RUBRIC Use the writing rubric to help students focus on the assignment requirements and for help with a quick assessment of their writing.

Do students' anecdotes

- tell about a time they were lonely?

- include details that help readers see, hear, and feel the experience?

- end with a closing sentence that ties things together?

Grammar, Usage, and Mechanics

At this point, you may want to teach a mini-lesson on adjectives and adverbs. If necessary, review examples of incorrectly used adjectives and adverbs. Supplement the examples in the book with these:

Incorrect: I ran quick and might have been the most fast runner in my grade.

Correct: I ran quickly and might have been the fastest runner in my grade.

V. WRAP-UP

Take a moment at the end of the lesson for students to reflect using the **Readers' Checklist**. Students will benefit from a short discussion of Mahfouz's **style**. What makes his sentences and paragraphs easy to read? What makes them difficult? Use their comments to help you plan for the lesson that follows on pages 170–177.

Assessment

To test students' comprehension, use the **Assessment** blackline master on page 213.

Name _____

VOCABULARY

Words from the Selection

DIRECTIONS Answer these questions that use words from the selection.

1. Is a <u>sheik</u> a male or female leader of an Arab family? _____

2. Is the <u>pavement</u> the finished or unfinished part of a road?

   _____

3. Is a <u>quarter</u> a section of a city or a section of a house? _____

4. What crime does someone have to commit to face an <u>execution</u>?

   _____

5. If your enthusiasm for a project has <u>waned</u>, has it increased or decreased?

   _____

Strategy Lesson: Greek Prefixes

A prefix comes at the beginning of a word. For example, the prefix *auto-* in *autobiography* means "self" or "of or by oneself." The words in the box all contain this same prefix. Choose the word that correctly fits in each sentence, and write it in the blank.

automatic = self-acting	**automobile** = vehicle self-propelled by an engine
autonomy = self-government; independence	**autocrat** = ruler who has unlimited power
autograph = person's signature	

6. Before going to the bookstore, we stopped at the _____ teller machine.

7. At the store, we asked a famous writer to _____ a copy of her book.

8. The book was a novel about a mythical king who was an _____.

9. Later, we skimmed a book about how the United States won _____ from Great Britain in the 1700s.

10. Eventually, Grandfather picked us up in his old _____.

Name _____

COMPREHENSION

Graphic Organizer

DIRECTIONS List on this chart some of the sensory words that Mahfouz uses in "Forgetfulness" and "An Unwritten Letter."

	"sight" words	"hearing" words	"touch" words	"taste" words	"smell" words
In "Forgetfulness"	flowing				
In "An Unwritten Letter"			shook		

Theme

DIRECTIONS Answer these questions about the two stories. Provide support for your answers.

What is the topic of "Forgetfulness"?

_____

_____

My support:

_____

_____

What is the topic of "An Unwritten Letter"?

_____

_____

My support:

_____

_____

Name _____

PREWRITING

Writing an Anecdote

DIRECTIONS To write an anecdote, follow these steps.

STEP 1. DECIDE ON A TOPIC. On the lines below, write the topic for your anecdote. (Your book asks you to write an anecdote about a time you were lonely.)

_____

_____

STEP 2. MAKE NOTES. Next make notes about the who, what, where, when, why, and how of your topic. Use this organizer.

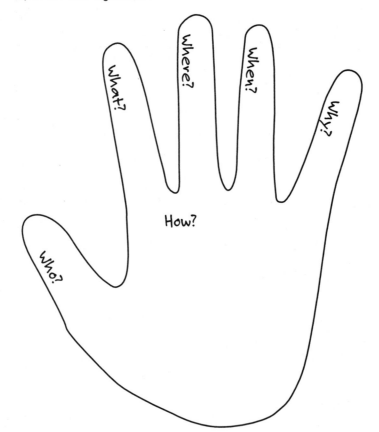

STEP 3. WRITE A TOPIC SENTENCE. Even a very short paragraph, such as an anecdote, needs a topic sentence. Write a topic sentence for your anecdote here.

_____

_____

STEP 4. WRITE AN ANECDOTE. Write your anecdote in your book on page 168.

Name _____

ASSESSMENT

Multiple-Choice Test

DIRECTIONS On the blanks provided, write the letter of the best answer for each question.

_____ 1. In "Forgetfulness," how long has the sheik been retired?
  A. more than 5 years   C. more than 15 years
  B. more than 10 years   D. more than 20 years

_____ 2. Why do most people fail to greet the sheik when he passes them?
  A. He is a mean man.   C. It is disrespectful to do so.
  B. He has a poor memory.   D. He is always in a hurry.

_____ 3. Why does the sheik leave his home every morning?
  A. He shops for groceries. C. He walks about getting exercise.
  B. He visits with friends. D. all of the above

_____ 4. What do you think the author's purpose is in "Forgetfulness"?
  A. to describe a person   C. to tell about a place
  B. to amuse   D. none of the above

_____ 5. In "An Unwritten Letter," what is the relationship between the three men?
  A. They are brothers.   C. They went to college together.
  B. They were childhood friends. D. They all work together.

_____ 6. What job did Sayyid al-Ghadban hold before his arrest?
  A. He was a lawyer.   C. He was a bouncer.
  B. He was a bartender.   D. He was unemployed.

_____ 7. What crime did al-Ghadban commit?
  A. He stole from a bank.   C. He refused to serve in the army.
  B. He kidnapped a child.   D. He murdered a dancer.

_____ 8. What punishment did al-Ghadban receive for his crime?
  A. death   C. 20 years in jail
  B. life in prison   D. none of the above

_____ 9. What does Hammam do for a living?
  A. He saves lives.   C. He works in the judicial system.
  B. He doesn't have a career. D. He is also a bouncer.

_____ 10. Why doesn't the narrator contact Hammam about his feelings?
  A. He doesn't have his address. C. He is ashamed to have lost contact with both men.
  B. Hammam already knows them.   D. He feels Hammam wouldn't be interested.

Short-Essay Test

Which character from these two selections would you most like to meet? Why?

A Man Reserves a Seat and Justice

Skills and Strategies Overview

THEME Naguib Mahfouz

READING LEVEL challenging

VOCABULARY
◇ frankness ◇ forged ◇ precautions ◇ madness ◇ induces

PREREADING word web

RESPONSE visualize

COMPREHENSION predict

PREWRITING sequence / storyboard

WRITING story / subject-verb agreement

ASSESSMENT depth

BACKGROUND

Since they have read the two Naguib Mahfouz stories in Lesson 17, students should now feel a little more comfortable with the author's distinctive style. Encourage them not to become distracted in their search for a message. In these two stories, as in much of his writing, setting, plot, and characterization take a back seat to theme. Students should continue to think of Mahfouz's writing as a series of snapshots that the author brings into focus through vivid description.

In the first selection, "A Man Reserves a Seat," Mahfouz describes an incident that clearly had a profound effect on him, although he never tells us who was there, how the accident happened, or what was the end result was. What's most important here is the question that Mahfouz seems to pose to readers: Is this really what life and death boil down to—a series of coincidences that can't be foreseen or controlled in any way?

In "Justice," Mahfouz is at his most enigmatic. We assume that he is the first-person narrator, but we have no idea what has brought about the lawsuit, or whether or not Mahfouz is in fact "one hundred percent innocent." What comment is Mahfouz trying to make about justice?

UNIT THEME In these two selections, Mahfouz explores issues relating to life, death, and justice.

GRAPHIC ORGANIZER The organizer below graphically illustrates the first Mahfouz story.

Sequence Organizer: Coincidence

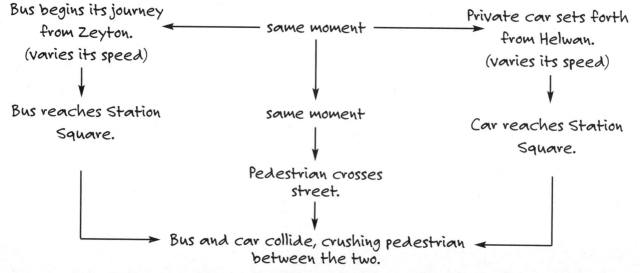

Bus begins its journey from Zeyton. (varies its speed) ← same moment → Private car sets forth from Helwan. (varies its speed)

Bus reaches Station Square. — same moment — Car reaches Station Square.

Pedestrian crosses street.

Bus and car collide, crushing pedestrian between the two.

BEFORE YOU READ

Before students begin reading, you might review with them some of the characteristics of Mahfouz's writing style. (Not all characteristics are apparent in these two selections, however.)

Mahfouz's Writing Style

- stream-of-consciousness
- minimal characterization
- sensory language
- simple sentence structure
- easy or average vocabulary

When students seem ready, have them do the prereading activity for this lesson, a **word web**. (Refer to the **Strategy Handbook** on page 40 for more help.)

Motivation Strategy

ENGAGING STUDENTS Tell students that "A Man Reserves a Seat" is about a coincidence, a sequence of events that results in an accidental happening but that seems to have been planned. Ask students to connect this theme to their own lives by describing for the class a coincidence that happened to them recently. What surprised them about the coincidence? How did they feel about it? Why?

Vocabulary Building

Help students use **context clues** as they read to figure out the meanings of difficult words, especially the key vocabulary words for this lesson: *frankness, forged, precautions, madness,* and *induces*. Ask students to circle these words in the text. Remind the class that context clues can be supplied through synonyms, through comparisons and contrasts, and through definition and description. For additional practice with these words, see page 218.

STRATEGY LESSON: ROOT WORDS As you know, a root is a base upon which a word is built.

root	meaning	word
bio-	life	
		biography
-graph	write	

Show students these words from the selection: *vivacious, extended, inspect, sequence,* and *pedestrian*. Ask them to find the roots for each in a dictionary.

For additional practice on this strategy, see **Vocabulary** page 218.

Prereading Strategies

Webs give students the chance to explore abstract words (such as *justice*) in a more concrete way. In a word web, students list phrases, situations, experiences, and emotions that they associate with the abstract word. The items they write on their webs can come from what they've read or seen or from their own ideas and experiences. When they've finished, students will have their own personal definition of the abstract word. They'll understand what the word means to them, which in turn will help them understand what the word means to the author.

Spanish-speaking Students

"Un hombre reserva un asiento" se trata de la incertidumbre de la vida y el poder último del azar. Dos hombres que viven en barrios opuestos conducen sus automóviles respectivos al mismo sitio. Salen a la vez y se encuentran con distintos obstáculos que les retrasan de un modo u otro. Sin embargo, llegan al mismo tiempo y se chocan. Un peatón se muere en el accidente. Mahfouz desarrolla esta idea de la injusticia de la vida en "Justicia." La selección se trata de la imposibilidad de determinar la verdad y juzgar justamente a otras personas.

II. READ

As students begin to read, have them note the little drawing of the bus and car in the **Response Notes**. Explain that each time they **visualize** a person or event from the story, you want them to make a sketch in the margin. This task will keep them focused on the reading while at the same time encourage them to use their imaginations to fill in the information that Mahfouz deliberately omits.

Response Strategy

QUESTION Questions are bound to come up whenever students read, but they will come up even more frequently when they read a writer like Mahfouz, who leaves so much for the reader to infer. It is important that students make note of their questions right away, so that they don't lose track of what they want to ask. Tell them to write their questions for the author, another reader, and you in the **Response Notes**. When they've finished reading, volunteers can read their questions aloud. Work as a class to find answers.

Comprehension Strategies

Making **predictions** keeps readers involved and interested in the story. As they read the two selections, students will make guesses about what they think will happen next. Many of their predictions will be far off the mark, but that's irrelevant. What's important is that students take a moment to think carefully about what has happened so far and what they think is likely to happen in the pages to come.

DIRECTED READING As an alternate comprehension strategy, you might conduct a directed reading of the two selections. This is an especially effective strategy to use with selections that you think will be hard for students to understand. During your directed reading of Mahfouz's work, you'll want to stop occasionally and ask questions that can help improve students' understanding of his theme. Even the simplest questions, such as "What is Mahfouz talking about here?", can move students a little closer to an understanding of his theme.

For more help, see the **Comprehension** blackline master on page 219.

Discussion Questions

COMPREHENSION 1. Who is killed in "A Man Reserves a Seat"? *(a pedestrian)*

2. Who is to blame for the accident? *(no one; it is bad luck and bad timing)*

3. What is the narrator of "Justice" angry about? *(He wants to prove his innocence in a legal action but is having trouble doing so.)*

CRITICAL THINKING 4. What does Mahfouz mean by the line, "Madness induces sorrow"? *(Refer student to page 173, where the quote appears, and have them make inferences about the line.)*

5. What is the tone of "A Man Reserves a Seat"? What is the tone of "Justice"? *(Remind students that clues about an author's tone can often be found in word choices. If they're having trouble thinking about the tone of these two selections, have them examine some of Mahfouz's word choices. The first selection is matter-of-fact. The second is less so.)*

Literary Skill

THEME The underlying meaning or main idea of a work is often called the *theme*. A theme is usually implied through character and events. Ask students to discuss the themes Mahfouz explores in the two selections. Remember that in a discussion of theme, agreement is not essential. What is important is how well students can support their interpretations with evidence from the text. Ask what the narrator's attitude seems to be about the two situations he describes. Is he making a comment about fate? about the madness of dealing with lawyers? or of obtaining justice?

III. GATHER YOUR THOUGHTS

The prewriting activities on page 175 ask students to reflect on what they have read. Students will complete the **plot sequence** of "A Man Reserves a Seat" and then comment on the author's theme in both pieces. Encourage the class to take its time with these two activities. Although the two stories are short, they are complex, and students should not be rushed.

Prewriting Strategies

BRAINSTORM On page 176, students plan **stories** about justice. Before they begin, students will want to review the webs they made on page 170. In addition, it might be a good idea to conduct a brief brainstorming session on possible topics for their stories. Allow students to help each other plan topics and consider story lines. Once they have a solid topic in mind, students should have no trouble planning the plots for their stories. Students can use the **storyboard** on page 176 or they can create a story pyramid using the **Prewriting** blackline master on page 220.

IV. WRITE

Set aside plenty of time for students to write. Some students may need help from you or others as they write their **stories**. Watch carefully for plots that meander or seem disjointed in some other way. Once they've finished their first drafts, students can revise their work using the **Writers' Checklist** as a guide.

WRITING RUBRIC Use the writing rubric to help students focus on the assignment requirements and for help with a quick assessment of their stories.

Do students' stories

- have a beginning, middle, and end?

- explore the topic of justice?

- Use correct subject-verb agreement?

Grammar, Usage, and Mechanics

At this point you may also want to introduce a mini-lesson on subject-verb agreement, which can be a problem area for many writers. Remind the class that the subject and verb of a sentence must work together, or agree. Singular subjects are always paired with singular verbs; plural subjects always require verbs that work with a plural subject. For example:

Incorrect: The car and the bus crashes.

Correct: The car and the bus crash.

V. WRAP-UP

Before leaving the unit on Naguib Mahfouz, take the opportunity to check the **depth** of students' understanding. Did his writing make them rethink some of their own ideas or experiences? If so, how? If not, then why didn't it? Students can use the questions on the **Readers' Checklist** as springboards for additional comments or discussion.

Assessment

To test students' comprehension, use the **Assessment** blackline master on page 221.

Name _____

VOCABULARY

Words from the Selection

DIRECTIONS Answer these questions that use words from the selection. Explain your answers.

1. If you express your feelings with <u>frankness</u>, are you being direct or vague?

   _____

2. When a signature is <u>forged</u>, is it copied or real? _____

3. Should you take <u>precautions</u> before or after crossing the street?

   _____

4. Is a person who is accused of <u>madness</u> thought to be crazy or sad?

   _____

5. If something <u>induces</u> a change, has it caused the change or stopped it from happening?

   _____

Strategy Lesson: Root Words

DIRECTIONS Read this list of common roots and their definitions. Then use what you've learned to write the meaning of the underlined words on the blanks.

Roots
vivere = to live
tendere = to stretch
specere = to look
sequi = follow
pedem = foot

6. The once <u>vivacious</u> man was lying motionless on the road beside the car.

   _____

7. As the driver <u>extended</u> his hand, he realized the pedestrian was dead.

   _____

8. Both drivers got out to <u>inspect</u> the scene of the accident. _____

9. The police officer asked questions about the <u>sequence</u> of events.

   _____

10. The <u>pedestrian</u> on the road was an innocent victim. _____

Name _____

COMPREHENSION
Graphic Organizer

DIRECTIONS Use this word web to explore the word *coincidence*. List words, phrases, and situations from the stories and from your own life that you think of when you hear this word. Then answer three questions about the word.

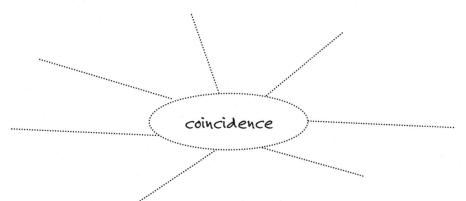

What is your definition of <u>coincidence</u>?

_____

_____

_____

What coincidence has happened to you lately? Describe it here.

_____

_____

_____

How does the word <u>coincidence</u> relate to "A Man Reserves a Seat"?

_____

_____

_____

Name _____

PREWRITING

Story Pyramid

DIRECTIONS Use this story pyramid to plan your story about justice. Think carefully about each line of the pyramid.

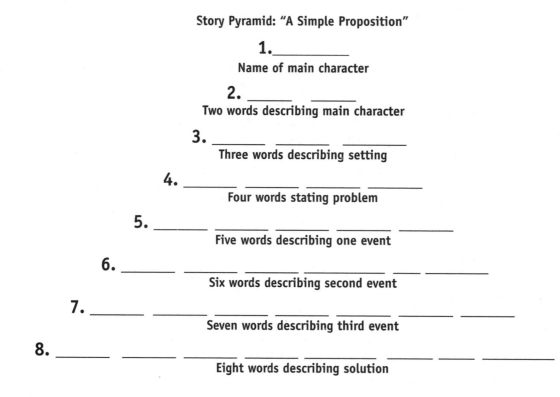

Story Pyramid: "A Simple Proposition"

1._____
Name of main character

2. _____   _____
Two words describing main character

3. _____ _____ _____
Three words describing setting

4. _____ _____ _____ _____
Four words stating problem

5. _____ _____ _____ _____ _____
Five words describing one event

6. _____ _____ _____ _____ ____ _____
Six words describing second event

7. _____ _____ _____ _____ _____ _____ _____
Seven words describing third event

8. _____ _____ _____ _____ _____ _____ ____ _____
Eight words describing solution

Name _____

ASSESSMENT

Multiple-Choice Test

DIRECTIONS On the blanks provided, write the letter of the best answer for each question.

_____ 1. What two vehicles are involved in the accident in "A Man Reserves a Seat"?

    A. a motorcycle and car   C. a motorcycle and bus

    B. a car and bus   D. a bicycle and car

_____ 2. How does the narrator feel about the accident?

    A. sad   C. scared

    B. happy   D. none of the above

_____ 3. Where does the accident occur?

    A. at a bus station   C. at a parking garage

    B. at a train station   D. at a parking lot

_____ 4. What damage was done to the bus?

    A. The front was scratched.   C. A headlight was broken.

    B. A tire was blown.   D. No damage was done to the bus.

_____ 5. Who died in the accident?

    A. The driver of the bus.   C. A man crossing the road.

    B. The driver of the car.   D. A passenger in the bus.

_____ 6. In the story "Justice," what is the narrator's first impression of the lawyer?

    A. He is happy with his frankness.   C. He is impressed with his knowledge.

    B. He doesn't like his personality.   D. He is unhappy with his answer.

_____ 7. What does the lawyer have to say about the conflict?

    A. The narrator is in the right.   C. Neither side is in the right.

    B. The opposing party is in the right.   D. Both are in the right.

_____ 8. To help resolve the problem, the narrator offers which idea to the opposing party?

    A. forget the whole thing   C. find someone they both have confidence in to review the facts

    B. call a judge   D. ask for a jury trial

_____ 9. What, among other things, is the narrator accused of?

    A. stealing a car   C. taking money

    B. threatening to kill someone   D. forging his signature

_____ 10. How does the narrator respond to the accusation?

    A. He ignores it.   C. He laughs at it.

    B. He cries about it.   D. He gets up and leaves.

Short-Essay Test

Is the tone of "A Man Reserves a Seat" the same or different from "Justice"? Explain.

Discrimination

Unit Background   **DISCRIMINATION** (pages 179–196)

Though Booker T. Washington (1856–1915) and Rosa Parks were born 57 years apart, they had much in common. Both suffered discrimination and became famous for their struggles to improve the lives of African Americans.

Born a slave in Franklin County, Virginia, Booker T. Washington never knew his father, an unidentified white man. His mother was a cook on a small plantation. When the Civil War ended, his mother took him and her three other children to Malden, West Virginia, to join her husband, a former slave who was working in the salt mines. Booker also worked in the salt mines and in the coal mines there as a boy. His schooling was irregular, but he gained enough education, partly with the help of the wife of a mine owner, that in 1872 he was admitted to Hampton Institute near Norfolk, Virginia. After his graduation with honors, he taught there and then was asked to start a school for black teachers in Tuskegee, Alabama. From there he went on to become an impassioned spokesman for African Americans.

The excerpt from his autobiography *Up from Slavery* is about his first days as a mostly part-time student in a school in West Virginia—part-time because he had to arise early, work until 9 A.M., and then attend school for only a few hours before going back to work.

Students may be acquainted with Rosa Parks's defiance of segregated seating on buses in Montgomery, Alabama. If not, the selection itself provides enough information on her courageous act and its consequences.

Teaching the Introduction

Page 179 shows a sign advertising a hotel in which "colored" people could stay, Booker T. Washington as a young man, Rosa Parks, and an incident during the first days of government-mandated school integration in the South.

Remind students that for many years African Americans who traveled in the South found it difficult to find a place to stay or a restaurant that would serve them. Black (and white) players on integrated sports teams from the North were often embarrassed because blacks were refused the same service provided to white team members.

1. Ask students whether they can name the achievements for which the following people are known: Jackie Robinson, Joe Louis, Marian Anderson, Frederick Douglass, George Washington Carver, Duke Ellington, Gwendolyn Brooks, Martin Luther King, Jr., Arthur Ashe, Alice Walker, Tiger Woods.

2. Ask students to discuss what makes some people become inspirations to others.

Opening Activity

Interested students might like to devise game-show type questions that require answering with the names of African Americans who have made significant contributions to American life and who continue to do so.

Ancestry

Skills and Strategies Overview

THEME	Discrimination
READING LEVEL	challenging

VOCABULARY

◆ perplexity ◆ privilege ◆ ancestry ◆ inherited ◆ reliance

PREREADING	anticipation guide
RESPONSE	predict
COMPREHENSION	retell
PREWRITING	opinion and support
WRITING	persuasive paragraph / commas
ASSESSMENT	meaning

BACKGROUND

Booker Taliaferro Washington (1856–1915) was an American educator who urged African Americans to try to improve their lives through education. Born the son of a slave in Franklin County, Virginia, Washington's childhood was all but destroyed by the back-breaking hours he worked in the salt and coal mines near his family's living quarters. After the Civil War, Washington was able to enroll in the Hampton Institute (now called Hampton University). He was so successful there that the school made him an instructor at age 19.

Washington's autobiography, *Up from Slavery* (first published in 1901), is considered one of the greatest autobiographies ever written. His compelling life story and self-help philosophy is said to have inspired generations of African-American leaders, including Marcus Garvey, Elijah Muhammad, Malcolm X, and Louis Farrakhan. In "Ancestry," an excerpt from the book, Washington recounts his first few days at the Hampton Institute.

UNIT THEME Booker T. Washington reveals his philosophy that the key to fighting discrimination is hard work and education.

GRAPHIC ORGANIZER You might prepare the left side of an organizer like this one, and have students fill in the right side.

Booker T. Washington

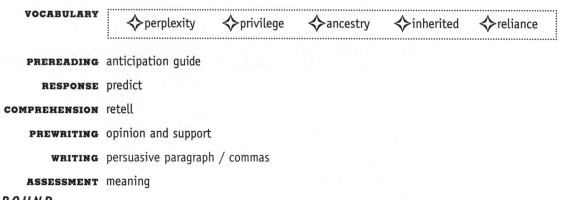

What he says . . .	What it shows about Washington . . .
"I have always felt proud, whenever I think of the incident, that my mother had strength of character enough not to be led into the temptation of seeming to be that which she was not—"	He was kind-hearted. —not impressed with worldly success —an adoring, loyal son
"I think there are not many men in our country who have had the privilege of naming themselves in the way that I have."	He was not impressed with worldly success. —took pleasure in simple things
"Years ago I resolved that because I had no ancestry myself I would leave a record of which my children would be proud, and which might encourage them to still higher effort."	He was determined. —driven —self-directed
"The world should not pass judgment upon the Negro, and especially the Negro youth, too quickly or too harshly."	He was kind-hearted. —forgiving

BEFORE YOU READ

Read through the introduction to the lesson on page 180 with students. Ask them to think about the theme of discrimination as they read "Ancestry." Then have them begin the prereading activity, an **anticipation guide**. (Refer to the **Strategy Handbook** on page 40 for more help.)

Motivation Strategy

Ask students to discuss examples of discrimination in American history. Over the centuries, what groups of people have been discriminated against and why? Even in the most general discussion, the type of discrimination Washington describes is likely to come up. Invite students to reveal what they know as a warm-up for reading the selection.

ENGAGING STUDENTS Explain that "Ancestry" explores one man's feelings about his heritage. Ask students: "Can a person's ancestry determine the type of person he or she becomes? What effect do our parents' and grandparents' history have on us today?" These questions will help students apply the topic of Washington's selection to their own lives.

Vocabulary Building

Washington's vocabulary in "Ancestry" will be challenging for some students, so it is particularly important that they apply what they've learned about using **context clues.** Remind students to start by looking for synonyms in the word's environment. These are the easiest context clues to spot and apply. Ask students to circle these key vocabulary words in the text: *perplexity, privilege, ancestry, inherited,* and *reliance.* Request that they use context clues to define each. For additional practice with key vocabulary, see page 228.

STRATEGY LESSON: PREFIXES As an additional vocabulary strategy, give students a list of words and then have them separate the prefixes from the roots. Words on your list might include these: *disagree, dismount, unacceptable, unplanned,* and *extend* (*ex-*, "out" + *tendere*, "to stretch").

For additional practice on this strategy, see the **Vocabulary** blackline master on page 228.

Prereading Strategies

Anticipation guides are easy to create and interesting for students to do. They work especially well with longer or more complex selections because they give students a "head start" on plot and theme work. As a part of the anticipation guide, students will make predictions about the selection. In most cases they'll rely on their own ideas and experiences to form their predictions. Almost without thinking about it, students will activate prior knowledge and make personal connections to the people, places, and themes the author explores in the selection.

K-W-L As an alternate prereading strategy, try using a K-W-L with students. A K-W-L will be particularly helpful with "Ancestry," since most of your students will have some knowledge of Booker T. Washington and discrimination. In the K column, students should write everything they know about the two topics. They can use the W column to note what they want to find out, and the L column to write what they learned from the article.

Spanish-speaking Students

"Ascendencia" viene de la autobiografía de Booker T. Washington, *Up from Slavery.* Muestra la actitud increíblemente positiva de Washington, que sufría racismo y opresión por ser negro. Explica que su pobreza y carecimiento de una ascendencia concreta le esforzaron e inspiraron a lograr mucho.

II. READ

> As you know, good readers respond to a text on three different levels: factually, interpretively, and evaluatively. Making predictions while reading can help with the first level, factual response. Remind the class to stop several different times during the reading in order to make **predictions** about Washington. Each time they make a prediction, they should write a note about it in the **Response Notes**.

Response Strategy

VISUALIZE Washington uses detailed description in several parts of his writing. As an alternate response strategy, have students visualize and sketch the events and situations he describes. These sketches will help them later, when it comes time to write a persuasive paragraph that relates to the selection.

Comprehension Strategies

Be sure students know that they'll need to stop occasionally in order to **retell** the events described. Retelling can help readers make connections that they might not have noticed the first time around. When they retell, students should be brief but thorough. They should focus only on the major events and ignore any minor details.

For more help, see the **Comprehension** blackline master on page 229.

Discussion Questions

COMPREHENSION 1. What type of writing is this? *(an autobiography)*

2. Who was Booker T. Washington? *(a famous American educator and leader)*

3. What "hat" problem does Washington encounter at school? *(He feels he needs a hat because the other students have one.)*

4. What "name" problem does Washington have? *(He starts school without a last name.)*

CRITICAL THINKING 5. How does Washington feel about his mother? *(Have students support what they say with direct quotations from the selection.)*

6. What is Washington's attitude toward his ancestry? *(Again, students will need to support what they say with evidence from the reading.)*

Literary Skill

WORD CHOICE To introduce a literary skill with this lesson, you might teach a brief lesson on word choice. Explain that an author's word choices can reveal a great deal of information about him or her. Washington's formal language and sophisticated sentence structures show him to be a thoughtful, well-educated, and contemplative man. For example, he uses the word *confronted* instead of *faced* and says he was "in deep perplexity" instead of saying he was "confused." His word choices serve to reinforce the importance of his message. He has something serious and vital to say, and he says it with serious, important-sounding words.

III. GATHER YOUR THOUGHTS

After they finish reading, students will record their thoughts about ancestry and a name on an organizer. In order to do this, they'll need to form an **opinion** on this issue: Does a person's ancestry or name have a strong influence on his or her life?

Prewriting Strategies

GROUP DISCUSSION As an additional prewriting strategy, hold a group discussion about Washington's essay and his views on ancestry. A large- or small-group discussion will be particularly helpful to students who have struggled a bit with this selection. During the discussion, ask factual and inferential questions that can help students see Washington's point of view and the type of support he offers.

Have students use the **Prewriting** blackline master on page 230.

IV. WRITE

Before they begin writing, you might take a moment to explain the characteristics of a **persuasive paragraph.** A persuasive paragraph is one that presents information to support or prove a point. It expresses an opinion and tries to convince the reader that the opinion is correct or valid.

When you feel they are ready, ask students to write a persuasive paragraph using the opinion they wrote on the chart on page 185. Remind them to offer three or more clearly worded facts, examples, and statements to support their opinions.

WRITING RUBRIC Use the writing rubric to help students focus on the assignment requirements and for help with a quick assessment of their writing.

Do students' paragraphs

- begin with their opinion statements?

- offer support in the form of facts, examples, and statements from the reading?

- stay focused on the topic of ancestry?

- use commas correctly?

Grammar, Usage, and Mechanics

Have students use the **Writers' Checklist** as a guide. Students should know that commas are used to set off transition words, parenthetical expressions, contrasted words, "yes" and "no," and to seperate coordinate adjectives. For example:

Incorrect: Yes Booker T. Washington was a famous educated leader.

Correct: Yes, Booker T. Washington was a famous, educated leader.

V. WRAP-UP

At the end of the lesson, allow time for students to consider whether "Ancestry" was **meaningful** to them. Explain that it is not enough to say a piece meant nothing. Are the author's ideas silly or out-of-date? Do students have a hard time connecting to the author's message? These questions, along with the questions on the **Readers' Checklist**, can help students reflect on what the text meant to them.

Assessment

To test students' comprehension, use the **Assessment** blackline master on page 231.

Name _____

VOCABULARY

Words from the Selection

DIRECTIONS To help improve your vocabulary, answer these questions about five words from the selection. Then write the meaning of the underlined words on the lines.

1. If you are deep in perplexity are you confused? _____

2. When you are given a privilege, are you excited or disappointed?

   _____

3. Does your ancestry have to do with your family or friends? _____

4. If you inherited a house, is it a gift or a loan? _____

5. On whom did you place your reliance when you were young?

   _____

Strategy Lesson: Prefixes

DIRECTIONS Study the prefixes and their meanings in the box. Then write the prefix, the root, and the meaning of each word.

un- = not	dis- = opposite of, lack of, not, lessen	ex- = out

	prefix	+	root	=	meaning
6. uncomfortable	_____	+	_____	=	_____
7. disappear	_____	+	_____	=	_____
8. discourage	_____	+	_____	=	_____
9. extend	_____	+	_____	=	_____

10. Write a sentence that shows you know the meaning of the word *disappear*.

_____

_____

Name _____

COMPREHENSION
Brainstorming
....

DIRECTIONS With a writing partner, brainstorm a list of four or more quotations from Washington's essay that explore the topic of ancestry. (You can use these quotations as support in your persuasive paragraph.) Then answer two questions about the selection.

My Brainstorming Notes

1.

2.

3.

4.

5.

Booker T. Washington thinks a person's ancestry is . . .

very important   sort of important   not important at all
                        (circle one)

I agree disagree with his opinion.

(circle one)

Name _____

PREWRITING

DIRECTIONS Follow these steps to write a persuasive paragraph.

STEP 1. WRITE AN ANECDOTE. Write an anecdote that shows the power of ancestry and a name. Your anecdote can come from your own life, or it can be a story you heard somewhere else. (See pages 167–168 of your book for a lesson on writing an anecdote.)

My anecdote about ancestry: _____

_____

_____

_____

STEP 2. WRITE AN OPINION STATEMENT. Next write your opinion statement. Use this formula:

A specific topic + a specific opinion = a good opinion statement.

My opinion statement: (ancestry) + (_____) = _____

STEP 3. GATHER SUPPORT. Now gather support for your opinion. Your support will come from facts, examples and experiences, and from the text itself.

fact #1 (from the text): _____

_____

_____

fact #2 (examples and experiences from Washington's life or your own life): _____

_____

_____

fact #3 (Washington's statements—use quotes from the text): _____

_____

_____

STEP 4. WRITE. Write your persuasive paragraph on page 186–187. Open with your anecdote. Then give your opinion statement and support. End with a closing sentence that says your opinion statement in a slightly different way.

Name _____

ASSESSMENT

Multiple-Choice Test

DIRECTIONS   On the blanks provided, write the letter of the item that best answers each question or completes each statement.

_____ 1. How did Washington's mother solve his hat problem?

  A. She made a hat for him.
  C. She bought a store hat.
  B. She gave him her hat.
  D. She borrowed a hat.

_____ 2. How did Washington feel about his mother's solution?

  A. embarrassed
  C. guilty
  B. proud
  D. angry

_____ 3. What is the tone of this selection?

  A. angry
  C. calm
  B. sad
  D. excited

_____ 4. How did Booker get the last name "Washington"?

  A. It was his father's last name.
  C. It was the name his teacher gave him.
  B. It was his mother's last name.
  D. It was the name he gave himself.

_____ 5. What does the "T" stand for in Booker T. Washington?

  A. Theodore
  C. Thorton
  B. Taliaferro
  D. Thomas

_____ 6. Because Washington had no ancestry of his own, he decided to . . .

  A. research where he came from.
  C. make his children proud of him in other ways.
  B. find another family to belong to.
  D. make it up.

_____ 7. According to Washington, what challenges do African-American young people face?

  A. obstacles
  C. discouragements
  B. temptations
  D. all of the above

_____ 8. Which of his family members had Washington never met?

  A. his grandmother
  C. his brothers
  B. his mother
  D. his aunts and uncles

_____ 9. Washington felt that young people can better resist temptation if they have . . .

  A. education.
  C. religion.
  B. a family history.
  D. a good job.

_____ 10. How did Washington feel about his childhood?

  A. regretful
  C. proud
  B. confused
  D. angry

Short-Essay Test

How did the events in Washington's childhood shape the man he would become?

Rosa Parks

Skills and Strategies Overview

THEME	Discrimination
READING LEVEL	average
VOCABULARY	

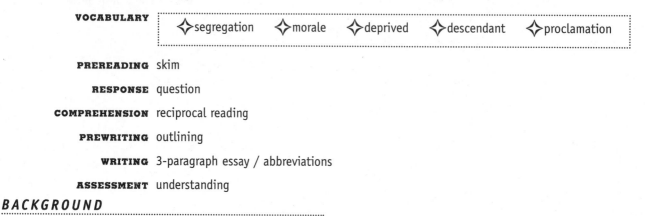

◇ segregation   ◇ morale   ◇ deprived   ◇ descendant   ◇ proclamation

PREREADING	skim
RESPONSE	question
COMPREHENSION	reciprocal reading
PREWRITING	outlining
WRITING	3-paragraph essay / abbreviations
ASSESSMENT	understanding

BACKGROUND

"The only tired I was, was tired of giving in." These are the words of Rosa Parks (born 1913), civil rights activist, who on December 1, 1955, refused to give up her bus seat to a white man. Parks's refusal and subsequent arrest sparked the Montgomery, Alabama, bus boycott that inspired civil rights activists nationwide.

In this selection, Rosa Parks tells her story in the same calm and dignified manner that she has lived her entire life. For the past 50 years or so, Parks has been speaking out against injustices great and small. Her bravery and fortitude continue to inspire men, women, and children around the world.

UNIT THEME Rosa Parks reveals the ugliness of discrimination in this true story of her refusal to give up her bus seat to a white man.

GRAPHIC ORGANIZER

Linear Spiral-String: "Rosa Parks"

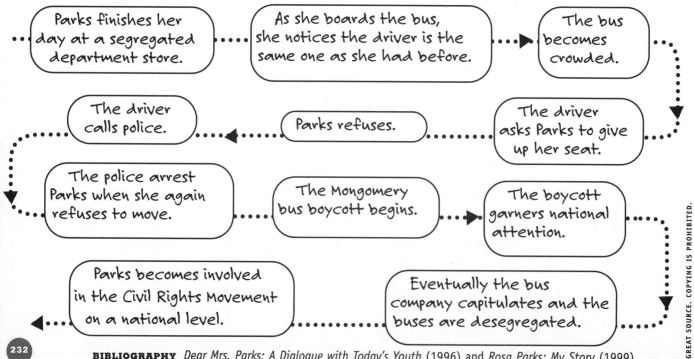

Parks finishes her day at a segregated department store.

As she boards the bus, she notices the driver is the same one as she had before.

The bus becomes crowded.

The driver calls police.

Parks refuses.

The driver asks Parks to give up her seat.

The police arrest Parks when she again refuses to move.

The Mongomery bus boycott begins.

The boycott garners national attention.

Parks becomes involved in the Civil Rights Movement on a national level.

Eventually the bus company capitulates and the buses are desegregated.

BIBLIOGRAPHY *Dear Mrs. Parks: A Dialogue with Today's Youth* (1996) and *Rosa Parks: My Story* (1999).

▌. BEFORE YOU READ

Read through the introduction on page 188. Clarify that students will **skim** the selection as a prereading activity. Have them first take a look at the fact sheet at the bottom of the page so they know what kind of information they'll be looking for during their skims. (Refer to the **Strategy Handbook** on page 40 for more help.)

Motivation Strategy

As an opening activity, ask students to tell you what they know about Rosa Parks. Write any questions they have about her on the board. Students can keep these questions in mind as they read the selection.

ENGAGING STUDENTS Explain that Rosa Parks is a woman who found the courage to speak out against discrimination. Ask students to think about a time they took a stand against discrimination or injustice. What happened and how did they feel? Help students connect the theme of the selection to their own lives. Encourage them to discuss examples of injustices they've seen at school, at home, in their towns, and on the news.

Vocabulary Building

Help students use **context clues** as they read to figure out the meanings of difficult words, especially the key vocabulary for this lesson: *segregation, morale, deprived, descendant,* and *proclamation.* Have students circle these words in the text. Although the footnotes define these words, students should try to use context clues to see if they can come up with meanings that are close to the ones in a dictionary. Remind them that synonyms and definitions in the form of appositive or explanatory phrases can function as context clues. For additional practice with these words, see page 236.

STRATEGY LESSON: SYNONYMS As an alternate vocabulary exercise, ask students to offer synonyms for these words from the selection: *struggle, alterations, appreciated, vacant, furious,* and *domestic.* Remind the class that learning the synonym for a word is like learning a shortcut to the word's full definition.

For additional practice on this strategy, see the **Vocabulary** blackline master, page 236.

Prereading Strategies

During a **skim**, students glance through the selection quickly and look for words and phrases that can reveal information about the topic. Skimming gives readers an idea of what they can expect during their close readings, and can alert them to words and ideas that might cause difficulty. If you like, work through the fact sheet on page 188 as a group after they've all finished skimming. This can help students see that everyone skims differently. Not everyone will catch every detail.

PREVIEW As an alternate prereading strategy, ask students to do a preview of "Rosa Parks." This also will help familiarize them with the topic and writing style of the interview. Ask them to read the first and last paragraph of the interview. Then have them look at the photos, vocabulary words, and interrupter questions. Ask: "What is the topic of this selection? Why would the author have wanted to interview this person? What do you think the most difficult part(s) of the article will be?"

Spanish-speaking Students

La decisión que tomó Rosa Parks a no moverse de su asiento en el frente de un autobús en 1955 cambió la sociedad en los Estados Unidos para siempre. En su entrevista con Brian Lanker, Parks describe su motivación por desobedecer las leyes racistas y las consecuencias de sus acciones. Ella había inspirado a miles de personas a lograr cambios sociales y legales. Su cuento es un ejemplo a todos de lo bueno que puede resultar de la acción de una persona.

II. READ

As students begin to read, remind them to write their **questions** and comments in the **Response Notes**. Each time they think of a question to ask, it means they are thinking critically about the meaning or message of the selection. When the entire class has finished reading, lead a group discussion of any questions that are still bothering students. Work together to find answers and discuss various interpretations.

Response Strategy

REACT AND CONNECT In addition to having students write their questions, you also might want to ask them to react and connect to what they're reading. This response strategy gives students a chance to note their immediate reactions to Parks's reminiscences. Sometimes a reader's first reactions and thoughts about a piece end up being the most insightful of all.

Comprehension Strategies

In their reciprocal readings of "Rosa Parks," pairs of students will alternate reading aloud to each other. Occasionally readers will interrupt in order to ask questions that will elicit factual and inferential responses. There are four types of questions used in a **reciprocal reading:** 1. questions that ask students to clarify the problem, characters, and setting; 2. questions that ask students to predict outcomes; 3. questions that ask readers to summarize the events; and 4. questions about the literature, author's message, and main idea.

For more help, see the **Comprehension** blackline master on page 237.

Discussion Questions

COMPREHENSION 1. Why was Rosa Parks so tired? *(She worked long, back-breaking hours and had a difficult trip to and from work.)*

2. Why did she refuse to give up her seat on the bus? *(She felt she had a right to sit there.)*

3. What did the bus driver do when Parks said she wouldn't get up? *(He called the police.)*

4. What did the police do with Parks? *(They arrested her.)*

CRITICAL THINKING 5. Why did the other African Americans stand behind Parks when she was arrested? *(Answers will vary. Possible: They too were tired of being pushed around and discriminated against.)*

6. What three descriptive words would you use to describe Parks? *(Answers will vary. Have students support what they say with evidence from the story.)*

Literary Skill

POINT OF VIEW You might take this opportunity to discuss point of view with students. Remind the class that point of view is the vantage point from which an author presents the events of a story. Ask students to think about the point of view of "Rosa Parks." Although the selection is an interview, the interviewer, Brian Lanker, omitted his questions. He chose instead to record what she said as she said it, with no editorializing. Lanker correctly assumed that Parks's voice would have a more powerful impact on readers.

III. GATHER YOUR THOUGHTS

The prewriting activities on pages 193–194 are designed to prepare students to write a three-paragraph essay about an important event. Students will begin by **summarizing** and **organizing** information about an important event in Rosa Parks's life—her refusal to give up her bus seat to a white man. First they'll complete an organizer that shows what she did. Then they'll read through the same information in outline form.

After they've finished reading the example, students will choose an event from their own lives to write about. They'll outline the event on page 194.

Prewriting Strategies

GRAPHIC ORGANIZER As an additional prewriting strategy, ask students to complete an organizer (similar to the one on page 193) that explores the important event they want to write about. Ask them to name the who, what, where, when, why, and how of the event. Then have them write a sentence summarizing why the event had such an impact on them.

Have students use the **Prewriting** blackline master on page 238.

IV. WRITE

Ask students to give their **three-paragraph essays** to a writing partner for review. Writing partners should check to make sure that the topic sentence is clear and that the support is adequate. Details should be vivid and interesting.

WRITING RUBRIC Use this writing rubric to help students focus on the assignment requirements and for help with a quick assessment of their essays.

Do students' essays

- contain a title, introduction, body, and conclusion?

- open with a topic sentence and close with a concluding sentence?

- stay focused on the important event stated in the topic sentence?

Students should take into account their partner's comments when they begin revising their essays. At this point, you may want to draw students' attention to the **Writers' Checklist**.

Grammar, Usage, and Mechanics

Teach a brief mini-lesson on abbreviations. Remind students that abbreviations are used only when necessary, although some abbreviations have become a part of standard English (for example, Dr., Mr., Ms., and Mrs.). Writers should abbreviate personal titles only when they are placed right before a proper name. For the most part, students should avoid using abbreviations for days of the week, holidays, months, states, and countries.

Incorrect: The dr. went to CO on the Tues. after Xmas.

Correct: The doctor went to Colorado on the Tuesday after Christmas.

V. WRAP-UP

Take a moment at the end of the lesson for students to reflect on their **understanding** using the **Readers' Checklist**. Its intent is to help students ask the kinds of questions good readers ask of themselves and to see that people read for a variety of purposes.

Assessment

To test students' comprehension, use the **Assessment** blackline master on page 239.

Name _____

VOCABULARY

Words from the Selection

DIRECTIONS Read these sentences from "Rosa Parks." Use context clues and your knowledge of the interview with Rosa Parks to figure out what the underlined words mean. Then write the meaning of the word on the line.

1. "The decision was made by the three of us, my husband, my mother, and me, that I would go on and use my case as a test case challenging <u>segregation</u> on the buses."

_____

2. "Mass meetings were keeping the <u>morale</u> up."

_____

3. "Some white people who were not wanting to be <u>deprived</u> of their domestic help would just go themselves and pick up the people who were working for them."

_____

4. "My desires were to be free as soon as I had learned that there had been slavery of human beings and that I was a <u>descendant</u> from them."

_____

5. "If there was a <u>proclamation</u> setting those who were slaves free, I thought they should be indeed free and not have any type of slavery put upon us."

_____

Strategy Lesson: Synonyms

DIRECTIONS Draw a line between the word in Column A that is a synonym of the word in Column B. The words in Column A are from the selection.

Column A	Column B
domestic	fight
6. struggle	angry
7. alterations	adjustments
8. appreciated	household
9. vacant	treasured
10. furious	empty

Name _____

COMPREHENSION
Reciprocal Reading

DIRECTIONS With a partner, work through the answers to these questions.

1. CLARIFY. Why was Rosa Parks asked to change her seat on the bus?

_____

_____

_____

2. SUMMARIZE. What was Rosa Parks's chief desire in life?

_____

_____

_____

3. PREDICT. Based on what you've read, what do you think Rosa Parks would say to people today who feel discriminated against?

_____

_____

_____

4. QUESTION. If you had the chance, what question or questions would you like to ask Rosa Parks?

_____

_____

_____

_____

Name _____

PREWRITING
Writing an Introduction
....

DIRECTIONS   The most important part of any essay you write will be the **introduction**. In the introduction, you might

1. grab your reader's attention with a story;

2. give the thesis for the essay;

3. introduce your support.

STEP 1.   WRITE AN ANECDOTE. Stories can capture a reader's attention like nothing else. As often as possible, begin with a brief anecdote that helps illustrate the point you want to make. (If you need help writing your anecdote, see pages 166–168 of your book.)

My essay topic: _____

An anecdote from my own life that relates to my topic:

_____

_____

_____

_____

STEP 2.   WRITE A THESIS STATEMENT. A thesis statement is a sentence that tells the purpose or main idea of an essay. Like topic sentences, thesis statements must be clear and direct. Use this formula to write a thesis statement.

Your topic + your ideas or feelings about your topic = a good thesis statement.

EXAMPLE: Rosa Parks + she is a person to admire = Rosa Parks is a woman we can all admire.

My thesis statement: _____

STEP 3.   INTRODUCE YOUR SUPPORT. Then tell your readers how you will support your thesis statement. Make the explanation one sentence long.

EXAMPLE: Rosa Parks is a woman we can all admire. Her most admirable qualities include her bravery on the bus, her leadership during the boycott, and her untiring work during the Civil Rights movement.

Sentence that introduces my support:

_____

_____

Name _____

ASSESSMENT

Multiple-Choice Test

DIRECTIONS On the blanks provided, write the letter of the best answer for each question.

_____ 1. How did Rosa Parks feel about African Americans having to go up North to find freedom?
A. hopeful
C. indifferent
B. resentful
D. none of the above

_____ 2. According to this selection, where did African Americans experience discrimination?
A. in hat stores
C. on buses
B. in shoe stores
D. all of the above

_____ 3. Where was Rosa Parks coming from when she got on the bus?
A. school
C. her job
B. her mother's house
D. a shopping trip

_____ 4. Who or what did she recognize when she got on the bus?
A. the bus number
C. the white man for whom she was asked to get up
B. the bus driver
D. a policeman

_____ 5. What tone of voice does Parks use when she says she will not give up her seat?
A. sad
C. angry
B. resentful
D. calm

_____ 6. When did Parks ride a segregated bus again?
A. the next time it rained
C. the next time she had to go a long distance
B. the next time it was really cold
D. never

_____ 7. How did Parks feel when others joined her cause?
A. appreciative
C. overwhelmed
B. jealous
D. scared

_____ 8. How did African Americans get to work during the bus boycott?
A. Black cab drivers drove them.
C. Some whites drove them to work.
B. They carpooled with each other.
D. all of the above

_____ 9. How does Parks feel about change?
A. It is dangerous.
C. It should be taken slowly.
B. It is necessary.
D. all of the above

_____ 10. When do you think this interview with Rosa Parks took place?
A. when she was a child
C. shortly after the bus incident
B. when she was in college
D. long after the bus incident

Short-Essay Test

Do you think Rosa Parks feels satisfied with the changes that have occurred over the years? Why or why not?

Images of War

Unit Background   IMAGES OF WAR (pages 197–218)

Two accounts of war are included in this unit, excerpts from *The Red Badge of Courage* (1895) and *The Cay* (1969). Although Stephen Crane had never been in battle, he was able to write movingly of the experiences of a young Civil War soldier, Henry Fleming, who is both frightened and horrified at what he learns of war. In fact, Crane was born in 1871, well after the Civil War. As a reporter, Crane did cover the Greco-Turkish War of 1897 and the Spanish-American War of 1898. His famous short story "The Open Boat" is based on his experience afloat in a dinghy after the gun-running ship he was on exploded in 1897.

Theodore Taylor was born in 1921 in North Carolina. He has worked as reporter, sports editor, press agent, and writer in Hollywood and has written fiction and nonfiction for young people and adults. His award-winning book, *The Cay*, grew out of a time he was stationed in the Caribbean while in the naval reserve.

Teaching the Introduction

Page 197 shows the dead on a Civil War battlefield and Union General Ulysses S. Grant. The map shows the location of Willemstad, setting for Taylor's book, and a surfacing submarine.

1. Ask students what they know about the Civil War. What were the two sides? Where were the battles fought? What do they know about the number of casualties? (More than 359,000 Union soldiers and 258,000 Confederate soldiers died.)

2. Students may not know that during World War II German submarines penetrated as far south as the Caribbean. The second paragraph of the excerpt from *The Cay* makes clear that the targets were oil refineries. After students study the map on page 197, ask why German U-boats would strike at Allied oil refineries.

3. Ask students how they think writers of fiction would find out about episodes of a war in which they did not participate. What kind of material would they research? (historical accounts, diaries, memoirs, letters)

Opening Activity

Since students are asked to write a review at the end of this unit, ask each student to bring in a short book review, or you might provide some short reviews of young adult books and make them available for students to browse through.

A Taste of War

Skills and Strategies Overview

THEME	Images of War
READING LEVEL	challenging
VOCABULARY	◇couriers ◇melancholy ◇tattered ◇sidle ◇industriously
PREREADING	picture walk
RESPONSE	react
COMPREHENSION	timeline / sequence
PREWRITING	brainstorming
WRITING	story beginning / subject-verb agreement
ASSESSMENT	depth

BACKGROUND

American author Stephen Crane (1871–1900) probably did more to advance the genre of literary realism than any other novelist in American literature. His first book, *Maggie: A Girl of the Streets,* is an uncompromisingly realistic view of a slum girl's descent into prostitution. The book became a sensation because of its subject matter and because it was so very different from the highly romanticized novels and stories that were popular during this period.

By the time he wrote his next novel, *The Red Badge of Courage,* Crane had perfected his realistic technique. In this novel of the American Civil War, Crane offers a detailed view of war. The story is told through the point of view of an ordinary solider—Henry Fleming—who is eager to demonstrate his patriotism and bravery in a glorious battle. When the slaughter actually begins, however, Henry is overwhelmed by fear and flees the battlefield. In this excerpt, Henry struggles with his feelings of fear and confusion about war and bloodshed.

UNIT THEME Stephen Crane offers an "eyewitness" account of a Civil War battle.

GRAPHIC ORGANIZER An organizer like this one can help students track events in the excerpt.

STORY TITLE "A Taste of War"

BEFORE A large Civil War battle has been fought. The youth's army is defeated.

BEGINNING The youth and his fellow soldiers march back from battle.

MIDDLE A tattered man approaches the youth and tries to engage him in conversation.

END The youth flees the tattered man and his endless questions.

SUMMARY A young man in uniform marches alongside a group of battle-weary soldiers. A wounded soldier approaches the boy and tries to engage him in a discussion of the unit's defeat. When the man asks where the boy has been wounded, the youth flees without responding.

BEFORE YOU READ

Read through the introduction to the lesson on page 198. Be sure students understand how valuable it can be to preview the art of a selection. Then have them do the lesson's prereading activity, a **picture walk**. (Refer to the **Strategy Handbook** on page 40 for more help.)

Motivation Strategy

In "A Taste of War," Stephen Crane gives readers a quick glimpse of the American Civil War. Work with students to create a "fact" list about this war. When was it fought? Who was involved? What was the outcome? Keep the list on the board for students to refer to as they write.

ENGAGING STUDENTS To help students connect Crane's story to their own lives, ask: "What kind of soldier would you be? Would you be brave or cowardly or something in-between? Why?" These questions will help prepare students for the ambivalence that Crane's protagonist feels.

Vocabulary Building

Help students use **synonyms** as a shortcut to memorizing the full definitions of unfamiliar or difficult words. Show students the key vocabulary words for this lesson: *couriers, melancholy, tattered, sidle,* and *industriously*. Ask students to circle the words in their texts. Have volunteers offer a synonym for each word. A quick vocabulary exercise like this one can help prepare students to read a selection that is full of unfamiliar vocabulary. For additional practice with key vocabulary words, see page 246.

STRATEGY LESSON: IDIOMS As an additional vocabulary lesson, you might spend some time discussing idioms. An idiom is a phrase or expression that means something different from the ordinary meanings of the words. For example, some people say "make like a tree" to indicate it is time to leave (leaf). For some students, especially students who speak English as a second language, idiomatic expressions are perplexing. You might offer this advice: "To understand an idiom, try picturing the action described." For example, if you visualize "talking across pickets" you get a picture of two people (neighbors) chatting across a fence. More than likely the visualization of the idiom will provide valuable clues about what the idiom means. Ask students to visualize these idioms: "He hung his head"; "Hold your tongue"; and "He was on thin ice." See how close they can come to defining what the idioms mean.

For additional practice on this strategy, see the **Vocabulary** blackline master, page 246.

Prereading Strategies

PICTURE WALK As a prereading strategy, students will do a picture walk of "A Taste of War." Have them tell you which pictures capture their attention and why. (Be sure to ask them if one or more of the pictures seem familiar. Students might recognize the photo of General Sherman on page 199, for example.) Also be sure that they read captions. What questions do they have about the captions? What do the pictures reveal about the conflict between the North and South during the war? Students can make notes about the art and their predictions on page 198.

Spanish-speaking Students

"Una prueba de la guerra" es parte de la novela famosa *The Red Badge of Courage*, escrita por Stephen Crane. Esta selección provee una vista de la realidad de la Guerra Civil, cuando soldados lucharon valientemente con las armas más avanzadas de la época, y sufrieron bajo el atrasamiento de la medicina. Un joven ingenuo que se ha entremetido en estas condiciones presencia el horror y la gloria de la guerra, e intenta entender su propio papel dentro de la lucha.

II. READ

Response Strategy

When students **react** to a selection, they explain how the selection makes them feel. This response strategy shows students that their individual responses to a reading can help them better understand the author's message. Encourage students to make detailed notes about their reactions to this excerpt. Do they have the same views as Crane did about war? Also remind students to make connections between what Crane describes and what they themselves have heard about war. Does any part of Crane's story seem familiar on a personal level? Have students heard stories about battles or war-related events that they'd like to share or write about later?

Comprehension Strategies

Clearly a **time line** or sequence organizer can be one of the most useful strategies that low-level students can use to understand a sequence of events. In the case of this excerpt, the timeline students create will be particularly handy because one of the most important events (the battle) occurs before the selection begins. Ask students to pay particular attention to the first organizer on page 200. The "Earlier" column is a place where students can record their inferences about what happened before the events described here. Encourage them to be creative in their inferences, although they should be able to support anything they say with evidence from the selection.

DIRECTED READING As an alternate comprehension strategy, try doing a directed reading of the selection. In a directed reading, the teacher or group leader reads the selection aloud, pausing every once in awhile to pose **stop and think** questions that can help students make factual and inferential responses. A directed reading allows you to see what is causing problems in the selection. Using students' feedback as a guide, you might want to speed up or slow down the pace of the reading.

For more help, see the **Comprehension** blackline master on page 247.

Discussion Questions

COMPREHENSION 1. What war are these men fighting? *(the American Civil War)*

2. Where are the men coming from? *(a battle)*

CRITICAL THINKING 3. Why does the tattered man talk to the youth? *(Answers will vary. Perhaps he is lonely or excited from the battle and hoping to relive it.)*

4. How does the youth feel about the tattered man? *(He doesn't know what to make of him and is not sure how to answer his many questions.)*

Literary Skill

DIALECT To introduce a literary skill with this selection, you might teach a short lesson on dialect. Explain to students that dialect is a form of speech characteristic of a class or region. Dialect differs from the standard language in pronunciation, vocabulary, and grammatical form. In *The Red Badge of Courage*, Crane uses dialect liberally in order to make his story seem as realistic as possible. He indicates the tattered man's dialect by spelling the man's words the way they would sound (*keerful* for *careful*) and having him use informal language and idioms ("yeh can't lick them boys"). Crane knew that many of the bravest, most decorated veterans from the Civil War were very much like the simple, uneducated men that the war-weary youth meets on his retreat from the battle. If students seem puzzled by idioms, you might ask them to complete the "Strategy Lesson: Idioms" exercise on the **Vocabulary** blackline master. See page 246.

III. GATHER YOUR THOUGHTS

On page 204, students will **brainstorm** what they know about the youth and the tattered man. Encourage them to refer to the story to be sure they correctly describe each person. On the left side of the page, students will record what the man is like. On the right side, students will say how they feel about the character.

On the following page, students will plan a new **story beginning** for "A Taste of War." Before they begin planning, remind the class that they'll need to use the same characters and stay with the same basic setting in their openers. Students may decide to describe how the characters look, how they walk, and so on. They may also want to give specific details about time and place, since Crane's description of setting is very general at this point in the novel. Encourage them to rely on prior knowledge about the Civil War in their descriptions.

Prewriting Strategies

JOURNAL ENTRY As an alternate prewriting strategy, have students write a journal entry for one of the two main characters in the selection. This activity will help them to better understand the "voice" of the character, his mood, thoughts, and emotions. Direct students to write about the character's day—his thoughts and feelings after the battle and long march.

Have students use the **Prewriting** blackline master on page 248.

IV. WRITE

On page 206, students are asked to write a new **story beginning** for "A Taste of War." Their new story beginning should provide a more detailed analysis of character and setting than is included in the pupil book. Remind them to use their planners to help them write.

WRITING RUBRIC Use this writing rubric to help students focus on the assignment requirements and for help with a quick assessment of their writing.

Do students' story beginnings

- offer details about both characters?
- include sensory details and dialogue?
- seem a good "fit" with Crane's "A Taste of War"?

Grammar, Usage, and Mechanics

After they've finished a first draft, draw students attention to the **Writers' Checklist** and consider teaching a brief mini-lesson on subject-verb agreement. Remind the class to think carefully about agreement when using verbs such as *is, has, were* and *are* with compound subjects. These verbs and their various forms often prove difficult for inexperienced writers. For example:

Incorrect: Both Northern and Southern soldiers was killed by disease.

Correct: Both Northern and Southern soldiers were killed by disease.

V. WRAP-UP

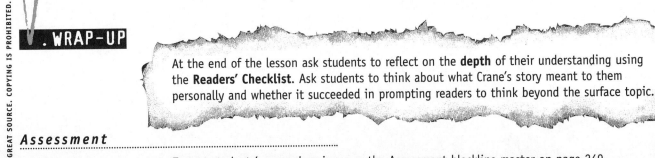

At the end of the lesson ask students to reflect on the **depth** of their understanding using the **Readers' Checklist.** Ask students to think about what Crane's story meant to them personally and whether it succeeded in prompting readers to think beyond the surface topic.

Assessment

To test students' comprehension, use the Assessment blackline master on page 249.

Name _____

VOCABULARY

Words from the Selection

DIRECTIONS Answer these questions that use words from the selection. Explain your answers.

1. Does a galloping horse <u>sidle</u> past you? _____

2. Do <u>couriers</u> deliver letters or food? _____

3. Is a <u>tattered</u> book old or new? _____

4. Would you want to hire a person who works <u>industriously</u>? _____

5. Who feels more <u>melancholy</u>, someone who cries or someone who laughs?

_____

Vocabulary Strategy: Idioms

An **idiom** is a phrase or expression that means something different from what the words actually say. For example, some people say *He's in over his head* to mean *He doesn't understand.*

DIRECTIONS Draw a line from the idioms in Column A to their correct meanings in Column B.

Column A

6. Hold your tongue.

7. Make up your mind.

8. She was walking on air.

9. He was talking across pickets.

10. He hung his head.

11. He kicked the bucket.

12. Use one of the idioms in Column A in a sentence of your own.

Column B

Decide.

He was ashamed.

Stop talking.

He was chatting with a neighbor.

He died.

She was very happy.

_____

_____

_____

Name _____

COMPREHENSION
Sketch a Place

Sometimes drawing a place can help you get ready to write about it.

DIRECTIONS   Draw the scene that Crane describes in "A Taste of War." Make your background as detailed as possible. Then answer some questions about the setting of the story.

where do you think "A Taste of War" takes place?

_____

what year do you think it is?

what time of the year is it? Is it spring, summer, winter, or fall?

Is it a sunny day or a cloudy one? (circle one)

what else can you "see" about the time and place?

_____

Name _____

PREWRITING
Plan a Story Opening

DIRECTIONS Use this story pie to plan what you will say in your new opening for "A Taste of War." Fill in as much information as you can and give as many details as you like.

Story Pie: A New Opening for "A Taste of War"

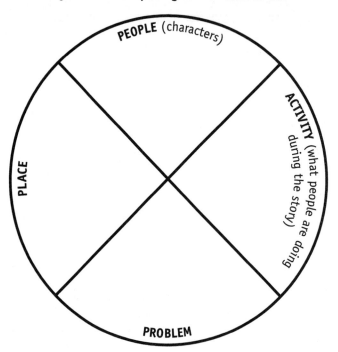

Write Dialogue

Next write some dialogue for your story opening. When writing dialogue, you need to consider these three questions:

- Who is there?
- What are they saying? (What topic are they discussing?)
- How are they saying it? (Are they angry? tired? sad?)

STEP 1. Which characters will be in your opening scene?

_____

STEP 2. What are the characters talking about?

_____

STEP 3. How are the characters talking? (Are they *muttering, laughing, murmuring, questioning, shouting, whispering, replying, giggling,* or *crying*?)

How they're saying it: _____

_____

Name _____

ASSESSMENT

Multiple-Choice Test

DIRECTIONS On the blanks provided, write the letter of the item that best answers each question or completes each statement.

_____ 1. What does the youth observe in the beginning of the story?
A. men marching to war
B. men coming back from a battle
C. a battle going on
D. none of the above

_____ 2. The tattered man and the youth hear about the battle from a . . .
A. sergeant.
B. prisoner.
C. drummer boy.
D. local inn-keeper.

_____ 3. How many wounds does the tattered man have?
A. none
B. one
C. two
D. many

_____ 4. How does the youth know the tattered man has a wound to the head?
A. He can't understand him.
B. He wears a blood-soaked rag.
C. He wears a bandage.
D. He wears a patch.

_____ 5. When the tattered man starts to talk to the youth, the boy . . .
A. questions him about the battle.
B. runs away.
C. ignores him completely.
D. is polite and walks faster.

_____ 6. What does the tattered man say about the day's battle?
A. His side ran out of ammunition.
B. The general was killed.
C. It was a good fight.
D. none of the above

_____ 7. What is the tattered man's attitude toward the army?
A. He loves the army.
B. He hates the army.
C. He is puzzled by the army.
D. He is saddened by the army.

_____ 8. What does the tattered man want to know about the youth at the end?
A. the year he joined the army
B. his age
C. where he is from
D. where he is injured

_____ 9. How does the boy respond to the man's last question?
A. He starts to cry.
B. He yells at the man.
C. He slides through the crowd.
D. He answers quietly.

_____ 10. What word best describes the youth?
A. nervous
B. angry
C. cheerful
D. regretful

Short-Essay Test

Explain why you think the boy runs away from the tattered man.

War Comes to Our Island

Skills and Strategies Overview

THEME Images of War

READING LEVEL easy

VOCABULARY

◇Caribbean ◇pontoon bridge ◇horizon ◇binoculars ◇torpedo

PREREADING walk-through

RESPONSE question

COMPREHENSION clarify

PREWRITING topic sentence and supporting details

WRITING review / titles

ASSESSMENT style

BACKGROUND

Theodore Taylor's novel *The Cay* is a powerful novel of prejudice, love, and survival. In *The Cay*, 11-year-old Phillip Enright, who lives with his family on the Dutch island of Curaçao, is forced to flee his beloved island when World War II moves too close for comfort. Phillip's parents decide that he and his mother will travel by boat to stay with relatives who live in Virginia.

On their way to Virginia, however, their boat is torpedoed by the Germans. Phillip is blinded and ends up adrift on a life raft with an elderly West Indian native named Timothy. Eventually, Phillip's distrust of the old man turns to love and admiration. Timothy's simple message that all friendships are colorblind makes this novel memorable to young people and adults alike.

In this excerpt from *The Cay*, Phillip and his friend Henrik learn that the war is dangerously close. Although first they think of it as a big game, the boys soon learn that war is terribly dangerous.

UNIT THEME Two young boys learn the lesson that war is very serious business.

GRAPHIC ORGANIZER This organizer can help to provide background for "War Comes to Our Island."

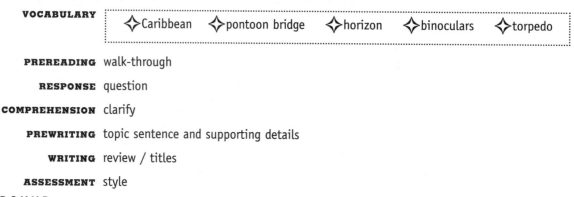

1939	1940	1941	1942	1943	1944	1945
Germany invades Czechoslovakia and Poland. Britain, France, Australia, New Zealand, and India declare war on Germany.	Germany invades Denmark, Norway, Belgium, and France. Japan and Italy join forces with Germany to form the Axis Powers. Allied Powers fight back but suffer terrible losses.	Germany eventually takes control of the Soviet Union. Allied powers continue to wage war against the Axis Powers. Japan bombs Pearl Harbor. The United States joins war effort.	Battles on all fronts.	Allies invade Italy; Allied Powers wage war in Russia. Their victory is a turning point in the war.	Allied Powers invade Normandy, France.	United States captures Nuremberg, Germany. Germany surrenders. United States bombs Hiroshima and Nagasaki, Japan. Japan surrenders.

BEFORE YOU READ

Before you begin, you might give students a brief overview of the key events of World War II. Explain that the action of "War Comes to Our Island" takes place in 1940, after Germany has invaded Denmark. When you feel students are ready, turn their attention to the prereading activity for the lesson, a **walk-through**. (Refer to the **Strategy Handbook** on page 40 for more help.)

Motivation Strategy

In "War Comes to the Island," two boys learn how scary war can be. Ask students to discuss war movies they've seen and books they've read. What are their impressions of war? What makes it so frightening?

ENGAGING STUDENTS To help them connect the theme to their own lives, ask students to complete this sentence: "I think war is _____." Then have them explain their answers. When they've finished reading the selection, ask the class if anyone wants to change the way they completed the sentence. If some students do, find out what changed their minds.

Vocabulary Building

The most efficient way to uncover the meaning of an unfamiliar word is to examine it in context. It's quicker and easier than turning to a dictionary. Good readers know that writers often leave clues about a word somewhere in the word's environment. Sometimes these clues appear in the same sentence; other times they can be found in the preceding or following sentences. Ask students to practice defining these key vocabulary words in context: *Caribbean, pontoon bridge, horizon, binoculars*, and *torpedo*. Although each of these words is footnoted at the bottom of the page, students should check the footnote only as a last resort. First they should try to define on their own. Ask students to circle the vocabulary words in the text. For more help with vocabulary work, see page 254.

STRATEGY LESSON: PREFIXES AND SUFFIXES Help students learn the definitions for common prefixes such as *bi-* and *fore-*; and common suffixes such as *-less, -est, -ness,* and *-ful*. Explain that prefixes and suffixes can give clues about the meaning of the word in addition to information about how the word should be used in a sentence. Encourage them to practice with these words from the selection: *darkness, moonless, oldest, binoculars*, and *peaceful*.

For additional practice on this strategy, see the **Vocabulary** blackline master, page 254.

Prereading Strategies

Doing a **walk-through** before reading can help familiarize students with the topic of the selection. This is a particularly valuable strategy to use when you know that the topic will be an unfamiliar one, such as life in Curaçao during World War II. Remind students to look at each photo and caption carefully. Have them record their responses on the chart on page 208. Also ask them to note any pictures they think are particularly interesting or puzzling. You may want to discuss these before students begin their close readings.

PICTURE WALK As an alternate prereading strategy, ask students to do a picture walk. Have them tell you what the pictures remind them of. Based on what they've seen, what do they predict the selection will be about? When they've finished reading, they might return to the pictures and explain what connections they see between the art and the story.

Spanish-speaking Students

"La guerra llega a nuestra isla" viene de la novela *The Cay*, de autor Theodore Taylor. Como la anterior, esta selección examina el terror e inmensa atracción a la guerra. Es el año 1942 durante la Segunda Guerra Mundial, y los Nazis acaban de conquistar Holanda. Aunque está ubicada en el Carribe, lejos de las batallas en Europa, la isla holandesa de Curaçaosche está en peligro de un ataque de los Nazis. Para dos jóvenes de la isla que han guiado sus vidas soñando con luchar y jugando a juegos de guerra, el ataque pendiente es algo emocionante y aterrorizante.

II. READ

As students begin to read, walk through the process of responding to literature. Tell students that they are to **clarify** the main events, and point out the example given in the **Response Notes**. Then ask students to begin reading. Remind them to make a note of important events. They'll use these notes to complete their story frames.

Response Strategy

QUESTION Questions such as "What's going on here?" and "What is he talking about?" are a reader's way of talking himself or herself through a selection. Encourage students to make a note when they catch themselves asking a question. Also have them note how they went about answering each question. Questions that remain unanswered at the end of the reading can be addressed by the whole group.

Comprehension Strategies

Students are asked to fill in **story frames** as they are reading "War Comes to Our Island." Story frames can help students understand the sequence of events in a story. As an added benefit, story frames can prod the reader into thinking carefully about elements of setting, character, and plot. Encourage students to reread their story frame notes once they've finished the selection. They may find that they need to make small revisions to their thoughts and ideas.

PREDICTIONS As an alternate comprehension strategy, ask students to make predictions as they read Taylor's story. Making predictions is an excellent strategy for low-level or reluctant readers because it helps them become engaged in what they're reading. Prediction questions ask students to consider outcomes and encourage them to ponder issues such as character motivation. If you like, have students stop at each story frame interrupter and make two predictions, one about character (Phillip or Henrik) and the other about the action.

For more help, see the **Comprehension** blackline master on page 255.

Discussion Questions

COMPREHENSION 1. Where does the story take place? *(on the island of Curaçao, which is off the coast of Venezuela)*

2. Why do Phillip and Henrik go to the pontoon bridge? *(They are curious about the invasion. They want to see what war looks like.)*

3. Who is Henrik and what's he like? *(He is Phillip's friend. He's a little more self-confident than Phillip and a little more brash.)*

CRITICAL THINKING 4. At what point does Phillip realize that his island really is at war? *(Answers will vary. Accept reasonable responses that can be supported with evidence from the story.)*

5. Does Phillip regret the events of his day? *(Again, remind students to support their interpretations with evidence from the story.)*

Literary Skill

CLIMAX If you'd like to introduce a literary skill with this lesson, you might discuss the characteristics of a plot's climax with students. The climax is the point of the highest dramatic tension or a major turning point in a literary work. It is the most decisive moment in the plot. In most stories, books, and plays, the climax occurs somewhere near the end. In "War Comes to Our Island," the climax occurs when Phillip realizes that his trip to the Queen Emma bridge was foolish and dangerous. Phillip's admission of his mistake comprises the falling action of the plot.

III. GATHER YOUR THOUGHTS

The goal of these prewriting activities is to help students decide whether or not they liked Taylor's story so that they can write a thoughtful **review** of it. You'll notice that students are asked to evaluate the story in terms of its plot, characters, setting, and theme. In most literature reviews, these four elements are discussed in some detail.

Prewriting Strategies

SUPPORTING DETAILS Remind the class that it is never enough to simply say that a story is "bad" or "good." The reviewer needs to support his or her opinion with evidence from the selection. If, for example, students say that the plot of Taylor's story is weak, then they'll need to find two or three places in the text that they see the plot falling apart for one reason or another. The same is true for their critiques of character, setting, and theme.

For additional practice, have students use the **Prewriting** blackline master on page 256.

IV. WRITE

Set aside plenty of time for students to write their **reviews**. If you like, have students discuss their opinions before actually writing about them. This may help them fine-tune what they want to say in their reviews.

WRITING RUBRIC Use the writing rubric to help students focus on the assignment requirements and for help with a quick assessment of their writing.

Do students' reviews

- open with a clear opinion statement?

- discuss one or more of the major elements of the story: plot, character, setting, and theme?

- support the opinion statement with evidence from the story?

Grammar, Usage, and Mechanics

When they've finished a first draft, turn students' attention to the **Writers' Checklist** on page 217. This information will be important since they'll be referring to Taylor's story throughout their reviews. You might take this opportunity to teach a mini-lesson on writing titles. Remind the class that quotation marks are used for titles of chapters, poems, short stories, and articles. Italics or an underscore are used to indicate the titles of books, films, long poems, magazines, and newspapers. For example:

Incorrect: War Comes to Our Island is an excerpt from "The Cay."

Correct: "War Comes to Our Island" is an excerpt from *The Cay*.

V. WRAP-UP

Take a moment at the end of the lesson for students to reflect on Theodore Taylor's writing **style** using the **Readers' Checklist** as a guide. Ask them to ponder such questions as these: "Is the story well-written? What might the author have done differently to improve the writing?" This quick assessment activity will give students the chance to act as editor of a published work. This will help boost their confidence and show them that their opinions are valid—that what they say really does matter.

Assessment

To test students' comprehension, use the **Assessment** blackline master on page 257.

Name _____

VOCABULARY

Words from the Selection

DIRECTIONS Underline the word or words that provide context clues to the meaning of each vocabulary word.

1. "I wanted to go . . . to Fort Amsterdam where I could look out to sea."
   "The whole world was at war, and now it had come to us in the warm, blue <u>Caribbean</u>."

2. ". . . I was standing on the famous <u>pontoon bridge</u> . . ."
   "The bridge is built on floats so that it can swing open."

3. "It was all so real that sometimes we could see the tall masted ships coming over the <u>horizon</u>."

4. "Men with <u>binoculars</u> had them trained toward the white caps, and everyone was tense."

5. "Don't you know they could shoot a <u>torpedo</u> up here and kill you all?"

Strategy Lesson: Prefixes and Suffixes

DIRECTIONS Underline the prefixes and circle the suffixes in the numbered words. Then use each word in a sentence that shows you know what it means.

prefixes	suffixes
bi- = two	*-ness* = quality or condition of
fore- = before, earlier	*-less* = without
	-ful = full of
	-est = used to show the highest degree of comparison

EXAMPLE: <u>fore</u>(cast)   predicting something before it happens

6. darkness

_____

7. moonless

_____

8. oldest

_____

9. binoculars

_____

10. peaceful

_____

Name _____

COMPREHENSION
Graphic Organizer

DIRECTIONS Decide what you liked and didn't like about "War Comes to Our Island." Use this chart to keep track of your ideas. Be sure to explain your reasons.

What I liked about the story	What I didn't like about the story	My reasons

If you had written the story, what (if anything) would you have done differently with . . .

the plot
_____

_____

the characters
_____

_____

the setting
_____

_____

the theme
_____

_____

Name _____

PREWRITING
Writing a Review
....

DIRECTIONS In a review, you need to

√ offer readers information about the selection you are reviewing;

√ tell your opinion of the selection;

√ offer support for your opinion;

√ say whether or not you can recommend the selection.

STEP 1. OFFER INFORMATION. Open your review with some facts about the selection. Tell the story's title and the author's name, and then offer a brief plot summary.

story title: _____

author's name: _____

what the story's about: _____

_____

_____

_____

STEP 2. TELL YOUR OPINION. Write an opinion statement that tells if you did or didn't like the story. (The opinion statement should be the first sentence of your review.)

My opinion statement: _____

STEP 3. OFFER SUPPORT. Then support your opinion of the story. Your support should come directly from the story.

support #1: _____

_____

support #2: _____

_____

support #3: _____

STEP 4. MAKE A RECOMMENDATION. Say whether or not you want to recommend the story. This will be your closing sentence.

My closing sentence: _____

_____

Name _____

ASSESSMENT

Multiple-Choice Test

DIRECTIONS On the blanks provided, write the letter of the item that best answers each question or completes each statement.

_____ 1. The story takes place on an island off the coast of . . .
   A. Mexico.   C. France.
   B. Japan.   D. Venezuela.

_____ 2. What news does Phillip wake up to?
   A. A lake tanker has been blown up.   C. An American sub has been spotted off shore.
   B. There is war in Germany.   D. A German sub has been spotted off shore.

_____ 3. How does Phillip react to the news of the day?
   A. He's excited.   C. He's frightened.
   B. He's saddened.   D. He's angry.

_____ 4. What news does his mother share with Phillip?
   A. They will be leaving town.   C. Soldiers are in the streets.
   B. School is closed.   D. There is no food.

_____ 5. To prepare for war, Phillip's mother does everything except . . .
   A. stock up on extra water.   C. put extra blankets in the cellar.
   B. check the food supply.   D. put blackout curtains in place.

_____ 6. How old are Phillip and Henrik?
   A. 14   C. 18
   B. 13   D. 11

_____ 7. What do the boys see at the Queen Emma pontoon bridge?
   A. German U-boats in the harbor   C. Ships are preparing for war.
   B. Ships and boats are still.   D. Ships and boats have been destroyed.

_____ 8. How does Henrik know so much about the war?
   A. He watches it on TV.   C. He reads about it in the newspaper.
   B. His uncle is in the navy.   D. His father is connected to the government.

_____ 9. Who does Phillip hope will come and protect their island?
   A. the German navy   C. the Aruban navy
   B. the American navy   D. the Brazilian navy

_____ 10. How does Phillip feel at the end of the story?
   A. curious   C. scared
   B. angry   D. sad

Short-Essay Test

Explain how Phillip's attitude toward war changes from the beginning of the story to the end.

Isaac Asimov

Unit Background   **ISAAC ASIMOV** (pages 219–238)

This unit contains a short story by Isaac Asimov and an Asimov essay containing some tips for would-be writers.

Born in Petrovichi, U.S.S.R., Isaac Asimov came to the United States as a child with his parents. They settled in Brooklyn where his father owned and operated a candy store. Asimov's interest in science fiction started when he was a boy, and his first published short story was "Marooned Off Vesta" (1939).

Asimov obtained a Ph.D in biochemistry from Columbia University and became a full professor at Boston University in 1979. He wrote nearly 500 books—science fiction, biblical studies, mysteries, and nonfiction—and a sampling of his titles gives some idea of the range of his works: *I, Robot* (1950) *The Intelligent Man's Guide to Science* (1960, rev.1965), *Asimov's Guide to Shakespeare* (1970), *Isaac Asimov's Treasury of Humor* (1971), *The Bicentennial Man and Other Stories* (1977), and *Foundation's Edge* (1982). He worked for eight years on what become known as the *Foundation Trilogy*, works about a galactic empire. He won many Hugo and Nebula awards, the former given by the World Science Fiction Society and the latter by the Science Fiction and Fantasy Writers of America.

Teaching the Introduction

Photographs on page 219 show a NASA command center, Asimov, the heavens, and rocket scientists.

Isaac Asimov

Isaac Asimov

Isaac Asimov (1920–1992) was born in Russia and moved to the United States at age three. He studied and taught biochemistry before becoming a full-time writer in 1958. Asimov's interest in science carried over into much of his writing—nonfiction, novels, essays, and short stories. Asimov is recognized as one of the greatest science fiction writers ever.

ISAAC
THE FINAL
GOLD
SCIENCE FICTION COLLECTION
ASIMOV

219

1. Students may equate science fiction with bug-eyed monsters, but science fiction also deals with the possibilities of future wars and with technology as the Asimov story in this unit does. If any of your students are fans of science fiction, ask them to tell what they enjoy about stories, movies, or television programs that belong to the science-fiction genre. How big a part does technology play in the science fiction they know about?

2. In his essay on writing science fiction, Asimov says that one has to "know science." Ask students to talk about what kind of science they think a science-fiction writer needs to know. (Asimov's field was biochemistry, the science dealing with the chemistry of living matter.)

3. Some science-fiction writers, unlike Asimov, have criticized technology. Ask students to think of technology in their lives or of some aspects of technology today. Are there grounds for criticizing surveillance cameras, call-waiting, robots, the Internet, communication satellites, and Mars and Moon landings? If so, what are these grounds?

Opening Activity

Ray Bradbury, Arthur C. Clarke, and Isaac Asimov have all written stories that are easy to read. If students are familiar with works by these authors, ask them to tell the rest of the class what they know. Alternatively, ask students to write down one thing they have learned in a science class. Then ask them to tell how this learning might be used in a science-fiction story.

Frustration

Skills and Strategies Overview

THEME Isaac Asimov

READING LEVEL challenging

VOCABULARY

◇ beckoned ◇ analysis ◇ premium ◇ simulation ◇ bearable

PREREADING word web

RESPONSE question

COMPREHENSION reciprocal reading

PREWRITING quickwrite

WRITING journal entry / commas

ASSESSMENT ease

BACKGROUND

Isaac Asimov, one of the most highly successful and prolific writers of science fiction of all time, started his career as an instructor of biochemistry. Asimov used his extensive knowledge of biochemistry and related scientific fields to write about machines, organisms, and other beings that were highly detailed and utterly believable. It is for this reason—because of his emphasis on realism—that Asimov's stories and novels hold such strong appeal for readers. Every science-fiction story he wrote had a believable edge to it. His events and characters are on the fantastic side, but not so fantastic that the reader can't ask: "I wonder if . . . ?" or "Could this really be . . . ?"

"Frustration" is a short story taken from one of Asimov's more than thirty books. Interestingly, Asimov wrote this story in 1990, a few years *before* computers became commonplace in homes and offices. Even so, the war-mongering computer he describes in the story has capabilities that go beyond even what computers of today can do.

UNIT THEME Isaac Asimov asks an interesting thematic question: Eventually, who will run the world: humans or the machines that humans have invented?

GRAPHIC ORGANIZER Collection cards can help student researchers keep track of information when they go to the library or the Internet. For example, if you were to ask students to research the differences between the computer in "Frustration" and today's computers, students' collection cards might look something like this:

Collection Card	
Topic: Computers of 1980–1990	
Important Details:	
What they can do:	compute facts
	tabulate results
	create statistical
	programs
	talk to other computers
What they can't do:	word processing is
	difficult or impossible
	feel self-righteous
	start wars?
Who uses them?	scientists
	government officials
What do they use them for?	research
	national security
Summary of information:	
My information came from:	

Collection Card	
Topic: Computers of today	
Important Details:	
What they can do:	compute facts, tabulate
	results, create
	statistical programs
	talk to other computers
	word process
	talk
	start wars?
What they can't do:	think
	feel self-righteous
Who uses them?	almost everyone
What do they use them for?	almost anything
Summary of information:	
My information came from:	

BEFORE YOU READ

Read through the introduction to the lesson with students. Ask what Asimov books and stories they've read. Have volunteers explain to the rest of the class what Asimov's writing is like. Then have students turn to the prereading activity, a **word web**. (Refer to the **Strategy Handbook** on page 40 for more help.)

Motivation Strategy

In "Frustration," Asimov ponders an important question: Can a computer start a war? Ask students to give their own answers to this question. Have them support what they say with information from outside readings.

ENGAGING STUDENTS Explain that Asimov's story is in part about the possibility of the destructive power of technology. What do students know about this topic? What examples do they have from their own lives? Have they had a computer or car disaster, or a technology-related problem at school or at the mall? Ask students to tell their stories. The stories they tell may help them connect the topic of Asimov's writing to their own lives.

Vocabulary Building

Help your class learn the definitions for some common **suffixes,** including, *-tion, -able, -ly,* and *–ed.* Remind students that a suffix in a word can tell them how the word should be used in a sentence. As they read Asimov's story, have students watch carefully for highlighted words that contain suffixes. Ask them to try and define these words using context clues. They might notice these key vocabulary words: *beckoned, analysis, premium, simulation,* and *bearable.* Ask students to circle these words in the text. For additional practice with suffixes, see page 264.

STRATEGY LESSON: PREFIXES Tell students that the prefix *counter-* means "in opposition to; against; in return." For example, a counterattack is a return attack or an attack against another attack.

For additional practice on this strategy, see the **Vocabulary** blackline master, page 264.

Prereading Strategies

Word webs are important exercises for students because they help to improve vocabulary, which in turn can improve students' understanding of a text. Focusing on an abstract concept such as "self-righteousness" can also serve to sharpen students' critical thinking skills. To help them get started with the web on page 220, ask students to take a moment to think about the words in the middle and then, without pausing, write the images, ideas, examples, documents, and people that come to mind when they hear these words. Later, you might ask students to share their webs.

READ-ALOUD As an alternate prereading strategy, ask students to do a read-aloud of the first several paragraphs of the story. A read-aloud can ease reluctant readers into a story and hopefully arouse enough curiosity that they'll want to continue reading on their own. For this read-aloud, choose a reader who will read with expression. Ask students to follow along in their books, making notes in the **Response Notes** about words or sentences that interest or puzzle them.

Spanish-speaking Students

Se conoce a Isaac Asimov como un escritor de literatura de ciencia ficción. En "Frustración" el autor describe un mundo en lo cual los ordenadores son componentes imprescindibles en la vida diaria, especialmente en los negocios y la política. El gobierno quiere usar los ordenadores para determinar las mejores circunstancias para empezar una guerra y para asegurar una victoria. Un mundo guiado por las conclusiones de los ordenadores parece bastante asustante, pero como uno de los personajes indica, es mejor que ser guiado por un ser humano impulsivo.

II. READ

Response Strategy

As students begin to read, remind them to make comments in the **Response Notes** that will help them **clarify** the events or people that Asimov describes. Their comments might include notations, reactions, and questions for the author.

Comprehension Strategies

In a **reciprocal reading**, pairs of students alternate reading aloud to each other. Occasionally the reader will interrupt in order to ask questions designed to elicit factual and inferential responses. Four types of questions are used in a reciprocal reading: 1. questions that ask students to clarify the problem, characters, and setting ("What kind of war is Hargrove interested in waging?"); 2. questions that ask students to predict outcomes ("What do you think Gelb will do with information he has learned?"); 3. questions that ask readers to summarize the events ("What is Hargrove's computer capable of doing?"); and 4. questions about the literature, author's message, and main idea ("What message does Asimov have for his readers?").

DOUBLE-ENTRY JOURNAL As an additional comprehension strategy, you might have students create a series of double-entry journals that explore their reactions to Asimov's story. This comprehension strategy can encourage active response to a text. For a double-entry journal, students find statements, quotations, ideas, or events in the selection, record them, and then note their thoughts and feelings. To help students get started, you might ask them to respond to these two quotations from the story:

- "We've got a world to run, space to develop, computerization to extend."

- "There won't be a war. There's no realistic combination of events that would make the computer decide on war."

For more help, see the **Comprehension** blackline master on page 265.

Discussion Questions

COMPREHENSION 1. Who is Hargrove? *(Secretary of Foreign Affairs)*

2. Why does he want a war? *(He wants dominion over the entire world.)*

3. What kind of war is he talking about? *(a war run by computers instead of humans)*

4. Why does Jonsbeck agree to work on the Hargrove project? *(He needs the job.)*

CRITICAL THINKING 5. How does Gelb feel about Hargrove's ideas? *(Ask students to support their ideas with evidence from the selection.)*

6. What does the final line of the story mean? *(Have students review their webs on page 220 before answering this question. You might also ask them whether they agree that self-righteousness plays a role in the decision of whether or not to wage a war. Their responses may lead to some interesting discussions.)*

Literary Skill

SCIENCE FICTION You might take this opportunity to discuss the genre of science fiction with students. Explain that science fiction is fiction that deals mainly with the impact of actual or imagined science upon society or individuals. The earliest science-fiction work is perhaps Mary Shelley's novel *Frankenstein, or The Modern Prometheus* (1818), although most scholars believe that Jules Verne's novels (1864–1874) marked the beginning of science fiction as a literary genre.

In recent years, science-fiction writers (Asimov included) have tended to focus on these subjects for their stories: future colonies on Earth; interstellar travel; technology out of control; and the possibility of intelligent life in other worlds.

III. GATHER YOUR THOUGHTS

In Part IV, students will write a journal entry that reflects their thoughts on the causes of war. The prewriting activities on page 226 will help prepare them for this writing assignment. First, students will summarize what they know about Asimov's story. In particular, they'll **summarize** what they read about the plot, setting, main characters, and theme.

After that, students will do a **quickwrite** about war. The directions ask them to think about Asimov's claim that war is caused by self-righteousness. Students should try to respond to this idea in their quickwrites. Before they begin, be sure they review their web work on page 220. You might also have students ask any lingering questions they have about the concept of self-righteousness.

Prewriting Strategies

TOPIC SENTENCES After students have completed their quickwrites, you might ask them to write topic sentences that clearly state their ideas about the cause (or causes) of war.

Have students use the **Prewriting** blackline master on page 266.

IV. WRITE

In their **journal entries,** students should explore in some detail what they see as the cause or causes of war. Before they begin, you might have them read over their **quickwrites** on this subject. Ask them to circle any phrases or sentences that they want to remember. They may be able to incorporate some of their quickwrite ideas into their journal entries.

WRITING RUBRIC Use the writing rubric to help students focus on the assignment requirements and for help with a quick assessment of their writing.

In their journal entries, do students

- reflect on the causes of war?

- use specific details?

- demonstrate a knowledge of history, politics, or current events?

Grammar, Usage, and Mechanics

When students have finished their first drafts, ask them to revise using the **Writers' Checklist** as a guide. At this point you may want to teach a brief mini-lesson on commas. Ask students to pay particular attention to commas in a series and how commas are used in dialogue. For example:

Incorrect: Gelb shook his head "Peter! This is an enormous exciting and innovative idea!"

Correct: Gelb shook his head, "Peter! This is an enormous, exciting, and innovative idea!"

V. WRAP-UP

Take a moment at the end of the lesson for students to reflect on whether they found the story **easy.** Using the **Readers' Checklist,** have students tell you what, if anything, they found difficult about Asimov's writing. Their comments about the story may help you decide which reading and writing strategies to emphasize when they read "Hints" (pages 228–238).

Assessment

To test students' comprehension, use the **Assessment** blackline master on page 267.

Name _____

VOCABULARY

Words from the Selection

DIRECTIONS Underline the suffixes in three of the words below. Then use each word in a sentence of your own.

Suffixes
-tion = act or process of
-able = can be
-ed = past tense

EXAMPLE: automa<u>ted</u>. The office is completely automated.

1. simulation _____

2. bearable _____

3. analysis _____

4. beckoned _____

5. premium _____

Strategy Lesson: Prefixes

The prefix *counter-* means "in opposition to; against; in return." Write the word from the list at the right that fits in each sentence.

counterclaim

counterproductive

counterclockwise

counterdemonstration

counteract

6. If you get a shot, it will probably

_____ the flu.

7. Do not wind that timepiece

_____.

8. Revising a paper after the school year has ended

would be _____.

9. When the player was sued, he filed a

_____.

10. While those who opposed the law marched down

the street, a _____ was held in

front of the mayor's office.

Name _____

COMPREHENSION
Venn Diagram

DIRECTIONS Use this Venn diagram to compare and contrast your ideas about war to Hargrove and Jonsbeck's. Write some conclusions on the lines below.

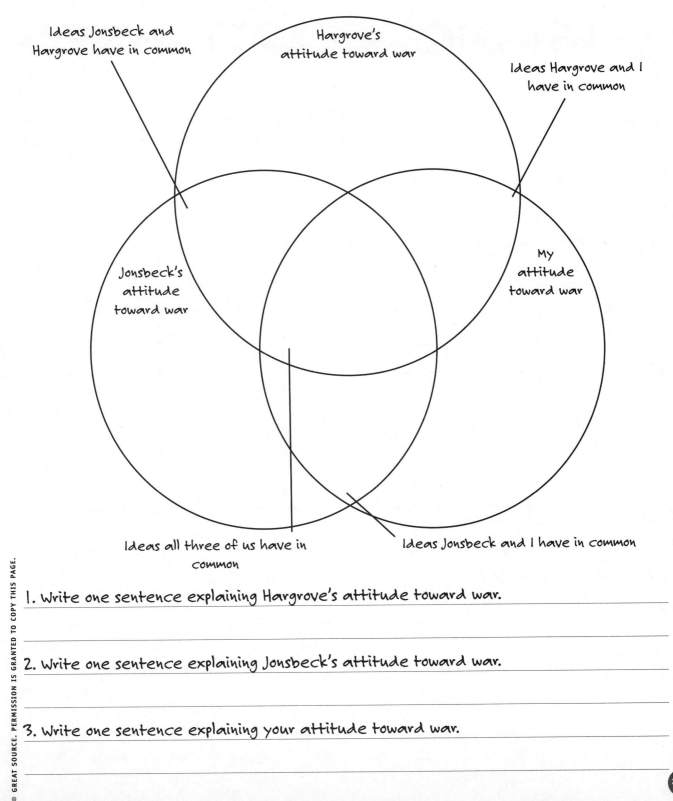

Ideas Jonsbeck and Hargrove have in common

Hargrove's attitude toward war

Ideas Hargrove and I have in common

Jonsbeck's attitude toward war

My attitude toward war

Ideas all three of us have in common

Ideas Jonsbeck and I have in common

1. Write one sentence explaining Hargrove's attitude toward war.

_____

_____

2. Write one sentence explaining Jonsbeck's attitude toward war.

_____

_____

3. Write one sentence explaining your attitude toward war.

_____

_____

Name _____

PREWRITING
Graphic Organizer
....

Directions Get together in a small group. Work together to fill out this chart about war. If you don't know an answer, assign a group member to look for information in a library.

Name of war	When was it?	What caused it?	Who was involved?	What was the end result?
the American Revolution				
the War of 1812				
the American Civil War				
World War I				
World War II				
the Korean War				
the Vietnam War				

Use the information from your chart to help you answer this question:

I think wars are caused by

Here's what I mean

Name _____

ASSESSMENT

Multiple-Choice Test

DIRECTIONS On the blanks provided, write the letter of the item that best answers each question or completes each statement.

_____ 1. "Old Man" Hargrove is . . .
A. the Secretary of Foreign Affairs.
C. The President of the United States.
B. the Secretary of Agriculture.
D. a Navy Admiral.

_____ 2. What job does Jonsbeck have?
A. He is a captain in the Navy.
C. He is a computer programmer.
B. He is a secretary.
D. He is the President of the United States.

_____ 3. Who is doing the fighting in the story?
A. the three men
C. the major world powers
B. computers
D. the United States and Europe

_____ 4. According to Jonsbeck, if countries would cooperate, they could focus on . . .
A. running the world.
C. extending computerization.
B. developing space.
D. all of the above

_____ 5. What does Hargrove plan to do with the information he gets from the computer?
A. keep it as a last resort
C. get the government to agree to war
B. threaten other countries
D. none of the above

_____ 6. In this war, who decides whether the benefits outweigh the casualties?
A. the computer
C. Jonsbeck
B. Hargrove
D. no one

_____ 7. How does Gelb feel about what Hargrove and Jonsbeck are up to?
A. excited
C. sad
B. terrified
D. confused

_____ 8. Why does Jonsbeck feel nothing will come from Hargrove's plan?
A. The world is at peace now.
C. Computers will never give the OK for war.
B. Computers tend to break down.
D. The government won't take this seriously.

_____ 9. According to Jonsbeck, what does the computer lack?
A. a sense of competition
C. the ability to fight an imaginary war
B. a sense of self-righteousness
D. nothing at all

_____ 10. Which character disapproves of using computers in war?
A. Hargrove
C. Gelb
B. Jonsbeck
D. all of the above

Short-Essay Test

What would you say are the problems with Hargrove's plan?

STUDENT PAGES 228–238

Skills and Strategies Overview

THEME	Isaac Asimov
READING LEVEL	average
VOCABULARY	◇ exceptions ◇ surgeon ◇ supersede ◇ interweaving ◇ deftly
PREREADING	web
RESPONSE	mark
COMPREHENSION	word attack
PREWRITING	brainstorm
WRITING	science-fiction story / capitalization
ASSESSMENT	enjoyment

BACKGROUND

"Hints" is an essay Isaac Asimov wrote in response to requests from young people who wanted advice on how to break into the field of science-fiction writing. What's interesting about this essay is that Asimov seems a bit more light hearted—a bit more wry—than he is in his stories. His language is colloquial, and his style is chatty. He's going to "spill the beans" in this essay and tell would-be writers exactly what they need to know.

As you might expect, Asimov doesn't mince words when he offers advice. Nor does he mollycoddle readers. He wants the world to know that his career is a tough one, and the reasons he succeeds so well are because he works very, very hard. Rather than hold up false promises, he explains that it is OK for a writer to simply give up after too many failures. Some people just cannot write, he says, so what's the point of trying and trying to get published if it is never going to happen? It is all a matter of knowing your limitations and realizing your strengths.

UNIT THEME Isaac Asimov gives some useful advice to students who are considering writing science fiction for a career.

GRAPHIC ORGANIZER

Bibliography Other books by Asimov include these: *Isaac Asimov: The Complete Stories* (1990); *The 21st Century in Space* (1996); and *Asimov's Chronology of Science and Discovery* (1994).

BEFORE YOU READ

Read through the introduction to the lesson with students. Be sure they understand that "Hints" is an essay and not the science fiction story they might be expecting. Then have them begin the prereading activity, a **web** that explores their thoughts about how to write. (Refer to the **Strategy Handbook** on page 40 for more help.)

Motivation Strategy

ENGAGING STUDENTS In "Hints," Isaac Asimov offers some advice to young people who want to make a career of writing science fiction. Ask the class: "How many of you have ever thought of a career in writing? What are the benefits and drawbacks of being a professional writer?" Students' comments will likely tie in with some of the points Asimov makes in his essay.

Vocabulary Building

Learning **synonyms** can help a new writer build vocabulary. Good writers have at their fingertips a large vocabulary that they can call on if they get stuck for a word. They know that using the same word over and over again makes for writing that is dull and uninspired. Have students get into the habit of automatically thinking of a synonym or two for words that they'd like to use in their own writing. You might have them practice by writing synonyms for these key vocabulary words, all of which are footnoted in Asimov's essay: *exceptions, surgeon, supersede, interweaving,* and *deftly*. Ask students to circle these words in the text. For more vocabulary work, see page 272.

STRATEGY LESSON: WORD ANALYSIS Students have learned a number of strategies for defining new words, analyzing word parts, and understanding word origins. To help students review some of these strategies, assign the **Vocabulary** blackline master, page 272.

Prereading Strategies

The purpose of the **web** on page 228 is to help students consider what they already know about the topic of Asimov's essay before they begin reading. Encourage them to incorporate advice they've learned in school and in their reading, in addition to writing techniques that they've developed on their own. When they finish "Hints," students can create a new web that incorporates advice from Asimov's essay.

QUICKWRITE Ask students to think about the writers they've read in this book. Which one did they like the best? Have them do a one-minute quickwrite in which they describe the author's style— what they liked about it and any aspects of the style that they think are worth emulating. The comments they make in their quickwrites will help them make more thoughtful analysis of the advice Asimov gives in his essay.

Spanish-speaking Students

En "Pistas," Isaac Asimov ofrece unas sugerencias a escitores prospectivos de la ciencia ficción. Es un ensayo bastante chistoso, implicando, por ejemplo, que ser autor es más noble que ser presidente de los Estados Unidos, pero sus pistas e ideas tienen mucho valor. Asimov no teme de retratar la realidad del mundo literario, presentando sus beneficios y sus problemas.

READ

Before students begin, remind them to **mark** or **highlight** the text as they are reading. They should make a note of anything they think is interesting, puzzling, confusing, or important. They should note their comments for the author and the questions they have about the work. Be sure they understand that marking a text and making notes can help them read more carefully.

Response Strategy

REACT AND CONNECT Many of your students will want to note their responses to Asimov's ideas, especially his tongue-in-cheek comment about non-writing professions. Have them give their reactions to his comments and connect what he says to their own skills as a writer. Their personal reactions will help them decide which pieces of advice to follow when they go to write their own science-fiction stories.

Comprehension Strategies

Word-attack strategies can help broaden students' vocabulary and provide them with new ideas for what to do when they encounter a word that they don't know. The word-attack strategies in this lesson include two recommendations: use word parts or context clues whenever you encounter a new word. Both of these strategies have been explored in some detail in the Vocabulary Building sections of this book.

DIRECTED READING As an alternate comprehension strategy, try doing a directed reading of Asimov's essay. This strategy can help reluctant or low-level readers better comprehend what the author says. Read the essay aloud to students, stopping every half page or so to ask a question that helps students see the point Asimov makes. Questions such as "What is he saying about rejections slips here?" and "What advice does he give to people who just can't write?" can help students build toward an understanding of his major points.

For more help, see the **Comprehension** blackline master on page 273.

Discussion Questions

COMPREHENSION 1. Who is Isaac Asimov? *(He is a well-regarded science fiction writer.)*

2. Why did he write this essay? *(He wrote in response to requests that he give some tips for writing science fiction.)*

3. What are his four main tips? *(Know your subject; be prepared to work hard; be patient; be reasonable.)*

CRITICAL THINKING 4. What examples of humor can you find in the essay? *(Answers will vary. Have students return to the text so that they're able to give specific examples.)*

5. Which piece of advice do you approve of most? *(Ask students to fully explain their ideas.)*

6. Which piece of advice do you *disapprove* of? *(Ask students to fully explain their ideas.)*

Literary Skill

HUMOR To introduce a literary skill with this lesson, you might take a moment to discuss humor in Asimov's essay. Of course, there are all type of reasons why a writer might choose to inject humor into a piece of writing. Some writers can't help it; they are just naturally funny. Others have to work at it a bit. Like all good writers, Asimov knew that humor could make a piece more enjoyable to read and easier to understand. Asimov made some strong points in his essay, but he tempered them with a bit of humor. This makes some of his painful ideas—for example, that some people really can't write—easier to swallow.

III. GATHER YOUR THOUGHTS

Prewriting Strategies

On page 235, students are asked to **brainstorm** a web similar to the one they made before reading the selection. This time, however, they'll be focusing on possible ideas for a science-fiction story. Encourage students to work together on this activity.

The second half of page 235 asks students to fill out a character organizer about a character they might use in a science-fiction story of their own. In addition to the questions listed on the organizer, consider having students answer these questions about their character:

1. What does he/she look like?

2. What does he/she act like?

3. How do other characters feel about him or her?

4. How do I feel about him or her?

Have students use the **Prewriting** blackline master on page 274.

IV. WRITE

Set aside plenty of time for students to write their **stories**. Remind them to use the story planners they created on pages 235 and 236.

WRITING RUBRIC Use the writing rubric to help students focus on the assignment requirements and for help with a quick assessment of their writing.

Do students' stories

• include details about setting?

• have a plot that is easy to follow and understand?

• contain well-developed, believable characters?

• include a bit of "real" science?

Grammar, Usage, and Mechanics

After students have finished their drafts, have them revise using the **Writers' Checklist** as a guide. At this point you might want to teach a mini-lesson on capitalization. Remind the class that the names of specific buildings, monuments, companies, and groups are capitalized, as are the names of ethnic groups, languages, planets, continents, countries, states, and cities.

Incorrect: When I go to south america, I'll be sure to take my spanish dictionary.

Correct: When I go to South America, I'll be sure to take my Spanish dictionary.

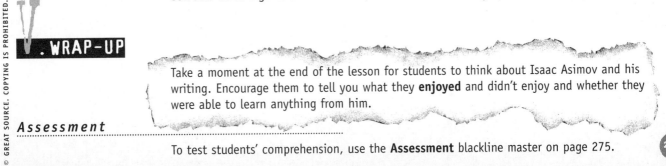

V. WRAP-UP

Take a moment at the end of the lesson for students to think about Isaac Asimov and his writing. Encourage them to tell you what they **enjoyed** and didn't enjoy and whether they were able to learn anything from him.

Assessment

To test students' comprehension, use the **Assessment** blackline master on page 275.

Name _____

VOCABULARY

Words from the Selection

DIRECTIONS Substitute a synonym from the word box for the underlined word or words.

◇ exceptions   ◇ surgeon   ◇ supersede   ◇ interweaving   ◇ deftly

1. A good writer uses vocabulary and grammar <u>skillfully</u>. _____

2. Luck will never <u>take the place of</u> hard work when it comes to writing.

   _____

3. One must work toward <u>blending together</u> many of the writing rules when composing a good story. _____

4. There are no <u>exclusions</u> to the rule that there is no magic formula for becoming a great writer. _____

5. A writer uses tools, just like a <u>doctor who operates on people</u>.

   _____

Strategy Lesson: Word Analysis

DIRECTIONS Write the word from the list at the right that correctly answers each question.

6. Which word has a prefix that means "between"?

   _____   patient

7. *Magnus* is Latin for "great." Which word has this Latin root? _____   reject

8. *Jacere* is Latin for "to throw." Which word means "to throw back"?   dialogue

   _____

                                                    interweaving

9. Which word means both "willing to put up with waiting" and "a person being treated by a doctor"?_____   magnificent

10. Which word has a root that means "speech"?

    _____

Name _____

COMPREHENSION

K-W-L

DIRECTIONS Complete this K-W-L organizer about Isaac Asimov and his writing style. Use the K column for what you know about the author and the L column for the things you learned from reading "Frustration" and "Hints." Use the W column to make notes about what you still want to learn.

What I Know	What I Want to Know	What I Learned

Isaac Asimov taught me this about science fiction:

_____

_____

Isaac Asimov taught me this about writing:

_____

_____

Name _____

PREWRITING
Sketch and Write

Drawing and writing go hand in hand. When you draw, you add details so that your reader can see the object. In writing, your details also help your readers "see" what you are describing.

DIRECTIONS Draw the setting for your science-fiction story. Add plenty of details.

DIRECTIONS Now write the details that you just drew. Write the setting of your story in the center of the web. Then describe how the place looks, sounds, smells, feels, and even tastes. List as many words as you can.

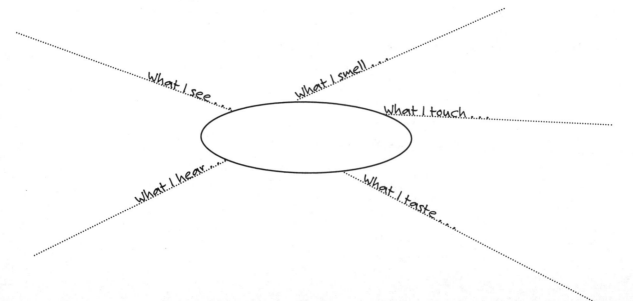

Name _____

ASSESSMENT

Multiple-Choice Test

DIRECTIONS On the blanks provided, write the letter of the item that best answers each question or completes each sentence.

_____ 1. How does Isaac Asimov feel about revealing some of his trade secrets?
   A. He is reluctant to share.
   B. He has no hints to share.
   C. He wants to share some useful principles.
   D. He would prefer you learn on your own.

_____ 2. According to Asimov, if you want to write, you need to master . . .
   A. vocabulary.
   B. spelling.
   C. grammar.
   D. all of the above

_____ 3. To become a better writer, Asimov suggests you . . .
   A. attend classes on writing.
   B. read the works of the masters.
   C. read books on how to become a better writer.
   D. go to writing conferences.

_____ 4. Asimov says that to have a good science-fiction career, you should . . .
   A. study science on your own.
   B. read the newspaper.
   C. major in science at college.
   D. be a professional scientist.

_____ 5. Asimov also suggests that to become a good writer, you must . . .
   A. follow his advice to the letter.
   B. concentrate on nonfiction.
   C. work at the job.
   D. get a tutor.

_____ 6. What kind of hope does Asimov give for selling your first novel?
   A. no hope at all
   B. almost no hope
   C. some hope
   D. a lot of hope

_____ 7. If you continue to write and don't seem to be getting better, Asimov suggests that you . . .
   A. keep trying.
   B. take more classes.
   C. find another career.
   D. none of the above

_____ 8. According to Asimov, what's one of the hardest things about being a writer?
   A. It is hard to think of new ideas.
   B. It can be very lonely.
   C. It is impossible to find an editor to read your work.
   D. It is very hard to make a living at it.

_____ 9. Of these professions, which does Asimov think is most important?
   A. a surgeon
   B. a writer
   C. Chief Justice of the Supreme Court
   D. President of the United States

_____ 10. What was Asimov's purpose in writing this essay?
   A. to argue
   B. to puzzle
   C. to teach
   D. none of the above

Short-Essay Test

Which of Isaac Asimov's writing hints do you find most helpful? Why?

HIGH SCHOOL: THE BAD AND THE GOOD

II. Read

Why does Anam stop wearing her hejab in public?
(Anam stops wearing her hejab in public so as not to draw attention to herself.)

What world events caused harassment of Muslim students?
(the Gulf War and the bombing of the World Trade Center)

How were these Muslims affected by the "kidding" of the other students?
(Some Muslims fought back when they were treated viciously, while others simply ignored the "kidding.")

Vocabulary

1. no. There is no proof that a rumor is true.
2. interest. A flirtation is paying attention to someone in a romantic way.
3. on your head. A hejab is a wrap worn across the face and around the head.
4. try to solve one. Compromises are issues settled by each person giving up a demand.
5. for your body. Chemotherapy is treatment of a disease by chemicals.
6. explosion-implosion
7. escalate-decrease
8. petty-important
9. complaints-compliments
10. vicious-kind

Assessment

1	B	6	D
2	C	7	C
3	C	8	D
4	C	9	A
5	A	10	B

FINDING PATRICK

I. Before You Read

LISTENER'S GUIDE

Where does the action take place?
(The action takes place in Kenya.)

When does the action take place?
(The action takes place in 1993.)

Who is Patrick?
(Patrick is a herdsman from a small village in Kenya.)

What kind of life does Patrick have?
(Patrick leads a simple life tending his father's cattle. He may not enroll in any of the country's universities because he failed to earn enough points on an exam.)

Vocabulary

1. herdsman
2. depart / departure
3. marathon
4. manage / management
5. develop / development
6. devastated
7. rewarded
8. hauled
9. resisted
10. rebuke

Assessment

1	B	6	B
2	A	7	D
3	D	8	C
4	A	9	D
5	B	10	C

IT'S QUIET NOW

II. Read

TITLE
("It's Quiet Now")

CHARACTERS
(The narrator, children, police)

PROBLEM
(The apartheid laws in South Africa have made life intolerable and miserable for the people of color.)

MAJOR EVENTS
(Students have been protesting the government's unfair and racist laws. The Mayor's house was burned down, along with PUTCO vans.)

OUTCOME
(The violence and uproar are so routine that they have left little impact on the population. The people eat and live in silence, trying to enjoy as much peace as possible.)

Assessment

1	D	6	C
2	A	7	D
3	A	8	A
4	B	9	D
5	D	10	C

Vocabulary

1 to riot in the streets. An activist is in favor of direct action.
2 a geographical place. In South Africa, townships are where black people live.
3 a brief sentence. A slogan is a motto.
4 talking. When you disrupt, you break up or cause disorder in.
5 government officials. They are elected to make laws and manage a city or town.
6 An informer is probably someone who reveals secret government information.
7 Transfixed probably means "unmoving."
8 Grumbling probably means "complaining."
9 Drizzle probably means "rain."
10 The authorities are probably people in charge, maybe police.

SURVIVAL

I. Before You Read

Names
Granny, George, Florah

repeated words
mealie meal, garbage, Alexandra, digging

Vocabulary

1 soliciting
2 eviction
3 malnutrition
4 perishables
5 expectantly
6 (a) trash
7 (d) rubbish
8 (b) twisted
9 (c) bad situation
10 (b) large crowd

phrases from beginning and end of each paragraph
"To prevent us from starving . . ."
". . . black people were burdened with their own survival."
"The Mlothi provided us with many items we could not afford. . . ."
". . . families fought over rights to dig up white people's leftovers."

Who and what is "Survival" about?
"Survival" is about the strife and hardship that black families endured under the racist laws of apartheid in South Africa. It is specifically about one boy's struggles and observations.

II. Read

What is the plight, or situation, of this family?
(The family is impoverished and malnourished.)

What are some of the health problems of digging for food in a garbage dump?
(Digging for food in a garbage dump can cause disease, infection, and injury because of the unsanitary and dangerous conditions of the food and dump.)

What were the two main problems the Mathabane family members faced?
(The two main problems the family members faced were the threat of starvation and eviction.)

Assessment

1	D	6	B
2	D	7	D
3	A	8	D
4	C	9	B
5	A	10	A

III. Gather Your Thoughts

RECOGNIZE IMPORTANT INFORMATION
"Survival" shows that life for black Africans under apartheid was unfair, extremely difficult, and degrading.

HOW IT FEELS TO BE COLORED ME

I. Before You Read

Students' answers will vary.

WHAT'S ZORA NEALE HURSTON'S STORY?

Who's involved?
Zora Neale Hurston
Eatonville residents
Tourists

What's happening?
Hurston describes
her childhood in
Eatonville and
experiences later in life.

When and where does it take place?
The story takes place
in Florida in the early
1900s.

Vocabulary

1 take risks
2 happy
3 disapproved of
4 appearing
5 various things
6 circumference
7 circumnavigate
8 circumvent
9 circumscribe
10 circumlocution

II. Read

In your own words, what did Hurston like about being on the front porch?
(Hurston liked watching and talking to the people who passed by.)

How did Hurston's feelings about herself change once she moved to Jacksonville?
(Hurston realizes that she is no longer the beloved Zora of Eatonville. While she knows she is colored and somewhat oppressed by a racist society, she is determined to take on the world.)

How have Hurston's ancestors helped her?
(Hurston's ancestors have helped energize and inspire her to be the best she can be.)

Describe in your own words how Hurston feels at Barnard.
(Hurston feels colored at Barnard. She stands out among the majority white population of the school.)

Why do you think Hurston tells the story about the jazz club?
(Hurston tells the story about the jazz club to show how being colored also enlivens her soul with rhythm in a way that some white people have never had the pleasure of feeling.)

Assessment

1	B	6	B
2	C	7	B
3	C	8	C
4	D	9	A
5	A	10	D

THE EATONVILLE ANTHOLOGY

II. Read

What words would you use to describe Mrs. Roberts?
(greedy, unsatisfied, needy)

Why do you think Hurston tells the story of Mrs. Tony Roberts?
(Hurston tells the story to show how pleading and begging don't always yield rewards.)

What is funny or unusual about "Turpentine Love"?
("Turpentine Love" is unusual because it tells the unlikely circumstances under which a woman is cured of a chronic condition and then able to marry.)

What is unusual about the man in "The Way of a Man with a Train"?
("The Way of a Man with a Train" is unusual because the subject of the story is frightened by trains.)

Vocabulary

1-5 Students' sentences will vary.
6 piece
7 pain
8 meat
9 passed
10 away

III. Gather Your Thoughts

COMPARING AND CONTRASTING

MRS. ROBERTS
Greedy
Uneducated
Beggar

JIM MERCHANT
has a good humor
loving
lucky

live in Eatonville
all are unusual characters with
unusual stories

Easily frightened
Unworldly
OLD MAN ANDERSON

Assessment

1	C	6	A
2	A	7	B
3	B	8	D
4	C	9	A
5	D	10	C

VISIT TO AFRICA

III. Gather Your Thoughts

(Students' answers will vary.)

MAIN IDEA:

The main idea of "Visit to Africa" is that life is precious and fragile.

SUPPORTING DETAIL: "On the third day, Guy, on a pleasure outing, was injured in an automobile accident."

SUPPORTING DETAIL: "Admittedly, Guy lived with the knowledge that an unexpected and very hard sneeze could force the fractured vertebrae against his spinal cord, and he would be paralyzed or die immediately. . . ."

SUPPORTING DETAIL: "He hadn't lived long enough to fall in love with this brutally delicious experience."

SUPPORTING DETAIL: ". . . we had been each other's home and center for seventeen years. He could die if he wanted and go off to wherever dead folks go, but I, I would be left without a home."

Vocabulary

1. fatuous-infatuation
2. invert-vertebrae
3. sumptuous-consumed
4. patriot-expatriate
5. Student sentences will vary.
6. obscene-indecent
7. cavorting-prancing
8. copious-abundant
9. plump-chubby
10. melodious-harmonious

Assessment

1	B	6	A
2	A	7	B
3	C	8	D
4	D	9	A
5	D	10	B

DEAR TIA AND PAPA

II. Read

(Students' answers will vary.)

Vocabulary

1. denial-di NI l
2. presence-PREZ ns
3. nostalgia-nah STAL juh
4. piercing-PEERS ng
5. sacred-SAY krid
6. stampede
7. cafeteria
8. mariachi
9. burrito
10. chocolate

Assessment

1	B	6	B
2	D	7	D
3	A	8	C
4	D	9	A
5	C	10	C

THE GUEST WHO RAN AWAY

I. Before You Read

(Students' answers will vary)

What did you find out from reading the title and author's name?
(The author is from Tunisia.)

What did you learn from reading the first paragraph?
(The Bedouin is a generous host and welcomes strangers.)

What characters are involved?
(a traveler and a Bedouin)

II. Read

Why does the woman eat all of the chicken? What does this tell you about her?
(The woman eats all of the chicken because she can't resist the temptation. This indicates that she is selfish.)

Why does the woman lie to the guest?
(The woman lies to the guest because she is too embarrassed and proud to admit she has eaten the food.)

III. Gather Your Thoughts

USE GRAPHIC ORGANIZERS (Students' answers will vary.)
Character Attribute Map

#1 Easily tempted

#2 Greedy

the woman

#3 Proud

#4 Liar

Vocabulary

Students' paragraphs will vary.
1 flee-fled
2 give-gave
3 run-ran
4 leave-left
5 teach-taught
6 fly-flew
7 ride-rode
8 drive-drove
9 fight-fought
10 choose-chose

Assessment

1 B   6 D
2 A   7 C
3 A   8 A
4 C   9 D
5 C   10 D

THE PRICE OF PRIDE AND HOW SI' DJEHA STAVED OFF HUNGER

I. Before You Read

STORY
"The Price of Pride"

"How Si' Djeha Staved Off Hunger"

WHAT THE CONFLICT ACTUALLY IS
- A Bedouin bargains for the return of his kidnapped son.
- A Bedouin seeks food and shelter from a stranger.

II. Read

1. a Bedouin's son is stolen

2. The Bedouin decreases the ransom each day

3. The kidnapper returns the child, who the Bedouin now sees as blemished and dishonored.

1. Si' Djeha approaches another traveler in the desert, hoping to be invited to a meal.

2. Si' Djeha talks with the fellow traveler, pretending to know about his family and home. The traveler doesn't offer food.

3. Si' Djeha lies to the traveler, saying his family and home have fallen apart. The traveler races home and Si'Djeha eats his food.

What, in your own words, was "How Si' Djeha Staved Off Hunger" about?
("How Si' Djeha Staved Off Hunger" is about a traveler who resorts to trickery in order to eat.)

III. Gather Your Thoughts

(Students' answers will vary) **A. DISCUSS AND REFLECT**
What is the conflict in the plot of "The Price of Pride"?
(The conflict in the plot of "The Price of Pride" is securing the return of the Bedouin's stolen son.)

What is the conflict in the plot of "How Si' Djeha Staved Off Hunger"?
(The conflict in the plot of "How Si' Djeha Staved Off Hunger" is Si' Djeha's own need to eat.)

Vocabulary

1 kidnapper
2 crier
3 dwindled
4 captor
5 parched
6 kidnap + er = person who kidnaps
7 travel + er = person who travels
8 compassion + ate = having compassion
9 merci + ful = showing mercy
10 Students' sentences will vary.

Assessment

1 C   6 D
2 A   7 B
3 B   8 A
4 C   9 D
5 D   10 A

PUERTO RICAN PARADISE

II. Read

TAKE NOTES
Write 3 things that Momma remembers from her life in Puerto Rico.

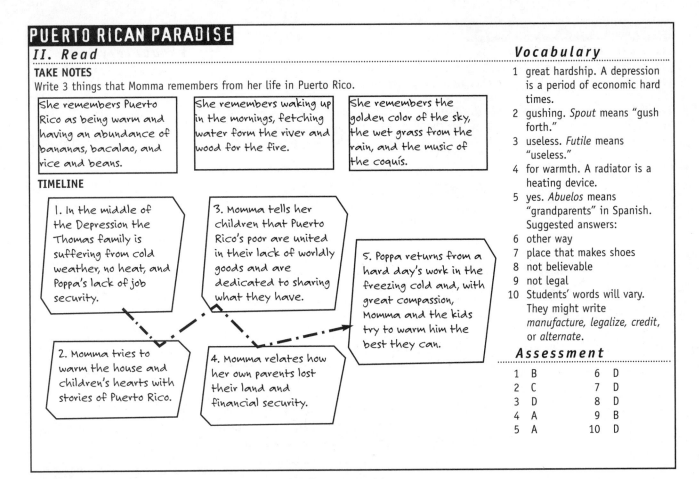

She remembers Puerto Rico as being warm and having an abundance of bananas, bacalao, and rice and beans.

She remembers waking up in the mornings, fetching water form the river and wood for the fire.

She remembers the golden color of the sky, the wet grass from the rain, and the music of the coquís.

TIMELINE

1. In the middle of the Depression the Thomas family is suffering from cold weather, no heat, and Poppa's lack of job security.

2. Momma tries to warm the house and children's hearts with stories of Puerto Rico.

3. Momma tells her children that Puerto Rico's poor are united in their lack of worldly goods and are dedicated to sharing what they have.

4. Momma relates how her own parents lost their land and financial security.

5. Poppa returns from a hard day's work in the freezing cold and, with great compassion, Momma and the kids try to warm him the best they can.

Vocabulary

1 great hardship. A depression is a period of economic hard times.
2 gushing. *Spout* means "gush forth."
3 useless. *Futile* means "useless."
4 for warmth. A radiator is a heating device.
5 yes. *Abuelos* means "grandparents" in Spanish. Suggested answers:
6 other way
7 place that makes shoes
8 not believable
9 not legal
10 Students' words will vary. They might write *manufacture, legalize, credit,* or *alternate.*

Assessment

1	B	6	D
2	C	7	D
3	D	8	D
4	A	9	B
5	A	10	D

IF YOU AIN'T GOT HEART, YOU AIN'T GOT NADA

II. Read

(Students' answers will vary.)

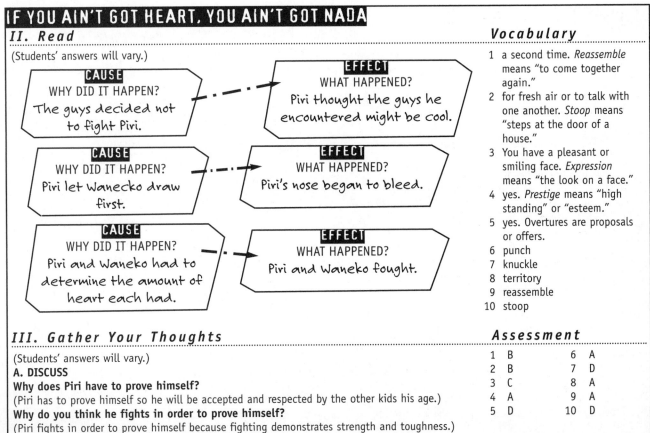

CAUSE WHY DID IT HAPPEN? The guys decided not to fight Piri.

EFFECT WHAT HAPPENED? Piri thought the guys he encountered might be cool.

CAUSE WHY DID IT HAPPEN? Piri let Wanecko draw first.

EFFECT WHAT HAPPENED? Piri's nose began to bleed.

CAUSE WHY DID IT HAPPEN? Piri and Waneko had to determine the amount of heart each had.

EFFECT WHAT HAPPENED? Piri and Waneko fought.

Vocabulary

1 a second time. *Reassemble* means "to come together again."
2 for fresh air or to talk with one another. *Stoop* means "steps at the door of a house."
3 You have a pleasant or smiling face. *Expression* means "the look on a face."
4 yes. *Prestige* means "high standing" or "esteem."
5 yes. Overtures are proposals or offers.
6 punch
7 knuckle
8 territory
9 reassemble
10 stoop

III. Gather Your Thoughts

(Students' answers will vary.)

A. DISCUSS

Why does Piri have to prove himself?
(Piri has to prove himself so he will be accepted and respected by the other kids his age.)

Why do you think he fights in order to prove himself?
(Piri fights in order to prove himself because fighting demonstrates strength and toughness.)

Assessment

1	B	6	A
2	B	7	D
3	C	8	A
4	A	9	A
5	D	10	D

HER LIFE WAS NOT A JOKE

I. Before You Read

ANTICIPATION GUIDE
After Reading
1. False
2. False
3. True
4. False
5. True

II. Read

(Students' answers will vary)
What are 3 things Greene tells you about Helen Keller?
1. Helen was born in Alabama in 1880.
2. She developed a disease when she was 19 months old that made her blind, deaf, and mute.
3. With the help of teachers, Helen learned to read Braille and to speak.

What would you say are Helen Keller's 3 most important achievements?
1. Helen learned to read Braille and to speak.
2. Helen was admitted to Radcliffe College, one of the most respected institutions in the country.
3. Helen wrote many books and became a role model for people around the world.

Vocabulary

1 manual
2 flailed
3 advocating
4 prestigious
5 rampant
6 sight + less = without sight
7 prestige + ious (or ous) = having prestige
8 govern + ment = act of governing
9 buffoon + ish = resembling a buffoon (clown)
10 sound + less = without sound

III. Gather Your Thoughts

ORGANIZE IDEAS

What she has done

Helen has learned to read Braille and to speak. She has graduated from college and published many books.

What she is like

Helen is blind, deaf, and mute. She is persevering and diligent.

How Bob Greene feels about her

Bob Greene feels Helen should be recognized and praised for her accomplishments and contributions to society. He thinks she is a role model for everyone, not someone to be made fun of.

Assessment

1	B	6	A
2	A	7	D
3	C	8	A
4	B	9	B
5	D	10	C

ONE MORNING

I. Before You Read

1. "'Hi, Mom. The paper arrived yet?' I said, pouring cereal into a bowl."
2. "By the age of 12, he was free and travelling the world in his crusade against the horrors of child labor."
3. "Surely slavery had been abolished throughout the world by now."
4. "Why was nothing being done to stop such cruelty?"

II. Read

(Students' answers will vary)
Write 2 things the author has told you so far.
1. Craig reads the comics every morning before heading off to school.
2. Craig is surprised when he reads about a victim of child labor.
What 3 things happened to Iqbal Masih?
1. Iqbal Masih was sold into slavery at the age of four.
2. Iqbal was freed eight years later and began to speak out against child labor.
3. Iqbal was killed by people who some believe to be members of the carpet industry.
What did Craig Kielburger do after reading Iqbal's story?
1. Craig asked his mother if she had read the story.
2. Craig thought intently about the article all day and wondered how child labor could possibly exist.
3. Craig decided to research the subject at the library.

Vocabulary

1 curious
2 hard to get out
3 weaving
4 shocking
5 no
6 maimed-crippled
7 trek-journey
8 hauled-dragged
9 defied-disobeyed
10 crusade-campaign

Assessment

1	C	6	C
2	C	7	D
3	B	8	C
4	A	9	C
5	B	10	A

GRAPHIC ORGANIZER
Who? Craig Kielburger → **Read What?** a newspaper article about a victim of child labor → **How did it affect him?** Craig was shocked and intrigued by the story. → **What did he do?** Craig researched child labor at the library. → **In the end, how did he feel?** Craig felt saddened and disturbed by the very existence of child labor.

THE KNIGHT IN PERSON

II. Read

(Students' answers will vary.)

Why were knights superstitious?
(Knights were superstitious because the life expectancy of knights in those days was short.)

How did the knights feel about how they looked?
(Knights were very concerned about their appearance and took great care in looking well.)

What did knights do to take care of their physical appearance?
(Knights took baths in hot, perfumed or oiled water to take care of their physical appearance.)

What does their concern about their looks tell you about knights?
(Their concern about their looks indicates that they were vain and that they lived in a society which placed great emphasis on maintaining good appearances.)

Vocabulary

1 healthy
2 no
3 holding or grasping something ("hair" in the selection)
4 barber
5 to protect yourself
6 medieval
7 physique
8 cholera
9 omens
10 medallions

III. Gather Your Thoughts

Assessment

1	D	6	C
2	A	7	B
3	B	8	D
4	A	9	B
5	C	10	D

DETAIL 1
Knights exercised a lot.

MAIN IDEAS
Knights were concerned about their looks

DETAIL 2
One knight destroyed a neighbor's land when he was criticized for the way he looked.

DETAIL 1
Some knights washed and styled their hair to make it shiny.

C. WRITE A TOPIC SENTENCE

The "Knight in Person" is an article about medieval knights that describes their life-style.

THE VICTORIOUS FEUDAL KNIGHT

I. Before You Read

(Students' answers will vary.)
1. "Victorious Feudal Knight" means a knight of the middle ages who was successful.

II. Read

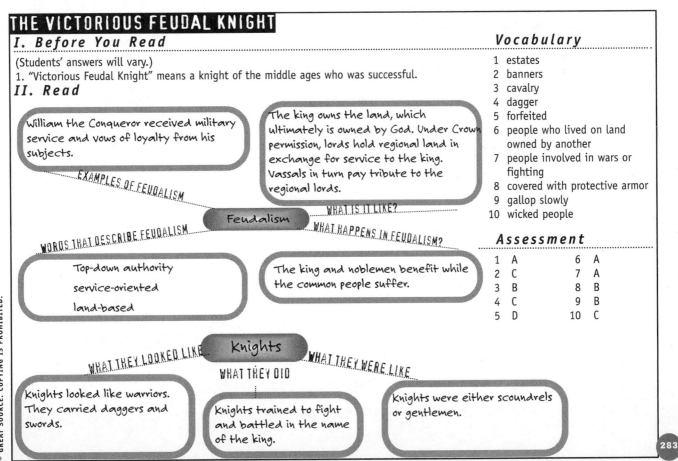

William the Conqueror received military service and vows of loyalty from his subjects.

The king owns the land, which ultimately is owned by God. Under Crown permission, lords hold regional land in exchange for service to the king. Vassals in turn pay tribute to the regional lords.

EXAMPLES OF FEUDALISM

WHAT IS IT LIKE?

Feudalism

WORDS THAT DESCRIBE FEUDALISM

WHAT HAPPENS IN FEUDALISM?

Top-down authority
service-oriented
land-based

The king and noblemen benefit while the common people suffer.

WHAT THEY LOOKED LIKE

Knights

WHAT THEY WERE LIKE

WHAT THEY DID

Knights looked like warriors. They carried daggers and swords.

Knights trained to fight and battled in the name of the king.

Knights were either scoundrels or gentlemen.

Vocabulary

1 estates
2 banners
3 cavalry
4 dagger
5 forfeited
6 people who lived on land owned by another
7 people involved in wars or fighting
8 covered with protective armor
9 gallop slowly
10 wicked people

Assessment

1	A	6	A
2	C	7	A
3	B	8	B
4	C	9	B
5	D	10	C

FORGETFULNESS AND AN UNWRITTEN LETTER

II. Read

READER'S LOG

"He has forgotten relatives and neighbors, students and the rules of grammar" means that in his old age, the man is losing his memory and understanding of basic concepts.

Vocabulary

1 male
2 finished
3 section of a city
4 murder
5 decreased
6 automatic
7 autograph
8 autocrat
9 autonomy
10 automobile

Assessment

1	D	6	C
2	B	7	D
3	C	8	A
4	A	9	C
5	B	10	D

A MAN RESERVES A SEAT AND JUSTICE

I. Before You Read

fair   truth   innocent until proven guilty
law   justice
jury   what goes around comes around

III. Gather Your Thoughts

(Students' answers will vary.)

A. REVIEW

THE PLOT OF "A MAN RESERVES A SEAT"

FIRST, a bus leaves Zeytoun.

NEXT, a car leaves Helwan.

THEN, they both arrive at Station Square at the same moment and collide.

FINALLY, a man crossing the square on his way to the station is crushed between the bus and car.

B. REFLECT

1. What does "A Man Reserves a Seat" say about justice?

(It says that justice is not always served. Although all three characters have made plans to go somewhere, none of them counts on getting in an accident. The man who dies certainly never considers the idea of not making it to the seat he has reserved.)

2. What does "Justice" say about justice?

("Justice" says that justice is not solely based on truth and fairness. Rather, it has much to do with point of view and skillful creation of the truth.)

Vocabulary

1 direct. *Frankness* means "openness in expressing one's feelings."
2 copied. *Forged* means "copied in order to deceive."
3 before. Precautions are actions taken to prevent possible danger.
4 crazy. Madness is craziness or an unstable state of mind.
5 caused a change. *Induces* means "brings out" or "causes."
6 lively
7 stretched out
8 look at
9 order in which things happened
10 person on foot or walking

Assessment

1	B	6	A
2	D	7	D
3	B	8	C
4	C	9	B
5	C	10	D

ANCESTRY

II. Read

(Students' answers will vary.)

Retell in your own words what has happened so far.

(Booker T. Washington has described his pride in a homemade cap that his mother sewed for him as a child. He learned to value his humble background and resist the temptation to keep up false appearances.)

Vocabulary

1 yes. *Perplexity* means "confusion."
2 excited. A privilege is a special right or benefit.
3 family. People who make up your line of descent or heritage are your ancestry.
4 gift. *Inherited* means "received after someone's death."
5 Student answers. Reliance means "dependence."
6 un + comfortable = not comfortable or uneasy
7 dis + appear = not appear or stop being seen
8 dis + courage = lessen the courage of
9 ex + tend = stretch out
10 Students' sentences will vary.

Assessment

1	A	6	C
2	B	7	B
3	D	8	B
4	B	9	C
5	D	10	D

ROSA PARKS

I. Before You Read

Facts about Rosa Parks

Rosa lived . . . in Montgomery, Alabama.

When Rosa Parks shopped, she . . . endured unfair treatment from salespeople and often had to purchase the things she had touched.

Rosa Park's job was . . . as a seamstress in a department store.

When Rosa Parks got on the bus, she . . . sat in the section reserved for white passengers.

II. Read

(Students' answers will vary.)

What's the bus driver saying to Rosa Parks?

(He is saying that she should move to the back of the bus to avoid legal problems and conflict with the other passengers.)

Why might Rosa Parks's action have made white people feel "more free"?

(Her action may have made white people feel more free to follow their own non-racist convictions and not suffer the stigma of promoting civil rights.)

How would you describe what Rosa Parks did?

(Rosa Parks helped jump-start the fight for civil rights by refusing to obey the racist laws that deemed her an inferior person.)

Vocabulary

1 separation from others or from a main body or group
2 state of mind
3 prevented from having
4 person who comes from particular ancestors
5 public announcement; declaration
6 struggle-fight
7 alterations-adjustments
8 appreciated-treasured
9 vacant-empty
10 furious-angry

III. Gather Your Thoughts

What Rosa did

She refused to give up her seat to white people on the bus.

How others feel about her

Many people feel she is the reason why black people achieved equal legal status with whites.

What she thinks

Rosa thinks that the struggle for equality will continue and that people must act to get what they want and deserve.

Assessment

1	B	6	D
2	D	7	A
3	C	8	D
4	B	9	B
5	D	10	D

A TASTE OF WAR

II. Read

Time line (Students' answers will vary.)

EARLIER
What occurred in the hours before
this group of soldiers started walking?
(The soldiers fought in battle, where many
were wounded.)

EARLIER
What is implied by the comment, "Th'
boys ain't had no fair chanct up t' now . . ."?
(The comment implies that it was impossible
for the soldiers to have won before.)

FIRST
What did the boy from Georgia predict would
happen when the fighting started?
(He predicted that the soldiers would run
away once they heard gunshots.)

FIRST
What question did
the wounded man ask
the youth?
(He asked where the youth
had been wounded in
battle.)

NEXT
How did the youth feel
when asked, "Where yeh
hit"? Why?
(The youth felt panicked
and nervous because he had
not fought in the war.)

NOW
How would you describe the
soldiers now?
(The soldiers are marching.
They are dirty, wounded, and
sad.)

FUTURE
What does the wounded man
think will happen in the future?
(The soldiers will win and show
the others what they're really
like.)

NOW
What did happen, according
to the wounded man, when the
fighting started?
(He said that his boys did not
run, but fought instead.)

LAST
How did the youth respond?
(The youth stammered. He
picked at the button on his
shirt and slipped through the
crowd.)

Vocabulary

1 no. *Sidle* means "move slowly."
2 letters. Couriers are messengers.
3 old. *Tattered* means "ragged."
4 yes. *Industriously* means "diligently."
5 someone who cries. *Melancholy* means "sad."
6 Hold your tongue.-Stop talking.
7 Make up your mind.-Decide.
8 She was walking on air.-She was very happy.
9 He was talking across pickets.-He was chatting with a neighbor.
10 He hung his head.-He was ashamed.
11 He kicked the bucket.-He died.
12 Students' sentences will vary.

Assessment

1	B	6	A
2	A	7	A
3	C	8	D
4	B	9	C
5	D	10	A

WAR COMES TO OUR ISLAND

II. Read

(Students' answers will vary.)

Story Frame #1
Who or what arrives first? What happens next?
(German submarines appear first. The main character is sleeping in his house. Then the Germans
attack an oil refinery on Aruba and then six small lake tankers. Next one submarine was seen.)

Story Frame #2
Why didn't Phillip have school that day?
(Phillip did not have school because the Germans had attacked his island.)

Story Frame #3
Where did Phillip and his friend go?
(Phillip and his friend, Henrik van Boven, went to the old fort.)

Story Frame #4
What did Phillip and Henrik find at the fort? Why didn't they stay there?
(The two boys found soldiers at the fort who told them to go home.)

Story Frame #5
What causes the boys to become frightened?
(An army officer warned the boys that they could be killed. Then, the boys looked out at the
sea. They were used to seeing it filled with boats; today it was empty.)

Vocabulary

Students will probably underline these words:
1 sea, blue
2 standing on, built on floats
3 tall masted, over
4 trained toward the whitecaps
5 shoot, kill
6–10 Students' sentences will vary.

Assessment

1	D	6	D
2	D	7	B
3	A	8	D
4	B	9	B
5	C	10	C

FRUSTRATION

II. Read

(Students' answers will vary.)

What is Jonsbeck's job?

(He is a computer programmer.)

What can you tell about the society described in this story?

(The future society relies heavily on computers.)

Why does Hargrove favor war? Will he succeed?

(Hargrove favors war because he thinks it will produce quick improvements.)

Jonsbeck says "Computers place a greater value on human lives than human beings do themselves. . . ." What does this mean?

(Human beings do not think that their lives are worth that much. Computers think that life is worth more than people do.)

What is "Frustration" about?

("Frustration" is about life in the future. Asimov describes a world in which technology reigns supreme and guides people's actions. Fortunately for humankind, however, technology lacks the necessary emotions to start wars.)

Vocabulary

1-5 Students' sentences will vary.
6 counteract
7 counterclockwise
8 counterproductive
9 counterclaim
10 counterdemonstrate

Assessment

1	A	6	A
2	C	7	B
3	B	8	C
4	D	9	B
5	C	10	C

III. Gather Your Thoughts

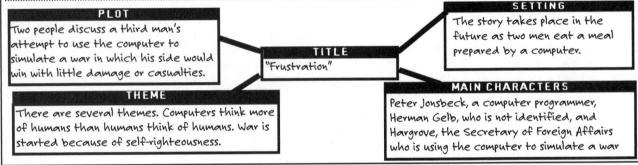

PLOT
Two people discuss a third man's attempt to use the computer to simulate a war in which his side would win with little damage or casualties.

TITLE
"Frustration"

SETTING
The story takes place in the future as two men eat a meal prepared by a computer.

THEME
There are several themes. Computers think more of humans than humans think of humans. War is started because of self-righteousness.

MAIN CHARACTERS
Peter Jonsbeck, a computer programmer, Herman Gelb, who is not identified, and Hargrove, the Secretary of Foreign Affairs who is using the computer to simulate a war

HINTS

II. Read

WORD ATTACK

Tip 1: <u>Correspondents</u> means people who communicate by letter.

Tip 2: What does the word <u>prosaic</u> mean? (boring, dull, lacking imagination)

What do you think the word <u>painlessly</u> means? (without pain, easily)

Look at the word <u>persevere</u> on the previous page. What do you think it means? Say it slowly to yourself.

(to persist in a purpose, an idea, or a task in the face of obstacles or discouragement)

Vocabulary

1 deftly
2 supersede
3 interweaving
4 exceptions
5 surgeon
6 interweaving
7 magnificent
8 reject
9 patient
10 dialogue

Assessment

1	C	6	B
2	D	7	C
3	B	8	D
4	A	9	B
5	C	10	C

Index

PE signals a pupil's edition page number.

TG signals a teacher's edition page number.